Contents

Foreword

John Knagg OBE

Recognising the role of English in today's world and responding to demands in society, governments and educational authorities around the world have, in recent decades, made serious efforts to improve the teaching and learning of English in their schools, universities, and communities. Whether these reform programmes were implemented at national, regional, municipal, or institutional level, and whatever the levels of success they have achieved, they can, taken together, provide us with a substantial body of experience and knowledge about the best way to conceive, design, and implement English language projects.

The British Council has built up substantial experience and expertise in the field of educational reform, with particular reference to the teaching and learning of English. Our hope is that this book will contribute to the successful implementation of future reforms. It is designed to be a book of practical value; a resource which will help all those involved in projects, including political decision makers, educational policy advisers, project and institutional leaders and managers, teachers, and specialist consultants. We hope that all these groups will be able to draw from the experiences and insights described in this volume and that this will add real value to their projects. Indeed, if we have been truly successful, the collection should become a valuable part of the educational reformer's toolkit.

Educational reform, like other forms of social change, is a process, not an event, and one that usually takes years, not weeks or months. We hope that our book will provide salutary lessons for those looking for quick results, underlining in particular the fact that time taken to involve all stakeholders in a reform process pays dividends in terms of achieving lasting impact. By the same token, educationalists need to be sensitive to the political dimension of reform programmes, which can involve the investment of large amounts of public money and time, and to understand the pressure that policy makers are under to demonstrate quick results. While the tensions inherent in this potentially contradictory relationship will not go away, we feel that a shared understanding of other stakeholders' agendas is essential, if the best outcomes are to be obtained.

Similarly, in any educational change programme, adapting the behaviour of teachers in the classroom and sometimes challenging the expectations of students, their parents, and wider society are not easy tasks. It is also important that different elements in the educational equation be tackled in parallel, if lasting impact is to be expected. For example, the initial training of teachers and testing and assessment systems are key elements that have to be addressed, alongside the curriculum, textbooks and other resources, and the orientation of serving teachers.

The changing role of English in the world is the main factor driving the increased interest in these projects. More and more, English is seen as a basic skill necessary for organisations wishing to operate internationally and for individuals who wish to improve their employment prospects and engage with the wider world. This internationalisation of English means that the language no longer 'belongs' to people in the traditional English-speaking countries, if indeed it ever did.

This book responds to the British Council's overall mission to work with peoples around the world to increase international understanding and respect. We live in a beautiful, diverse, and sometimes dangerous world. Part of the beautiful diversity is the 7,000 languages that we human beings speak. Each one of these languages carries a rich and glorious culture with it, and many of my colleagues at the British Council have had their lives enriched by contact with these cultures and languages. While English may be the leading international language in the late 20th and early 21st centuries, we must not forget that the languages that matter most are those in which we speak to our grandparents and grandchildren. It is these languages which embody our particular cultures and constitute an essential part of our personal identity. I hope that this diversity will flourish.

John Knagg OBE
Head of Research and Consultancy, British Council

Acknowledgements

A collection of this kind depends on the work of a large number of people, and all deserve a vote of thanks. First, and obviously, I would like to thank the authors whose work you will find in this volume. Their willingness to engage with the project, the quality of their contributions, and their promptness in responding to deadlines have made the whole process both rewarding and enjoyable. Two other people deserve a special acknowledgement. They are the British Council commissioners and managers of this project, Adrian Odell and John Knagg. Working in the background, they have ensured the intellectual consistency of the end product and the smooth development of the whole project. Without them (as in so many projects), nothing would have happened! I would also like to thank John McGovern for his invaluable advice in the early stages of the development of this book and Donald Watt for his meticulous copy editing. Thanks to the effort of all these people I have greatly enjoyed the preparation of this book. We hope that it will make a strong contribution to the field and that you, the reader, will enjoy reading it.

Christopher Tribble
Lecturer in Applied Linguistics, King's College London

Overview

Christopher Tribble

Introduction

The purpose of this book

Some 20 years ago, after a career as a language teacher in the United Kingdom and overseas, I moved from my job at Queen Mary University to take part in the setting up of British Council offices and programmes for the newly independent countries of Estonia, Latvia, and Lithuania. During what was a period of historic transformation, I had the good fortune to be the ELT project manager with responsibilities across the three countries and had a high degree of professional autonomy. I was initially slightly intimidated by the task I had taken on, as there appeared to be very few resources on which I could draw to help me shape the programme. Although I did eventually discover that systematic approaches to the design and implementation of projects (such as the Logical Framework) had been around since the 1970s (see World Bank 2005), and there was an emerging literature on approaches to the management and evaluation of innovation in ELT (for example, Brumfit 1983; White 1987; Kennedy 1988), at the outset I was not aware of this earlier experience. However, I had the good luck to be put in contact with John McGovern (then Director of the Institute for English Language Education at Lancaster University) and, following discussions with John and with Susan Maingay, the British Council Director, I started my three years in the Baltic States by conducting a baseline study of English language provision. This process, combined with extensive stakeholder consultation, made it possible for me to establish a set of robust priorities which carried us through the first years of our co-operation with language teaching policy makers and professionals in the three countries and which left an inheritance of institutions which are still functioning two decades later.

In my later experience as an evaluator, however, despite the many excellent interventions I have had to review, I have also come across a significant number of projects which have been either poorly designed, badly implemented, or inappropriately evaluated – and sometimes all three. It is our hope, in developing this book, that we can help those who are in the process of developing or approving project concepts, planning the implementation of new interventions, or designing their evaluation, to learn from successful practice – and to avoid some of the pitfalls that are reported here. To this end, we have deliberately avoided making the book overly scholarly and hope that it will communicate with interested professionals across the whole gamut of policy development and implementation.

This does not mean that there is an avoidance of theory in the contributions which follow, and this is as it should be. In one very strong sense, all projects are social theories, so theory is not something that we should avoid. In my own experience, I have found Pawson's (2003) comment that all project interventions are premised on a common hypothesis particularly helpful. Thus, if we accept that projects start with a working hypothesis, namely that 'if we provide these people with these resources, it may change their behaviour' (ibid. 471), then we are much better placed to begin to design both the implementation and evaluation of our interventions. To paraphrase Pawson (2003):

- projects are theories

- evaluation seeks to discover whether projects work

- evaluation is theory-testing.

As we shall see later in the case studies which follow, coming to an understanding of a project's theory of change (Connell and Kubisch 1998), can be one of the most fruitful starting points for a project design or an evaluation. If we know what theories the project planners have about what they hope to achieve (long-, medium- and short-term outcomes), how they expect to achieve them (inputs and activities), and why the proposed actions should deliver intended outcomes (rationale), we can begin to assess the utility and feasibility of their proposal and plan a sound basis for its evaluation.

So, while this book is not intended as an exhaustive summary of all previous research in the area, it is not a theory-free zone. What we have attempted to do is to offer a state-of-the-art survey of some key issues in ELT project design, implementation, and evaluation, and to complement these accounts with a set of case studies which give insights into grounded practitioner experience. We hope that our readers will feel that the theories which are introduced have relevance to their needs and that the practical experiences that are reported in the book provide them with new insights which will, in their turn, help them theorise and frame their own interventions in their own educational cultures.

Design and organisation

The book is organised into three main sections. The first, the present chapter, provides an overview of the whole book and its different components. The second section contains four specially commissioned chapters which provide overarching studies of the major issues and challenges which face those involved in the complex processes of innovation in ELT. These studies provide a coherent background for (and form links with) the third section, a collection of 21 case studies which report on experience of successful and less successful practice in the delivery of ELT projects worldwide. This third section is followed by a summarising chapter which is designed for the busy reader. This brings together a digest of the major lessons from experience offered by the different case studies. Although all those involved in preparing this collection would be very disappointed if our readers restricted their reading to this chapter, we also felt that it would be useful to provide this synthesis of key findings as a resource. It could, perhaps, be the first thing to share with colleagues who have not as yet read the whole volume.

As will become clear, the structure of the book, especially the organising of the case studies, draws on a well-accepted conceptualisation of projects, often called Project Cycle Management. Although a wide range of (sometimes conflicting) terminology is applied to the project cycle, a broad consensus has emerged in relation to its main components and their interrelations. Thus, most iterations of the project cycle include an initial phase of policy development and project identification, a design phase, an implementation phase, and a phase in which final evaluation takes place and the project benefits are handed over to those who will be responsible for the continuing management of new institutions and practices. There is some debate as to whether evaluation should be seen as a separate phase in the project cycle or as a set of practices which apply across the whole project cycle (the latter being my preferred position). An example of the project cycle is given in Figure 1 below:

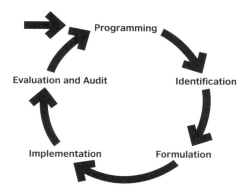

Figure 1: The project cycle (European Commission 2004: 16)

For the purposes of this book we have used four major elements of the project cycle as a basis for the organisation of different sections. These are: Policy and Design, Implementation, Monitoring and Evaluation, and Embedding and Dissemination. These map onto the EU project cycle as follows:

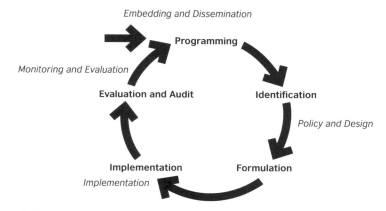

Figure 2: The project cycle and the sequencing of the case studies

In the following sections I will comment on each of the contributions. I will start with the four overarching reports and then move on to the 21 case studies. I hope that this set of brief abstracts will provide readers with a map which will guide them through the volume and which will help them find those resources which will be of most immediate use.

Issues in ELT change management

Five leading scholars, all with strong practical experience of central issues in the development of ELT projects, have written the four reports in this section. The reports offer a theoretical underpinning for the case studies which follow. By problematising the notions of innovation and the project, and by reviewing the challenges which face policy makers and implementers when designing interventions and evaluating the impact that these interventions have made, we hope to provide the reader with a fuller appreciation of the complexity of designing and delivering innovation in education. We also wish to provide accounts, based on current research, of what we can expect of an innovation in ELT and what the limitations of the project approach are in educational reform and renewal. If, as Pawson (2003) says, there is 'Nothing as Practical as a Good Theory', in what is a highly practical collection, we nevertheless feel that it is important to frame our account of practice with an appreciation of current theories on the management of innovation in general and innovation in English language education in particular.

Projects and programmes: Contemporary experience in ELT change management

Author: Rod Bolitho

Drawing on extensive experience as a project manager, consultant, and evaluator, Bolitho works with a conceptualisation of a project as 'a structured and time-bound intervention aimed at bringing about change at an identified level within an educational system' (Bolitho, this volume). Looking back over the last 30 years, he finds that far too many ELT projects have been either left incomplete, have failed to reach target audiences, or have been managed in an overcentralised or top-down way – despite their apparent espousal of democratic, open values. Fortunately, however, enough projects have led to positive change for Bolitho not to have altogether lost faith in the project as a way of managing interventions.

The rest of Bolitho's chapter is taken up with a review of how projects start, are managed, and end. In the first section, he considers the concept and nature of a project itself, a term as often misunderstood as it is clearly grasped and useful. He then goes on to examine the fast changing context for educational change and the difficulty those with a stake in education have in keeping pace with these wider developments. Despite the changes in the contexts for project development, Bolitho still holds that the starting points for change initiatives in education have not altered. These are: the curriculum, methodology, assessment, and materials. In the following section he subjects these to close scrutiny, arguing strongly for solid research as the essential foundation for success in a project, research which must always take into account the intercultural issues which can make or break a change initiative.

Bolitho's discussion of issues related to educational and intercultural contexts is important for our overall discussion (as we shall see in Kiely below), as any failure both to ensure a fit between the intervention and its context, and to take into account the interests of potential champions and opponents, will almost certainly foredoom a project to failure.

Bolitho concludes his chapter with a review of the procedures which are involved in getting change messages across to those who need to put them into practice and with an examination of the continuing problem of sustainability – and what this term might mean in practise. His chapter ends with some conclusions in the shape of a summary of what he feels we have learnt about change through ELT projects in the last 30 to 40 years.

Planning for success: Culture, engagement and power in English language education innovation
Author: David Hayes

Hayes situates his study within a context in which there is a general belief that success in English, right from school level, is a key factor in national competitiveness and is of paramount importance to national economies in a globalised world. This has led to governments making significant investments in programmes and projects designed to improve the teaching and learning of English in state schools across the age range, with the focus usually on implementing Learner-Centred Education (LCE) through Communicative Language Teaching (CLT) approaches. In many countries, however, these investments do not appear to have produced the changes to established patterns of classroom interaction to accord with new curriculum guidelines or to have raised student achievement as their funders intended.

For Hayes, an important part of the background to this process is the way in which educational reforms have become export commodities. Hayes highlights two issues: the lack of an appreciation of local educational cultures in the implementation of CLT approaches as part of educational reform, and the increasing attention paid to international comparisons of educational achievement. This latter tendency in particular can lead to 'a naïve belief among many policy makers and practitioners that policies and practices designed in one context can be unproblematically transported elsewhere' (Hayes, this volume).

To counter these tendencies, Hayes proposes a set of principles which should be drawn on in the design of an intervention. As will be seen elsewhere in the case studies, the relevance of many of these principles is borne out by the experience of those who have been directly involved in project implementation. In his argument Hayes stresses the importance of recognising the systemic nature of innovation and the importance of joined-up thinking, paying particular attention to the continuing (and all too often ignored) importance of listening to teachers; ensuring that there is adequate support during the process of implementation; and recognising the impact that issues of power and leadership have in managing innovation.

Hayes argues throughout that educational innovation is not value- or culture-free but must be considered in relation to the context in which it is to be implemented. He also comments that it is frequently the case that there is a failure to recognise how costly innovation can be, and the resources needed to implement it successfully are underestimated. Alongside the failure to understand the cost of innovation, we still continue to find that the impact of an innovation in one area of the system on other areas is not fully thought through or that the powerful effect of existing practise on the likelihood of an innovation being adopted is not adequately appreciated, particularly where there is a curriculum-testing mismatch. That this is still the case is disturbing, given the wealth of international experience which points to this lesson again and again. We can hope that this collection will make some contribution to remedying this situation. Certainly, if Hayes' final recommendations are understood and acted on, there is a better chance for the success of future interventions, both in ELT reform and across the whole school curriculum.

Understanding innovation in English language education: Contexts and issues

Authors: Denise E. Murray and MaryAnn Christison

Murray and Christison's chapter complements Hayes' study, stressing, as it does, that innovations which are successful in one context may have to be adapted (or even rejected) in another. They comment that contexts for English language education vary across the globe, and so policy development must be responsive to the local context. In their report, they discuss the nature of innovation and change, detail the various contexts for English language education around the world, and examine issues common to all contexts, but with responses which need to be local.

Drawing on current research in management science, Murray and Christison outline two issues that are central to innovation. The first is that of organisational cultures and structures. Here they identify two strongly contrasting traditions, the segmental and the integrative. They comment that:

> Segmentalist cultures suffocate change because they do not foster interaction across areas or encourage thinking 'outside the box'; instead they view ideas and problems in isolation. In contrast, integrative cultures see issues as part of the whole and experiment with different ways of addressing them. (Murray and Christison, this volume)

On the question of leadership, they identify three skills that are required for effective organisational leadership (and therefore effective project management leadership). These are: the interactional skills needed for the management of individuals and teams; the skill to facilitate groups and support others, as they learn how to facilitate their own teams and groups, as well as to confront conflict and build consensus; and finally, the strategic skill linked to understanding how change is designed and constructed in an organisation.

In the next major section in their chapter, Murray and Christison outline an account of what can be considered to be an innovation in ELT, focusing on the contexts in which ELT innovation might be required and the issues which they consider to be relevant for innovative interventions. These include: teacher knowledge and beliefs; teacher language awareness; level of English proficiency; knowledge about language; pedagogical expertise; subject matter expertise; and attitudes of content teachers to being responsible for language learning. In itself, this list offers policy makers an invaluable inventory of possible areas to which attention should be paid when educational renewal is on the agenda.

Murray and Christison complete their survey by considering a set of important implications for policy makers. Here they outline centrally important areas that should be included in any systematic policy review. They include: the quality and content of teacher education programmes; pre-service programmes to develop new teachers with appropriate knowledge and understanding; in-service programmes to develop current teachers' levels of expertise; teacher educators' ability to convey innovative approaches; and print, multimedia, and teacher-developed materials.

Designing evaluation into change management processes
Author: Richard Kiely

Kiely examines the role of evaluation in change management processes in English language teaching. He first outlines two purposes for evaluation in ELT projects. The first relates to accountability, that is, measuring or otherwise determining the success of the project in terms of the impact of the activities and resources introduced by the project. The second purpose relates to facilitating such success, through enhanced understanding of project activities, opportunities, and constraints. The accountability purpose orients evaluation towards rigorous, objective accounts of impact which sponsors and policy makers can have confidence in and the sector as a whole can draw lessons from. The development purpose situates evaluation ownership and activity within projects, where the focus is on understanding project processes and on advocacy for the success of these processes and overall project goals.

Kiely's discussion reflects key strands of the paradigm debate in programme evaluation generally and the ways these have shaped theoretical work on ELT project evaluation over recent decades. Linking these perspectives to constructs of stakeholding, innovation, and knowledge building in the ELT field, Kiely concludes by describing three characterisations of evaluation practise where a focus on understanding and developing project processes can, over time, contribute to the accountability agenda. The first is evaluation for development, where teachers and programme managers use the processes of evaluation to understand and explain the factors which shape learning opportunities. The second is evaluation for quality assurance, where the goal is to demonstrate to immediate and remote stakeholders that the programme is well managed and achieving its goals. The third is evaluation as situated practitioner research, where ELT professionals within projects devise studies which build knowledge relevant to the success of that project. In all cases these evaluation processes contribute to innovation and change which improve programmes and extend the skills and knowledge of teachers and other ELT professionals.

Kiely concludes that the challenge for evaluation is to engineer a merging of these different and sometimes competing agendas and processes, so that all programme stakeholders work together for successful innovation and change, for the improvement of programmes, for the building of integrated theories of ELT effectiveness, and, through these, for rigorous accounts of the value of investment in ELT.

The case studies

The 21 case studies have been grouped into the four major strands mentioned above: Policy and Design, Implementation, Monitoring and Evaluation, and Embedding and Dissemination.

POLICY AND DESIGN

Policy and design are the critical stages in a project, when contextual knowledge and professional judgement should come together to build a theory of change which will frame everything that happens during the elaboration of a project and which will provide the basis for continuing evaluative activities. As we will see, the process of policy formation and its interpretation as a project design is not always as effectively managed as it might be, but when it is successful, the project's chance of achieving sustainable outcomes is greatly enhanced.

Peacekeeping English

Author: Mark Crossey
Location: Poland
Period: mid 1990s

Crossey discusses the Peacekeeping English project (PEP), which started in the Baltic States of Estonia, Latvia, and Lithuania under the name of the 'Baltic Battalion ELT project' and was extended to a further five Central and Eastern Europe states, among them Poland, in late 1994. Funded by the UK Foreign and Commonwealth Office and Ministry of Defence and closely associated with NATO's Partnership for Peace programme, which also commenced in 1994, PEP Poland was originally designed to meet the perceived English language needs of the militaries of the NATO accession states of Central and Eastern Europe (CEE).

Crossey comments on factors which worked for and against the success of the project. On the success side he highlights:

- the use of three to four well-qualified UK ELT consultants working directly within the Polish Ministry of Defence and ensuring that the 'UK voice' on ELT reform was heard

- the good level of resourcing for PEP Poland at a time of great financial constraint

- the lack of competition from other suppliers (such as the US Defense Language Institute)

- a context of flux, which in some ways made change easier to effect, at least in terms of centralised policies and legislation.

The main weaknesses of the project he discusses are:

- an apparent lack of openness on the UK side, which had the unintended effect of politicising the project in its opening stages

- shortcomings in the initial scoping process, which created problems during the first three or four years of the project.

Crossey concludes that one of the major reasons why PEP Poland achieved so much impact was that it lasted for 11 years, i.e. it is one of the longest-running projects reported in these case studies.

Mismatched perspectives: In-service teacher education policy and practice in South Korea

Author: David Hayes
Location: South Korea
Period: 2006–10

Hayes reports on a major in-service teacher development project in South Korea and some of the limitations in design which have led to problems. The major problems with the project arise from divergent perspectives amongst teacher development providers and schoolteachers about the most productive forms of INSET (in-service education and training), and an absence of the kind of in-school follow-up which research indicates is crucial to maximising the impact of INSET. Under these circumstances, it has been difficult to achieve the level of desired impact. By basing the INSET programme on a deficit theory of teachers' knowledge and skills, educational administrators appear to have decided that teachers are lacking in some way that impedes their professional efficacy. This has proved to be the wrong starting point, as it is much more likely that an INSET programme will contribute to school improvement, if it provides teachers with the space to reflect upon their prior experience, and any new knowledge and skills introduced, and to create a collaborative professional learning environment for teachers. Hayes concludes that educational policy makers and administrators would do better to remove those constraints which research has identified as inhibiting successful development, most notably teachers' lack of time and opportunities to reflect on their own teaching and to share practise with their colleagues.

Designing a 'Language-in-Education' planning strategy

Author: Hamish McIlwraith
Location: Tunisia
Period: 2007–12

In this short case study, McIlwraith discusses the significant problems which the (often conflicting) terminology of projects can cause for projects which have been designed within one organisational culture, but which have then to be communicated in another. Although he is not able to offer a definitive solution to the problem, the discussion makes clear that this is an area to which all project planners should pay attention. Even though project management terminology may be felt to be accepted and uncontroversial in one context, this does not necessarily mean that it will not be challenged in another context; the terms remain open to subjective interpretation.

The ETeMS project: English for Teaching of Mathematics and Science

Author: Mina Patel
Location: Malaysia
Period: 2003–10

This case study focuses on the issues which can arise when a major policy to introduce English as the medium of instruction for a mainstream subject (in this case, mathematics and science) is implemented without sufficient preparation time. In the present instance, very experienced teachers, who had been teaching their subject in Bahasa Malaysia for over 20 years and were close to retirement, were now being asked to go on English courses. At the other end of the continuum, younger teachers, who had been taught through the medium of Bahasa Malaysia at school themselves, struggled with the concept of suddenly having to teach through another language. Patel reports how the problem was further compounded when the decision was made that, by 2008, all examinations should be solely delivered through English. Unfortunately, this change in language policy coincided with the introduction of a new ICT (information and computing technology) strategy for the teaching of mathematics and science. Although this was welcomed by some teachers, others feared it simply because they had had no experience of using technology in the classroom before this, and others relied on it heavily to make up for their own lack of language and pedagogy to teach their subjects through English. The combination of inherent contradictions in the policy and its implementation led to poor outcomes for students and the eventual official reversal of the policy.

Materials design and development in English for the world of work: Policy, strategies, and processes

Author: Mike Scholey
Location: Turkey
Period: 2006–09

In this case study, Scholey demonstrates how the best way to 'change the system' was to do it from within the classroom by means of a bottom-up approach, in a way that teachers could see and understand – i.e. what was changing and why. By focusing on new materials, policy makers were able to have an immediate impact on classroom teaching, to encourage teachers to reflect on the innovation, and to change their methodology and content.

Alongside the new teaching materials, specialist vocational teacher training in methodology was provided, so that there would be a core group of properly trained and committed English language teachers-cum-materials writers to be the key agents of change. In this way, real curricular and methodological innovation could be achieved through the production and piloting of high-quality vocational language learning materials, written by Turkish teachers, in Turkey, about Turkey, for Turkey.

Another important aspect of the project was that it made sure that key players – especially head teachers – were involved in decision making and that policy documents such as the logframe and timelines for resource input, which are often incomprehensible to stakeholders, were largely avoided during later stages of the project. In this way, clear and effective communication was established throughout the project's life. All this meant that, whenever a problem arose, large or small, it was dealt with rapidly and effectively, project team motivation and morale were maintained, and effective delivery of a successful innovation was achieved.

Mind the gap: Language policy reform

Author: John Simpson
Location: Rwanda
Period: 2008–11

Simpson reports how a national government has faced major challenges with the sector-wide establishment of English-medium education and in enabling all teachers and learners to become proficient in English. The initial language policy prioritising English as the medium of education led to a new configuration of roles and relations amongst the three languages, with Kinyarwanda the foundation for initial literacy, English the main language of learning, and French an additional language. However, those attempting to implement this policy met significant problems, including: the need for teachers to develop their language skills and ability to teach effectively in English; the lack of pupils' exposure to English, particularly in rural areas; a shortage of learning materials in English; and the language level of some textbooks being above the pupils' existing competence.

Although there existed a clear vision and sense of urgency for national development, Simpson comments on how these reforms may have been jeopardised by their number and – in a skills-deficit, resource-constrained context – the lack of capacity and funds to implement numerous large-scale changes concurrently. Thus, the drive to ELT reform as a means of helping to achieve the government's goal of fostering regional integration, including harmonisation of education systems and economic development, may have eclipsed the desirability of giving due weight to pedagogic considerations in policy formation, in particular to an understanding of the role of the first language in promoting early literacy and learning. It seems to be the case that if the pedagogic stream had been given fuller attention during policy formation, later reversals of policy might have been avoided.

Textbooks, teams, and sustainability

Author: Catherine Walter
Location: Russian Federation
Period: 2000–10

Walter reports on a major ELT textbook reform implemented by the British Council, in co-operation with the Russian Ministry of Education and numerous regional and local education authorities. The success of this project derived from its adherence to a set of core principles. These were the importance of embedding the project in a nexus of mutually supportive projects; the importance of constructing the project at all stages as a Russian-British partnership, with Russian partners taking the major role in the initiation of the project and the publication of the materials; taking great care in the selection, development, and management of the authors, and ensuring that the author teams were well distributed across the country and not just in the two major cities; and engaging regional and local educational communities.

By working in this way, the project was able to contribute to long-term change across vast geographic areas in a complex and rapidly changing political and social environment.

Redesigning a blended learning course: Introducing new technologies for ELT

Author: Claire Whittaker
Location: Bosnia and Herzegovina
Period: 2005–08

Whittaker's case study reports on the redesign process of a range of blended learning English language courses in the Armed Forces of Bosnia and Herzegovina (blended learning being defined as a combination of face-to-face, computer, and self-study modes in a single teaching and learning environment). The reform arose from a review in which it became clear that there was a need to standardise English language delivery and to provide learners with comparable learning opportunities.

The project was driven by a need to ensure long-term post-project sustainability and to benefit from the development of an internationally funded Peace Support Operations Training Centre (PSOTC) that provided education and training for junior officers in the region through the medium of English. Whittaker reports that one of the main reasons for the project's success arose from the way in which it was staged over a three-year period. This maximised the impact on the users (officer instructors, teachers, and learners), and allowed time for reflection and comment. This iterative approach to the redesign process created great scope for the project to be responsive to stakeholder needs and greatly enhanced long-term impact.

IMPLEMENTATION

During implementation, a project team has responsibility for providing the results that are specified in the project design, for monitoring and evaluating progress, and for adjusting the project plan where necessary. When project teams have the authority and competence to make decisions based on the evidence provided by systematic monitoring and evaluation and continuing consultation with stakeholders, project success is greatly enhanced.

Making it work: A case study of a teacher training programme

Author: Lin Hong
Location: People's Republic of China
Period: 2001–05

Lin Hong reports on the Primary English Teacher Training (PETT) project launched in Guangdong province in 2001 against the background of the rapid introduction of English as a first foreign language in primary schools nationwide. The aim was to train as many primary English teachers as possible to adapt to learner-centred communicative activities. In three years a total of 102 local trainers were trained, first at Guangdong Teachers College of Foreign Languages and Arts, and then at Lancaster University. They in turn cascaded to 4,800 primary English teachers in the province. Although the British Council's involvement ended in 2005, the cascade training is still taking place at the time of writing.

Lin Hong's study shows how important localising is for a foreign-funded training project. In many earlier projects in China, foreign trainers designed the whats and hows for a programme on the basis of their understanding of the local situation and context after a brief survey. This alienated local professionals and militated against sustainability of project benefits. She shows how PETT achieved its high impact on a large number of beneficiaries and its good sustainability, through effective localisation of ownership of the training process. By ensuring long-term institutional support for the training initiative, the cascade training had a high level of success – something that has rarely been achieved in other interventions in China.

Teacher Training Colleges

Author: Hanna Komorowska
Location: Poland
Period: 1990s

The early 1990s was a period of revolutionary change in the orientation of Polish society. Komorowska reports on a project in which (with British Council participation on the English language programme) a whole new layer of higher-education institutions was created. This was made up of 50 colleges with 1,500 places for students of English, 400 for students of French, and 450 for students of German. As in the case of other successful projects, luck had some part. For example, the decision to go for a three-year course of studies turned out to have been a good one. When the Bologna Process started in 1999, resulting in the introduction of three-year BA and two-year MA courses at universities, the fact of having the same length of study at colleges and for university BA courses facilitated smooth integration and ensured sustainability. Equally importantly, the project accepted variation in the programmes developed by individual colleges and was flexible in its model of commitment, so that it could respond to problems which arose during implementation. In this way, the project was able to respond innovatively to shortfalls in provision and to maintain quality despite complex conditions.

Komorowska demonstrates that by deciding not to wait for ideal solutions, co-operating with everybody (including former enemies), looking for critical opinion, and attempting to maintain the project through rewards rather than punishments, it was possible to provide a project which created institutions which continue to bring positive benefit to Polish society.

Change in Tamil Nadu

Author: Clare O'Donahue
Location: India
Period: 2009–11

Although the limitations of the cascade model are fully recognised, O'Donahue reports how a successful cascade was implemented by drawing on the previous experience of partner organisations and embedding strategies for minimising loss of impact during the cascading process within the implementation plan.

O'Donahue shows how the simple measures of agreeing partners' specific roles and fostering an environment of mutual respect and trust through regular consultations and meetings with key stakeholders led to a high level of success in the cascade. Listening to, acknowledging, and acting on suggestions discussed in these consultations led to buy-in from the key players and thence to long-term sustainable impact. Her observation that it is the people and not the policies that effect change is worth noting.

The Romanian textbook project: Learning together, driving reform

Author: Ruxandra Popovici
Location: Romania
Period: 1991–95

Popovici's case study reports on a Romanian Ministry of Education project, in partnership with the British Council Romania, to produce a new complete series of eight textbooks of English for secondary schools in Romania (grades 5–12) and to create local expertise in materials writing. She comments that the need to replace instructional materials that were outdated in content and methodology was urgent and recognised by the teaching community and the decision makers as a key part of the overall education reform agenda.

Popovici argues that the project was successful primarily because the new books were written locally. Even though the innovative ELT methodology that the books used challenged some of the deep-rooted traditional values of Romanian ELT, because the new textbooks were written by Romanian specialists, it was possible for the project team to convince teachers to adapt to new, almost revolutionary methodologies and approaches. This would not have happened if the project had been led by 'outsiders'.

Implementing the pilot stage of English in Action: Negotiating the route to sustainable improvement in ELT classroom practice

Author: Mike Solly and Clare Woodward
Location: Bangladesh
Period: 2010–19

Solly and Woodward report on the pilot phase of a nine-year project in Bangladesh. The project's purpose is 'to increase significantly the number of people able to communicate in English to levels that enable them to participate fully in economic and social activities and opportunities'.

Because many primary school teachers in Bangladesh receive no training before entering the classroom and have little English language understanding, children receive minimal modelling of good communicative language practice. To give the children and teachers access to clear and accurate English, all participating teachers in the pilot received an iPod loaded with classroom materials and provided with speakers. The materials on the iPod support the content of the textbooks and code-switches between Bangla and English to ensure that the children understand the context within which the English dialogues are set.

The dilemma in the project design was to find a sustainable balance between materials support and mediated support. Ultimately a blended approach was taken: materials on the MP3 players, hard-copy teacher guides, classroom materials, peer support in their schools, monthly 'cluster' meetings and classroom visits. Peer teacher facilitators (TFs), who also have contact with each other and with other English in Action (EIA) stakeholders via mobile phones, facilitate these meetings and classroom visits. In the latter stages of the pilot, SMS (short message service) was used to encourage teachers to try out activities in their classrooms and reflect upon successes and challenges.

On the basis of the piloting experiences and adjustments to the programme which Solly and Woodward report, the project's next phases are now premised on a robust model for materials delivery and a clearer set of relevant success indicators.

The Oman BA project: ELT change implementation, process or event?

Author: Martin Wedell
Location: Oman
Period: 1996–2008

Wedell's study deals with a project which began in 1996, when the Omani Ministry of Education (MoE) launched a major policy initiative Reform and the development of general education. Its goal was to create a ten-year system of basic education that would provide Omani citizens with the knowledge and skills needed to participate in the changing global and local economy and job market.

The case study focuses on one key strand of any ELT change initiative – the provision of contextually appropriate teacher support and development – and highlights some beneficial results for the outcomes of the initiative as a whole that can arise when implementation is (at least implicitly) recognised to be a process, not an event.

The project has achieved a high degree of success thanks to a set of particular features. These include the fact that the long-term stability of leadership and management in the project enabled the people involved on both sides to get to know each other well, develop good, trusting personal relationships, and so establish ever more effective communication systems. It also meant that there was sufficient time for the MoE (which commissioned and funded the project) to recognise that the project leadership was competent, and thus feel able to delegate ever more decision making to the project level. This, in turn, supported and enhanced relationships between leaders, which enabled more informed development of coherent systems such as summer/winter school monitoring and report systems. In addition, Wedell describes how throughout their studies all teachers taught four days a week at their schools. Structuring the project in this manner had positive effects on the success of the project. Teachers had ample opportunity to consider the appropriateness or otherwise for their own contexts of the ideas and practices that the programme introduced. The response from their teaching experiences generated through discussion during their weekly day-release sessions also contributed more or less directly to the teaching materials revision process, which was such a constant feature of the project.

MONITORING AND EVALUATION

Monitoring and evaluation are best seen as a process which starts before the project design has been completed (in the form of a baseline study) and which continues for some time after the last project product has been handed over to end users. Through systematic and focused monitoring and evaluation, the project team is able to improve its own processes and apply learning from earlier stages to activities in later stages in the completion of the project. Without such monitoring and evaluation, the chances for sustainable impact are dramatically reduced.

Measuring the impact of the PROSPER Project: A learning experience

Author: Mirela Bardi
Location: Romania
Period: 1991–99

PROSPER (Project for Special Purpose English in Romania) was set up in 1991 with the wider aim of improving the level of English proficiency of future personnel in key sectors of the Romanian economy and public life such as engineering, economics, public administration, and medicine, and with the immediate aim of upgrading and diversifying the teaching/learning of ESP (English for Specific Purposes) in major tertiary education institutions. Bardi focuses on the monitoring and evaluation of the project. This was the most complex and challenging project activity, with the study of impact being carried out over a period of three-and-a-half years (1996–99). The study aimed to capture evidence of expected and unexpected project impact on the teaching/learning process and on the major stakeholders involved.

Bardi's case study relates how the collaborative project culture of consulting and involving project members in decision making during implementation fed into and enhanced the evaluation design and delivery. What happened in Romania can be seen as a model for how to conduct participatory evaluation, with the project members designing the study framework and carrying out all the stages in the research process: drafting, trialling, and revising the instruments, collecting the data, and analysing and writing up the results. She concludes that, critically, the involvement of project managers in the research process increased the team's confidence in their ability to supervise the process competently, while making the managers themselves more knowledgeable about the demands of the research process and the needs of the team.

The challenge of monitoring and evaluation

Author: Lesley Dick
Location: Sri Lanka
Period: 2005–12

Dick's case study deals with an in-service programme for English language teachers in Sri Lanka, designed by the British Council and carried out in association with the Ministry of Education. Uniquely, in this set of case studies, the project has been funded by a Sri Lankan private-enterprise organisation, the Council for Business with Britain (CBB). A non-profit, non-political organisation focused on expanding bilateral trade links between Sri Lanka and the United Kingdom, CBB has HSBC as principal sponsor.

Dick comments on the importance of having a detailed monitoring and evaluation plan, complete with needs and objectives matched to data collection methods, and of having a schedule in place from project inception. A very careful definition of project scope (and therefore of evaluation scope) at the outset is also essential, as is a baseline evaluation in the opening stage of the project. She also stresses that data collected and human resources used should be exploited fully, that the data collected must be reliable, valid, and accurate, and that regular and good methods of communication are essential. In her conclusion, she comments that one of the unexpected benefits of regular monitoring has been that evaluators have become valuable mentors and a channel for support to the implementation team.

Understanding washback: A case study of a new exam

Author: Rama Mathew
Location: India
Period: 1988–95

The Curriculum Implementation Study (CIS) was part of a much larger Central Board of Secondary Education (CBSE) ELT Project. This large project focused on the needs of English Course A students (secondary-level English-medium students). Its main purpose was to improve teaching/learning of English in Classes IX and X, with a focus on the development of language skills in communicative situations. The special feature of the project was intensive involvement of teachers from CBSE schools in all aspects of curriculum development, i.e. designing the new syllabus, preparation of teaching materials, the new testing scheme and sample papers, and the training manual for orienting teachers to the new curriculum. The CIS was designed to review how the different aspects of the curriculum, the new textbooks, testing scheme, and teacher education unfolded in different types of classrooms, including the washback of the Board exam. One of its major purposes was to provide continuing support for a more effective implementation of the curriculum.

The CIS was highly innovative in the Indian context, because it was strongly insider-/teacher-oriented and involved teachers in the studying of the different aspects of curriculum-as-reality (how the curriculum unfolded in everyday classroom activities), as opposed to curriculum-as-intention (the syllabus/textbooks as documents) or curriculum-as-product (the language proficiency of students revealed through end-of-course exams). Additionally, the study was developmental, with built-in flexibility which allowed changes and extensions as and when a need was perceived.

Although the CIS can be considered to have been a success, the story of the main CBSE ELT project is less positive. The study revealed that the negative washback from the new exam significantly reduced the impact of the new curriculum, especially for weaker learners.

Redirecting a curriculum development project

Author: Mona Zikri
Location: Egypt
Period: 1975–91

With a focus on evaluation and monitoring, Zikri's study reports on Egypt's longest-running ELT programme. This ran from 1975 to 1991 and was sponsored by the British Council, the University of California at Los Angeles (UCLA), the Binational Fulbright Commission, and the Faculty of Education (FoE) of Ain Shams University. The curriculum development projects (CDPs) in this programme are classified as CDP I: materials development, CDP II: research, and CDP III: a staff development scheme.

The evaluation revealed that the project's change theory had three flaws: the adoption of a prescriptive approach recommended by the expatriate experts; the way in which the rationale for reform focused on product, not process; and the fact that the social context of the reform was not sufficiently recognised. Thus, the CDPs succeeded in developing curricula but failed on two fundamentals of reform: building ownership and improving capacities.

Zikri concludes that the elements which are crucial to project success are ownership, capacity development, and the incorporation of the social context through appropriate methodologies. Most importantly from an evaluation perspective, she argues that valid monitoring and evaluation systems should be in place from the earliest possible point in the project cycle so that they can inform project designers, implementers, and policy makers on how best to achieve the desired results.

EMBEDDING AND DISSEMINATION

If the design, implementation, and monitoring and evaluation of the project are successfully achieved, the possibilities of achieving long-term sustainability are greatly enhanced. When the project's fit with local culture is good and stakeholder ownership of the project's institutional outputs is strong, then the chance for achieving real changes in educational practice and results is high. Without this kind of cultural fit and stakeholder ownership, projects have little chance of bringing about change.

The English Language Teachers' Association (ELTA) project for newly qualified teachers

Author: Sue Leather
Location: Romania, Georgia, Macedonia, Azerbaijan
Period: 2005–08

Leather's case study considers a project which aimed to address the needs of newly qualified secondary-school teachers of English in Romania (where the project was 'owned'), Georgia, Macedonia, and Azerbaijan. The project was initiated in 2005 and handed over to local partners in April 2008. She comments that an important factor in the successful dissemination and embedding of the project in Azerbaijan was the effective matching of project aims and context. First, the teachers in the target group had very little classroom experience and were arguably more open to change than teachers who had been teaching in a particular way for many years. While these NQTs (newly qualified teachers) still had to fit in with their school cultures to an extent, their youth and relative lack of experience may well have enhanced their flexibility. Secondly, the carefully staged preparation of trainers and roll-out of the training during the implementation phase seem to have been successful in providing a good model of how the training could be managed. Finally, the monitoring and evaluation during the phase of the project which was supported by the British Council also ensured that the handling agencies and the trainers felt guided and supported, so that handover was made much easier.

Leather comments that this project achieved long-term sustainability of results by ensuring that it met a real need in the local context, that the right partners were chosen to take the project forward, that project resources were well suited to the real needs of the target group, and that there was a consistent, realistic approach to the completion of the project.

Embedding change in state education systems: The Paraná ELT project

Author: Christopher Palmer
Location: Brazil
Period: 1999–2002

Palmer's case study considers an ambitious three-year project, undertaken at the request of the State Secretary of Education, Paraná, Brazil, with funding coming from the World Bank. The project focus was on improving the language and teaching skills of teachers of English in the southern Brazilian state of Paraná. Key to the project's success was its careful contextual analysis in the design phase and its innovative approach to the use of distance learning methodology.

Palmer demonstrates how, on the basis of this work, the project was able to overcome a major issue of low professional self-esteem amongst English language teachers. He also shows how the project supported the development of a professional culture in which teachers became independent learners and, through the creation of a university supply network, were able to build their capacity to influence directly the development of the regional project. The challenge of size and reach was addressed by the adoption of a distance education approach, with periods of self-study interspersed with fortnightly meetings with tutors. The internet and radio English courses also helped to enhance the sense of managing one's own learning. The use of these resources brought the twin benefits of making teachers more independent in their learning and less dependent on the teacher trainer for input, and of giving teachers a sense of self-worth and achievement which will continue well beyond the project itself.

An early years bilingual schools project

Author: Teresa Reilly
Location: Spain
Period: 1996–2011

Reilly reports on a major Spanish Ministry of Education project delivered in partnership with the British Council. The Early Bilingual Education Project (EBEP) started in 1996 as a pilot in 44 state schools throughout Spain. Fifteen years later, there are 120 primary and secondary schools participating in it, with a total of 30,000 pupils aged between three and 16. The model developed through the project now serves as an example of good practice for regional governments in Spain which are developing similar programmes. As a result of the project, by the age of 16, the majority of participating pupils are proficient, literate English second language users, confidently able to communicate with age-appropriate native and non-native audiences.

Reilly comments that the project has achieved this success because there is strong political will and parental demand, a good partnership between the Ministry of Education and the British Council, and a major commitment to continuity. By combining these factors with an integrated curriculum, well-supported teacher provision and Continuous Professional Development (CPD), it has been possible to have a major, sustainable impact on a national education system.

Issues in ELT
change management

Projects and programmes: Contemporary experience in ELT change management

Rod Bolitho

Introduction

This chapter draws extensively on my own long-term involvement as a consultant on a number of projects and programmes in Europe and in Central and South Asia. I have also listened to and taken into account views of colleagues and in-country partners engaged in similar initiatives in other contexts.

It is much more difficult, in this second decade of the millennium, to identify a single structured model for the design of ELT projects than it was, say, 20 years ago. This difficulty is perhaps partly attributable to changing views of projects and what they can achieve. For the purposes of this study, I am sticking to a view of an educational project as a structured and time-bound intervention aimed at bringing about change at an identified level within an educational system.

In the eighties and nineties, we were still thinking and acting in terms of idealised frameworks which focused, in tune with the spirit of the times, on fixed timescales, measurable outputs, sustainability, and the dreaded risks and threats. Project after project in different parts of the world ended when the money ran out and the planned time came to an end. This sometimes resulted in resigned acceptance in the host community (among some professionals in Hungary, for example, where the post-1989 injection of funding gave short-lived impetus to the fast-track training of English teachers), in disappointment (which I sensed most acutely in Romania, where funding ran out long before English teachers were able to contemplate paying for their own professional development or to access European Union funds), or in ill-feeling (as in francophone Africa, when ELT professionals there realised that most of their share of the aid cake was being redirected for political ends to the newly 'liberated' countries of Eastern and Central Europe). In each of these cases, there has been a degree of regression to 'old' ways of teaching, preparing teachers, designing curricula, and preparing examinations. The impetus and incentives to maintain the level and speed of change were often simply lost in the battle for day-to-day survival which many teachers in these regions continue to face. I have also encountered teachers who were never touched by the planned changes because some of the projects which were launched in the nineties were far from inclusive in their coverage (often concentrating on a capital city elite) or relied on multiplier effects which never materialised, as change messages were diluted through several layers of cascading.

Ironically, too, at a time when learner-centred views of classroom practice were enjoying something of a revival, in part because of the rediscovery of Vygotsky's work and a renewed interest in the work of other progressive educational thinkers such as Dewey and Carl Rogers, educational projects remained essentially driven by and accountable to donors, even if some attempted to break this mould. In other words, even projects which advocated learner-centred and communicative approaches in ELT often had a centralised and top-down management structure.

In the rest of this paper, I will be reviewing in more depth a number of aspects of projects and programmes. I will first take a look at the concept and nature of a project itself, a term as often misunderstood as it is clearly grasped and useful. I will then go on to examine the fast-changing backcloth to educational change and the difficulty those with a stake in education have in keeping pace with these wider developments. However, the key starting points for change initiatives in education remain largely the same as ever – the curriculum, methodology, assessment, and materials – and in the following section I will subject these to close scrutiny. Having considered these fundamental issues, I will argue the case for solid research as the essential foundation for success in a project, and then go on to discuss intercultural issues, which can make or break a change initiative. In the final sections, I focus on the procedures involved in getting change messages across to those who need to put them into practice and the old chestnut of sustainability and what this term might mean in practice. At the end of the paper, I risk a few conclusions in the shape of a summary of what we have learnt about change through projects in the last 30 to 40 years.

Projects

Readers will, I hope, forgive me if I remind them of some of the earlier meanings and connotations of 'project'. It is a term much used in industry and construction in the United States of America, perhaps even more so than in the United Kingdom. The building of the Hoover Dam was consistently referred to as a 'project', as were the huge estates built to house workers in the industrial cities of the USA in the thirties and forties. More recently we have seen the term associated with innovation initiatives in industry and the corporate world. The influx of management practices into donor circles and educational institutions in the eighties and especially the nineties led to the adoption of the concept of a 'project' as an attractive way of packaging an aid-funded or otherwise sponsored intervention – attractive because of its neatness in terms of objectives, timescales, budget allocations, and deployment of manpower.

But the model did not always transfer easily. The language associated with projects (logical framework, outputs, deliverables, success indicators, assumptions, risks and threats, etc.) at first seemed alien to those involved in education, and frequently erected a conceptual barrier between those planning an intervention and those charged with implementing it. More tellingly, perhaps, there was only a very gradual realisation that a project model created to deal mainly with tangible and three-dimensional outputs was not ideally suited to change efforts that necessarily depend at least as much on process as on products, and with countless variables in terms of context, affective factors in stakeholders, status issues, and so on. As a result, in the nineties, the term 'process project' began to emerge, carrying the implication that good practice might involve changing course, realigning objectives, or modifying expectations during the lifespan of a project.

The changing context of educational change

There is no doubt that the wider context for a discussion of these issues has changed almost beyond recognition over the last 20 to 30 years. In particular, we have come to understand with greater clarity what Toffler (1970) and other early change gurus were warning us about in the last century: that the speed of change is constantly picking up and that we had better get used to dealing with its impact on all parts of our lives. This realisation has had, and continues to have, an influence on thinking about the purposes of education, including the teaching of English. In educating the citizens of tomorrow, we are told, we should be preparing them to cope with change in our increasingly globalised world. Among other things, this seems to mean laying emphasis on using language as a tool for communication and for accessing information and developing transferable skills such as critical thinking and learning how to learn. These features should be in evidence in the curriculum and in textbooks as well as in classroom practices.

We are moving increasingly towards what Wedell (2009) describes as an interpretive and dynamic view of the educational process, with emphasis on teachers as supporters of learners in their learning, and away from a transmission-based view, which sees the teacher as an imparter of a pre-existing body of knowledge. Or are we? It is easy to see why educational thinkers and planners are attracted by this post-modern view of what we are all involved in. Yet in most of the 10 or so countries that I have been actively involved in as a trainer or consultant over the last 20 years, the reality has usually looked very different.

One plausible explanation for this gap between thinking and practice has been put forward by Holliday (1994) and others who have pointed out the gap between western and developing world contexts, and consequently their respective educational beliefs and ideologies. But that is only one part of the story. There is – and this goes straight to one of the core themes of this paper – almost always a yawning chasm between strategic thinking and planning for educational change on the one hand, and what teachers and other education professionals actually do at classroom level on the other. This applies as much in the west as it does in any developing country.

Planning for and implementing educational change is difficult enough when it all takes place within the confines of a system in a given context, as we found out in the United Kingdom when the National Curriculum for schools was first introduced in 1988. It becomes doubly complicated when, as in many ELT projects around the world, a donor agency such as DfID (Department for International Development), the British Council, or the World Bank is involved. These agencies, whether they are 'gifters' or 'lenders' (Hunter 2009), always bring their own agenda and conditions to the planning table: there is usually no such sentiment as altruism at the apex of activity in a donor-recipient relationship, though it is (fortunately) often present in large measure in those involved in the detailed implementation of a project. Among the problems that this gives rise to are:

1. **The impulses for change.** Sometimes, donors' and recipients' priorities overlap or are even congruent. This happened to some extent in the post-1989 period in Central and Eastern Europe, when the political reform agendas at government level found resonance with the economic and political priorities of donor agencies. But this is not always the case and, in certain contexts, funding has not always been used as donor agencies have intended. There have been some well-documented instances, even in education and ELT, of acquiescence in the donor's agenda by recipient ministries simply as an expedient to obtain funding and to appropriate it for their own ends. However, DfID dealt a severe blow to ELT in the developing world in the nineties by redirecting its aid priorities to meeting the eight Millennium Development Goals, at the same time apparently failing to recognise the key role of English in working towards those goals.

2. **Conflicting time perspectives.** Wedell (op.cit.) and others have made the point that large-scale educational change requires a long-term view if it is to take root, anything from five years to a whole generation. Donor agencies, however, typically work to a limited time frame for projects, seldom more than four years from inception to exit. This would seem to lead to a view that it would be better for donors to limit their sponsorship to smaller-scale or local initiatives such as supporting training seminars in a particular district or seminars to teach teachers in a given context how to evaluate textbooks. However, probably for reasons related to impact, most aid agencies prefer to target larger-scale systemic change through their interventions.

3. **Value for money.** Feeding off an Anglo-American-led culture of accountability, many projects have been designed and implemented with a view to results and products that can be measured in quantitative terms at a given point in time. The dominant terminology in 'project-speak' still retains words such as 'outputs' and 'deliverables', as well as more familiar terms such as 'outcomes' and 'benefits' (see McIlwraith, this volume, for a discussion of these terms and their meanings in relation to each other). There is, as yet, no agreed way of assessing the value of 'process' in an educational project. Yet, from a recipient perspective, this is often where the value lies: projects can trigger dialogue among stakeholders, the revisiting of old problems, the uncovering of issues which need to be addressed, or fresh opportunities for professional development at different levels. If we take this just a step further, it is now recognised by at least some donor agencies that change itself is a process, rather than a measurable and time-bound outcome, which means that we should be looking at building provision for continuing change into projects, rather than seeking to quantify achievements in simplistic ways, for example by making absurd and ill-founded statements such as '2,500 teachers trained in implementation of the new

curriculum' (from a project report which fails to mention that all this training took place in one-day seminars which could do no more than scratch the surface of the in-depth training that would really have been needed).

4. **Top-heavy strategic planning.** Donor agencies need high-level clearance to get involved in initiatives at national level. This often leads to a majority of time spent in dialogue with education authorities and too little time in getting to know grass-roots views on matters relating to planned changes. Payback time in such cases usually comes later, when the planned changes trickle down to school and classroom level for implementation and teachers exercise their right to sabotage or ignore any aspect of the change they do not understand or agree with. However, without the political will from on high, a change project stands no chance of even passing first base, let alone succeeding.

5. **The role of local professionals and the cuckoos that arrive in their nests.** Local ELT professionals are often galvanised by the prospect of involvement in a project and by the arrival of an 'expert' appointed by the donor agency, especially if this offers the chance of a visit to the United Kingdom or another English-speaking country. In all too many instances, this initial enthusiasm declines pretty rapidly as the project comes to an end, the expert leaves, and funds for courses and visits run out. Zikri's account of ELT reform in Egypt (this volume) confirms how this can lead to 'short-termism' in the minds of both donor-appointed and local staff, and inevitably militates against sustainability.

6. **Those cuckoos.** UK donor-appointed project leaders are different in character these days from the ones who were active as trainers, Key English Language Teachers, and advisers in the last 30 years of the 20th century. At that time, these appointees were in post for the long haul and were deliberately embedded somewhere in the state education system of the recipient country. They were usually charged with the task of getting to know the system they were acting in from an insider perspective, and to this end they worked with counterparts who facilitated everything from ministry encounters to classroom observations. DfID's shift of policy away from ELT projects in the nineties to concentrate resources on key millennium goals such as poverty alleviation and equal opportunities for women had the unfortunate effect of sidelining a whole cadre of highly knowledgeable and versatile professionals with a history of involvement in project management, and ultimately led to a process of de-skilling in donor agencies, the effects of which are only now being felt. Many UK personnel charged with managing projects lack the kind of depth of perspective that was so valuable to their predecessors and it is usually left to local staff to compensate for this in both implementation and in follow-up. In some cases, this may even mean picking up the pieces. A further consequence has been a move towards outsourcing or buying-in of expertise on a consultancy basis, with mixed results in terms of achieving project objectives.

These issues form a kind of backcloth of experience to what is going on in projects today. There are, of course, some factors that remain current, either as areas of focus or as issues that affect success or failure in projects. In the following sections, I will attempt to pinpoint some of them and to highlight some examples of good practice.

Drivers of change and joined-up thinking

The four main points of entry for educational change are generally agreed to be the curriculum, methodology, textbooks and materials, and examinations. The most conservative of these areas, and at the same time the most powerful, is examinations. There is ample evidence from around the world that it is extremely difficult to push through change in any of the other three areas, if examination reform is neglected or even if it lags behind other changes. There is no real excuse for failing to take this into account at the design stage of an ELT project. Programme theory (Weiss 1997) offers a means of running a 'plausibility check' on objectives and expected outcomes, before time and expense are committed on the detail of implementation.

All the evidence in completed and current projects points to the need to synchronise efforts in all four areas, if a project is to succeed fully and have impact. The PKG project[1] in Indonesia in the eighties and nineties focused mainly on teaching methodology and was completely unconnected with the authorities responsible for curriculum, textbooks, and examinations (this from Brian Tomlinson, the project leader, in a personal communication, but see also Tomlinson 1990). Textbook reform projects in Russia, Romania, and Belarus, which I was involved in as lead consultant, all came up against heavily guarded interests, some of them in academia, in the areas of methodology and examinations, and also among local textbook authors. The laudably joined-up thinking that characterised ELTIP (English Language Teaching Improvement Project) in Bangladesh was frequently knocked back by often undeclared, but powerful, conservative influences in the areas of textbooks and examinations:

> *Although the project also wrote two influential course books (for grades 9 to 12), these and the revolution in methodology were, and are, doomed to slow progress without the reforms in national examinations. The oldest story in TEFL!*
> Former Project Team Leader, Bangladesh, in a personal communication

In textbook initiatives, there is often so much concentration on producing the materials themselves that the other dimensions can be overlooked:

> *Learners don't find our new books easy to use and teachers are also a bit confused. They are going to need training.* Belarusian textbook writer

> *The publishers have supplied the books but they haven't delivered on their promise to provide training. Teachers are just making the best of it.*
> School Director, Kurdistan Region of Iraq

In many systems, those responsible for these four main building blocks of change are in different departments of ministries and different locations, and an effort, as well as a directive from higher authority, is required to bring them all together in the same meeting to co-ordinate thinking and to reassure them about their roles in the change process. When this kind of co-ordination and joined-up thinking does

---

[1] Permantapan Kerja Guru: Strengthening the Work of Teachers

take place, it expedites all aspects of work towards success in a project. Achieving this requires leadership and commitment. An example of this can be found in the English Reform Project in Uzbekistan, which has addressed all aspects of teaching English and preparing English teachers in higher education institutions across the whole republic. This took time, and project managers were constantly listening to teachers:

> *Teachers can't focus on communication in their classes with these out-of-date textbooks. The new curriculum can't be put into practice without materials.*
> Senior English Teacher, Uzbekistan

As a result of this kind of input, the curriculum reform has now been underpinned by the provision of teaching and learning materials, the establishment of Professional Development Centres, the provision of training courses based on training packages produced within the project, and, significantly, an overhaul of assessment procedures. For an account of this, see Gulyamova and Isamukhamedova (forthcoming).

Good research as the foundation of successful change

Any change initiative needs to be founded on a clear understanding of the status quo and also of the reasons for undertaking the change. This is achieved through a research exercise commonly known as a baseline study. Good practice in baseline research (cf. Tribble 2000) takes into account a number of factors and perspectives which may (and probably will) turn out to be crucial to the success or failure of the change initiative. Wedell (op.cit.), for example, reports in-depth on an initiative in Eastern Europe in the nineties (designed to fast-track the initial training of teachers of English), which was rushed into place without the underpinning of a baseline study, and he goes on to describe the consequences. By contrast, the successful tertiary level ESP (English for Specific Purposes) Curriculum project in Ukraine in the 2000s was based on a thorough study carried out by a UK researcher in close co-operation with in-country project partners (British Council 2003). The new curriculum has been broadly welcomed in Ukrainian universities and is helping to drive up standards of English in undergraduate and graduate students across a range of discipline areas (Ministry of Education and Science of Ukraine 2005).

Data collection in baseline research for ELT projects may involve any or all of the following:

- interviews with and/or questionnaires to a range of primary and secondary stakeholders in the proposed change to gauge levels of interest in, attitudes to, and potential commitment to the proposed change

- classroom observation to gain a first-hand view of practices

- evaluation of teaching materials in use

- a critical review of existing curriculum documentation and examination practices

- sample institutional audits to assess staffing, resources, management structures, etc.

- collection of relevant statistical data on numbers of teachers, learners, etc., as well as on examination results and other relevant academic issues

- a study of key contextual issues that affect travel and communication such as availability of internet access and telephones, and accessibility of target locations.

The purpose of all of this is to establish where everyone and everything is at the start of the project and to assess the extent and potential impact of the change on people and institutions involved. On the basis of all of this, strategic planning of the project can commence with some degree of confidence. Baseline data also provides an essential basis for future evaluations, mid-term, end-of-project, and long-term impact evaluations. In short, there is no way around a thorough baseline study, if a change project is to have any chance of success.

The culture gap

Fullan describes 'reculturing' as the process by which 'teachers come to change their beliefs and habits' (2007: 25). In international ELT projects, the term takes on considerable additional dimensions. There is potential for intercultural dialogue and for degrees of misunderstanding not only in classroom practices and everything that underpins them, from societal and behavioural norms to authority structures, from values to language and the way terminology is used. Examples of this include the way in which terms like 'methodology' and 'syllabus' are understood differently in the West from the way they are understood in Eastern Europe, where methodology is seen as a serious academic discipline in its own right, and where there are no simple and easily understandable translations of 'syllabus' or 'curriculum'.

Reculturing manifests itself in ways as simple as the 'sorry, but that wouldn't work in my classroom' syndrome or as complex as a decision to terminate a project or close down a donor's operation in a particular country on the grounds of cultural incompatibility. What western agencies and consultants have been learning slowly and sometimes painfully over decades is that it pays to start off by getting to know the recipient culture intimately and in some depth, and to work with partners from where they are at the time the project is launched and not from where the donor consultants are or where the consultants want their partners to be. The kind of cultural dissonance manifested in this quotation, for example, has not been uncommon in the Russian Federation in recent years:

> We manage to forget, to cut off, the best things ever existing in our system of education and adopt the worst things from the West. (Russian Professor of Education, speaking at a conference on methodology and textbooks)

But it is not a new phenomenon, as this comment by Tomlinson in connection with the PKG project bears out:

The optimum classroom culture for foreign language learning might be at odds with the culture of the school and the culture of the society. This could lead to a conflict of values and objectives... (1990: 36)

The need to find a shared vision and an acceptable starting point applies at all levels, from the ministry to the classroom. It requires patience and sensitivity, but it allows donor and recipient partners to walk through the change process hand in hand, rather than resorting to the kind of pushing and pulling which only results in alienation. It works best where agencies such as the British Council (as in India) are prepared to commit key staff long-term to a particular context or project to allow them to become sufficiently immersed in the local cultural norms to earn their partners' respect and trust.

Change, then, as Handal and Lauvas (1987), Claxton (1989), and others have recognised, will never succeed, if it focuses simply on behaviour. Classroom teaching, textbook and curriculum writing, and examination procedures are in one very important sense a manifestation of the values, attitudes, beliefs, theories, and experience of those who design and deliver these behaviours and artefacts. This is the 'deep culture' of any educational system, and some of it goes back a long way in history, in some cases to medieval times and even beyond. If a change project does not penetrate into these deeper layers, it cannot succeed in the long term. It is also from these deeper layers that resistance to change emanates. Whether in learners, teachers, or managers, resistance is always a likely response, especially in the early stages of a change initiative and most frequently among the more experienced and long-serving members of a teaching community. If the proposed changes seem to be imposed, rather than negotiated, and if they threaten or are incompatible with beliefs, values, status, or any other deep-seated factors in those involved, the change will be stalled and, in extreme cases, rejected outright. Sikes (1992) discusses this interestingly. But there is good news about resistance too. In my experience, in project after project, people use resistance as a strategy to gain time and make sense of the proposed change, often taking up the position of a devil's advocate in order to probe and understand more fully what the change is about and how it is likely to affect their lives. Gulyamova and Isamukhamedova put it very clearly in their reflections on lessons learnt through the English Reform Project in their own context:

Change is a long-term process. It does not happen in one day and it never ends. For example, in Uzbekistan some deep-rooted traditional practices mentioned at the beginning of the article still linger on. Bringing about change is a slow process and you have to be prepared to deal with resistance. (forthcoming, 2012)

Once they have satisfied themselves that they can live with what is proposed, they are often even more fully on board than early adopters who required no convincing from the outset. Doubters and resisters can be very valuable in pushing for modifications and rethinks in the process of change as it evolves, and if the project framework is flexible enough, this can create benefits for everyone involved.

Change is soluble and dilutable

When it works well, educational change might usefully be conceived of as a kind of soluble substance, capable of being absorbed into an existing system and becoming an integral part of it, at the level of both thinking and action. People involved in it become immersed in it to an extent that it no longer feels like an alien import but is seen as a valuable stimulus in their professional lives. This kind of process is also sometimes described as organic change. But change is also dilutable, as this 'earthquake' model shows:

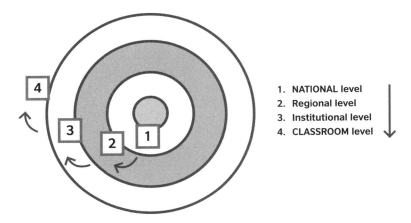

1. **NATIONAL level**
2. **Regional level**
3. **Institutional level**
4. **CLASSROOM level**

Figure 1: Change: The 'Earthquake' Model: Version 1

If the epicentre of change is located in a ministry or a national institution, that is where activity and momentum are likely to be strongest. If the structure of the project is based on dissemination or cascading from this centre of activity and on energy being transmitted through existing institutions at regional and sub-regional levels, there is every chance that change messages will be diluted and distorted by the time they reach the periphery of the earthquake zone (apologies for the mixed metaphors here). This has been a frequent criticism of cascade models. However, in some projects such as in the EWoW (English for the World of Work) project in Romania, activity and energy were generated initially at classroom level, with high levels of initial involvement of both teachers and learners, which in a very real sense put them at the epicentre of the project and thus reversed the flow in the 'earthquake' model:

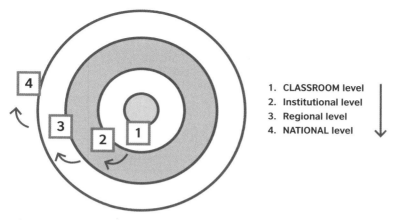

Figure 2: Change: The 'Earthquake' Model: Version 2

In cases like this, with noble bottom-up intentions, it is equally hard for good practice at classroom level to be disseminated as far as national level, where the impact might be heeded and lessons learnt. Dilution again! What we seem to have learnt – though it is not always evident in practice – is that we need to start change-oriented projects at both of these critical points, recognising stakeholder interests, and identifying and mobilising change agents at each level in a system. The major revision of the National Curriculum in the United Kingdom in the nineties gained much greater acceptance because there was wide consultation among teachers, who this time felt that they had had more of a say in its drafting and implementation. Examples of good practice in implementing the curriculum were subsequently recognised and highlighted in in-service training events across the country.

The real meaning of sustainability and capacity building

The need to build capacity and sustainability has long been a mantra in project design and implementation. But what kind of capacity and what form of sustainability? In the textbook projects of the 1990s and 2000s, local authors in Russia, Belarus, Romania (cf Popovici, this volume), and Uzbekistan were trained to produce contextually appropriate textbooks to match the demands of their respective curricula and to reduce dependency on products imported at considerable expense from British and American publishers. In each of these cases, some of the trained authors have continued to write, but also contribute to other projects as trainers or consultants. These are professionals who have found their voices and have shown a readiness to contribute to the longer-term development of ELT in their home contexts. In Uzbekistan, writers who produced training packages for in-service courses have gone on to be involved in testing and curriculum development projects, thereby making a major contribution to the development of ELT far beyond the brief they took on initially. This is the kind of capacity building that seems to make sense.

In the 1980s and 1990s, the notion of sustainability became associated with bricks and mortar and institutions, rather than just with people or ideas. This seems to have worked to some extent. On a recent visit to Sri Lanka, I was pleased to meet some resource centre co-ordinators who were able to report that their centres, set up under an aid project in the eighties and nineties, were still functioning effectively, in some cases despite the political unrest in their own region. These centres stand as change project products, and teachers in Sri Lanka still appreciate them.

A more modern view of sustainability is far less concrete but just as important. It is to do with sustaining those beliefs and values which underpin change and which recipient communities are asked to buy into when a project gets under way. These include a belief in the importance of change itself as a sustained and probably never-ending process in education, the same core value that underlies the contemporary notions of continuing professional development and lifelong learning in education professionals. This view probably needs to be part of the vision of project partners from the outset. It is about people, far more than concrete and clay.

Conclusions: What we have learnt about change

From the discussion above, it feels reasonable to offer a few conclusions about what can be learnt from previous experience in change management in the context of educational programmes and projects. I give these below as a list and hope that they will be, at best, useful and, at the very least, a starting point for further discussion.

1. Change is a process and not just a product. Change projects need to recognise this and to find ways of valuing and accounting for good process as well as outcomes. Part of an acknowledgement of this manifests itself through the degree of flexibility that is built into a project to accommodate evolving needs and priorities over the allotted timescale.

2. Projects targeting large-scale systemic change need to be seen as long-term undertakings. It may be better to see this kind of project as a means of kick-starting a change initiative, rather than seeing it through to a final conclusion.

3. A change project which starts without a baseline study and without a view of the planned change built on the baseline study is like a house built on sand – inevitably destined to collapse, and probably sooner rather than later.

4. Teachers are often the target of a change initiative, but they are also front-line change agents. They need to be involved in the project from the earliest possible stage and inspired to take ownership of the change.

5. Successful change projects are characterised by joined-up thinking between the key participants in the change process and by good communication both within the project and at the interface with all stakeholders with a legitimate interest in the change.

6. Donor consultants need to be ready to work on the terms of the recipient community rather than on their own terms and this implies immersing themselves in the realities on the ground in the host community.

7. Some of the routine lexicon of change projects, such as 'capacity building' and 'sustainability', needs to be re-examined and possibly redefined to take account of the way projects themselves are now being conceived and carried through.

8. As Fullan (2007) reminds us forcefully, change is all about people, and it stands or falls in direct relation to the impact it has on their lives. This is as true in ELT as it is in any other sector of education.

Planning for success: Culture, engagement and power in English language education innovation

David Hayes

Introduction

Developing proficiency in English amongst school students is of pressing concern to education ministries around the world. There is a general belief that success in English, beginning at the school level, is a key factor in national competitiveness and is of paramount importance to national economies in a globalised world. As an example, the 'Project Demand and Economic Analysis' for the Asian Development Bank 'Education for Knowledge Society Project' in Sri Lanka stated that:

> Given the major emphasis of the Project on improving English language and ICT skills, secondary and tertiary graduates will be more readily employable as their skills will more closely match labour demand in the private sector. (Asian Development Bank 2007: 51)

One of the 'Performance Targets/Indicators' was 'unemployment rates of educated youth reduced by 5 per cent from 2008 to 2012' (Asian Development Bank ibid.: 21). Similarly, in Thailand, the stated goal of the Ministry of Education is 'to build the capacity of Thai people to communicate in English language in order that they will be able to seek new knowledge by themselves and benefit their profession as well as international competitiveness' (Punthumasen 2007: 8).

These beliefs about the necessity for English are backed up by research which shows that, in some countries, proficiency in English, in the context of additive bilingualism, has been demonstrated to correlate positively with increased earning power for individuals (Posel and Casale 2011). Governments have, accordingly, made significant investments in programmes and projects[1] designed to improve the teaching and learning of English in state schools across the age range, with the focus usually being on implementing Learner-Centred Education (LCE) through Communicative Language Teaching (CLT) approaches. In many countries, however,

---

[1] For the purposes of this paper 'programmes' and 'projects' are synonymous. Though a programme is often conceptualised as of a larger scale than a project, there are enough instances of large-scale educational projects to render the distinction meaningless for most practical purposes.

these investments do not appear to have produced the changes to established patterns of classroom interaction to accord with new curriculum guidelines or to have raised student achievement as their funders intended (see, for example, Hu 2005 on China; Baker 2008 on Thailand; Kikuchi and Browne 2009 on Japan; Waters 2009 for a general review of innovation).

This effect – or lack of it – is not confined to innovations in English language education which prioritise LCE, as Waters and Vilches (2008) conclude for other subject areas of the Philippines Basic Education Curriculum, and Stronkhorst and van den Akker (2006) for science teaching in Swaziland. Similarly, reviewing 72 studies of the implementation of LCE in various curriculum areas which appeared in the International Journal of Educational Development, Schweisfurth (2011: 419) noted that 'the history of the implementation of LCE in different contexts is riddled with stories of failures grand and small'.

What lies behind this consistent pattern of failure? Schweisfurth (2011) identifies a number of barriers to implementation of LCE in general which can be applied to CLT in particular. First, the nature of the change expected is too great and the speed at which it is required to happen is too rapid. CLT/LCE is seen to be particularly demanding 'because of the profound shifts required in teacher-learner power relations, and due to the nature of teacher professional learning' (ibid.: 421), which is shaped by prior learning experience as well as sociocultural context. Secondly, in many countries, the resources to support innovation – school infrastructure, class size, teaching-learning materials, and teacher capacity – are severely constrained. Thirdly, innovations based on imported pedagogy are often opposed to local cultural values in various ways, particularly the role expectations of 'teacher' and 'student', and there may be a corresponding resistance to innovations perceived as western. Fourthly, change is driven by people who do not have to implement it, either donor agencies external to the context or educational administrators and policy makers internal to it.

As policy tends not to 'reflect joined-up thinking which takes into consideration all parts of the education system' (ibid.: 423), teachers find themselves being instructed to use CLT/LCE in the classroom, while, for example, success in high-stakes examinations is still determined by 'learners' ability to reproduce fixed bodies of knowledge' (ibid.: 423). In circumstances where teachers are judged by their students' performance in such examinations, it is little wonder that 'traditional' teacher-centred, knowledge-focused pedagogic practices align with the examination imperatives to win out over the learner-centred, communicative approaches mandated by curriculum innovations. In the face of this evidence of continual failure, where does the interest – or obsession – with CLT/LCE come from and why does it persist?

The export of educational reforms

CLT is seen by some as part of the 'linguistic imperialism' of the west (Phillipson 1992; 2001). In English language education worldwide, there has been widespread criticism of the deference accorded to native speakers[2] of the language and intense debate about western ideological influences on pedagogy (see, for example, Canagarajah 1999; Holliday 2005; Kabel 2009).

Western English language educators are seen, wittingly or unwittingly, to collude with commercial publishing interests to export CLT around the globe. The enduring worldwide popularity of western teacher-training manuals such as Harmer's (2007) *The Practice of English Language Teaching*, now in its fourth edition, and the global sales of textbooks such as the *New Headway* series published by Oxford University Press or the New Interchange series published by Cambridge University Press bear witness to this process, as does the fact that some version of CLT and a learner-centred curriculum for English is to be seen in state education systems in most countries. For example, the Papua New Guinea Lower Secondary Syllabus for English states that:

> *English is a practical subject and teaching and learning must reflect this. Learning will be done through practical activities; students will learn by speaking and listening, creative thinking and doing. […] The English Syllabus uses a student-centred approach as a vehicle to guide and facilitate students' learning.* (Department of Education 2006: 6).

Advocates of the malign effects of linguistic imperialism would not be surprised to learn that the syllabus was developed with outside assistance, in this case 'with the support of the Australian Government through the Curriculum Reform Implementation project (CRIP)' (ibid.: iii), or that there has been criticism of the way in which curriculum development has been handled. A recent blog by the head of the Department of Economics at the University of Papua New Guinea comments:

> *When the Australian consultants came in with their PhDs and masters degrees and earning their K200,000 salary packages, the local curriculum officers were quite overwhelmed and did not feel confident to question or challenge them.*

> *CRIP consultants took advantage of this situation to push the project through quickly and soon started producing policy documents like the National Curriculum Statement and Assessment Policy, which they claimed were written 'by Papua New Guineans for Papua New Guineans'.*

> *But it didn't ring true.*

> *From what I saw, the new OBE [Outcomes-based Education] curriculum documents seemed to be largely drafted by the Australian consultants with token input from subject advisory committees, then rubber stamped by Curriculum Unit, and printed with everybody's names inside to make it look like they were written by the Papua New Guineans.*

> *But they weren't. I know because I was there.* (Kora 2011)

---

[2] I acknowledge the contested nature of this term but retain it here, as it is still the most widely used in the literature.

Papua New Guinea is not alone in feeling that outside 'experts' do not pay sufficient attention either to stakeholders or to the context in which reforms have to be implemented. Gu (2005) analyses the experience of British Council projects advocating the use of CLT in Chinese universities and comments that:

As Chinese teachers saw it, what British specialists were lacking were cross-cultural adaptability and an understanding of the Chinese educational context.
(Gu ibid.: 292)

An understanding of the importance of context to educational innovation is also lacking in another of the major stimuli to educational innovation across the globe: the increasing attention paid to international comparisons of educational achievement. When one's own education system is deemed to be deficient in some way, it is perhaps natural to look to other, apparently more successful countries to determine the reasons for their success and to generalise from this to one's own context. The Programme for International Student Assessment (PISA) rankings have led many people to look to Finland, for example, which has had great success in these rankings, to uncover the underlying reasons for their accomplishments. Burridge (2010) reports that more than 100 delegations from other countries visited Helsinki in 2009 in order to find out the secrets of Finnish success in education. However, though there may indeed be something to be learnt from others' experience, the attempt simply to transfer 'best practice' in education from one country to another is a cause of failure in much innovation.

Any conclusions about what may be best practice in English language (or any other) educational innovation need to be framed within the constraints and opportunities of the context(s) in which the innovation is to be implemented, as well as within an understanding of the sociocultural and historical context of the system from which the innovative practices derive. In his discussion of 'the Finnish miracle of PISA', Simola (2005) focuses on these dimensions and cautions against 'comparative educational studies [being] turned into a political tool for creating educational policy or a mode of governance, rather than remaining in the realm of intellectual inquiry' (op.cit.: 456). He sees Finnish achievement as being the result of a whole complex of factors viewed in sociological and historical perspective, citing Välijärvi, Linnakylä, Kupari, Reinikainen, and Arffman (2002):

Finland's high achievement seems to be attributable to a whole network of interrelated factors, in which students' own areas of interest and leisure activities, the learning opportunities provided by schools, parental support and involvement as well as social and cultural contexts of learning and of the entire education system combine with each other. (op.cit.: 456)

In contrast to this situated understanding of educational achievement, Walker and Dimmock (2000: 157) note that 'there appears to be a naïve belief among many policy makers and practitioners that policies and practices designed in one context can be unproblematically transported elsewhere'. As we have seen, experience in a number of non-western contexts with the implementation of western-derived CLT/LCE indicates that this kind of transfer is indeed often problematic, rather than being the panacea expected (Gu 2005; Holliday 2005). Does this mean, then, that innovation in English language education is something that education ministries should avoid or that nothing can be transferred successfully from other contexts to one's own?

What makes for successful innovation?

Clearly, abstaining from innovation is not an option for most countries and the pressure of being measured in international comparisons is unlikely to lessen. Technology is driving change in many aspects of the global economy, as well as in wider society. All education systems need to respond to these changes to ensure that the students they educate are as well-equipped as possible to assume productive roles in society, as well as to realise fully their individual human potential (OECD 2001). A critical examination of programmes and projects to determine the factors which are most likely to lead to change, when an innovation is designed and implemented, and those which are most likely to result in stasis is, therefore, essential to inform the decision-making process of those educational policy makers and administrators who seek to innovate. Analysis of a number of these key factors follows.

Owing to inevitable restrictions of space, I shall confine discussion to four issues in effective programme and project design and implementation, viz. (1) the systemic nature of innovation; (2) grass-roots stakeholder involvement; (3) adequate support during the process of implementation; and (4) power and leadership in managing innovation.

The systemic nature of innovation – the importance of 'joined-up thinking'
As we have seen from Schweisfurth (2011), policy tends to ignore the fact that reform in one area has an impact on other areas of the system – there is no 'joined-up thinking'. To illustrate the importance of joined-up thinking, Hayes (2007) points out how a proposed policy change to the grade level at which English was to be introduced in Vietnam would reverberate across the whole grade spectrum and would also affect areas as diverse as teacher staffing levels, both pre-service and in-service teacher training, and curriculum and materials. Further, there are associated financial implications for the government, which must make additional resources available to accommodate the proposed changes. Hayes (2007: 50-51) comments:

> Changes are, however, not just necessary in the new grade levels in which English is introduced but throughout the entire system, as earlier introduction of a subject inevitably requires adjustment to the curriculum and materials in all subsequent grades. The follow-on implications of a decision to teach English earlier in the school cycle are profound. Once a decision has been made, then, to teach a language to primary school children, if failure as identified by Graddol (i.e. that children could be deterred from language learning in future years) is to be avoided, all manner of other factors come into play which are common to systemic educational reform for any subject area in the curriculum. These are, primarily:

- *ensuring that there are adequate numbers of teachers to teach the subject to the particular grades*

- *ensuring that these teachers are well trained for the task*

- *ensuring that instructional time is available in the curriculum for the teaching of the subject*

- *ensuring that curriculum materials and teaching-learning approaches are appropriate to the age group*

- *ensuring that adequate time has been allowed for the preparation of new curriculum materials*

- *ensuring that appropriate and timely in-service training is given to teachers in the use of the materials and teaching-learning approaches*

- *ensuring that adequate in-school advisory support is available to teachers as they implement the curriculum*

- *ensuring that appropriate evaluation procedures are in place to evaluate the effectiveness of the innovation*

- *ensuring that adequate material and financial resources are available to implement all of the above*

- *and, of course, ensuring that necessary adjustments are made to the curriculum and materials for all subsequent grades, and that teachers are given training to introduce them to these changes in the higher grades.*

The widening circles of impact from a change to the grade level at which a subject is first taught affect the entire school curriculum, as the factor 'ensuring that instructional time is available in the curriculum for the teaching of the subject' cannot be treated in isolation. If, for example, English is introduced as a compulsory subject at earlier grades, where does the time come from? Are other subjects to be given less time (at the risk of alienating teachers and others with an investment in those subjects) or is the school day to be extended (with all kinds of implications for schools and for parents who must accommodate the extension in their own personal and professional lives)?

In another example of widening impact, even where individual teachers do manage to overcome the cultural change factors which Schweisfurth (2011) identifies as contributing to failure, they may encounter resistance from other teachers who feel that new pedagogical behaviour does not fit with local accepted school norms. Hayes (1996) illustrates this kind of impact with the example of a Thai teacher who was keen to put into practice the CLT approach she had learnt on training courses, but whose classes were criticised by her colleagues for being too noisy, contrary to the local cultural norm of passive, obedient students listening intently as the teacher transmitted knowledge. The teacher spoke about her students and teaching in this way:

You know they're good students, very good, and they love me a lot. They like the way I taught them and they thought that English is easy when they study with me, and they can enjoy studying. But every time they study English, it's a problem, so they have to be very quiet. When I make a loud noise, when my students make a loud noise, when I come back to the staffroom ... I have to walk quietly. (Hayes ibid.: 181)

Here the teacher tries to remain true to her ideals, reinforced by the positive response from her students, but the reaction of her colleagues was such that, as Hayes (ibid.: 181) comments, 'after a "noisy" class she tried to make herself less noticeable by virtually tiptoeing into the staffroom'.

It is also surprising how often mismatches between mandated teaching-learning approaches and high-stakes examinations are cited as a cause of failure of pedagogical innovations. O'Donnell (2005: 305), for example, notes that for many teachers in Japan 'the main purpose for teaching English is to prepare students for university entrance examinations' and he concludes that the teachers he interviewed all believe:

...lasting change can only occur as entrance examination content changes along with the way teachers conceptualise how they can teach English. Teacher-participants argue that reform of the content of English university entrance examinations must occur in tandem with curricular reform, so that more teachers can be won over to the implementation of reform in their classrooms. (O'Donnell ibid.: 314)

Given that the importance of success in these examinations for students – and for teachers, who are judged by their students' success – is widely acknowledged in society, one wonders why educational administrators, who have themselves been through this very system, fail to see that reform of classroom pedagogy will not happen unless changes are made so that the examinations test students in a manner consistent with the way innovators propose that they should be taught. I share Wedell's (2009: 44) exasperation when he says, 'I find it difficult to understand how so many policy makers and their educational experts can remain so blind to their own educational cultures', of which high-stakes examinations are for many a very significant element.

The systemic nature of innovation: lessons from experience
The lesson to be drawn here is that those responsible for English language innovation must not think of it in isolation from other aspects of an education system, including the teaching and learning of other subjects. Innovators must take steps to ensure that their thinking is truly 'joined up', i.e.

- that they are aware of all the human and material resources required to implement the innovation

- that they understand its likely impact on the wider educational – particularly school – context into which it will be introduced, with respect to which evaluation needs to be an integral element of innovation design (see Kiely, this volume, for an extended discussion)

- that innovative pedagogy is in harmony with high-stakes examination procedures

- and that they have the necessary commitment of the people who are responsible for implementing the innovation at classroom level.

It is to this latter group – teachers – that we now turn our attention.

Grass-roots stakeholder involvement – the importance of listening to teachers

A cause of persistent failure in educational innovation is that it is driven by people who do not have to implement it (Schweisfurth 2011). Wedell remarks that:

> ...at national level educational-change policy makers and planners often seem able to delude themselves that it is not necessary to think about how the people affected by implementation will react to change, or about how the implementation process might be affected by the existing classroom conditions.
> (Wedell op.cit.: 45)

Yet, if 'educational change depends on what teachers do and think – it's as simple and complex as that' (Fullan and Stiegelbauer 1991: 117), then central to effective innovation is an appreciation of teachers' views of what will and will not work in their classrooms. Teachers are, as Murray and Christison (this volume) put it, 'the linchpins in the implementation process'. However, classroom teachers are rarely consulted about educational innovations when these are in the planning stages. Prapaisit de Segovia and Hardison (2009: 161) make this point for Thailand, noting that 'although the teachers played a major role in the reform, they were an untapped resource in the decision-making process'.

The practical outcome of this failure to consult those responsible for implementing innovations in the classroom can be observed in Hayes' (2010) case study of a teacher of English in north-east Thailand. The teacher spoke about the demands of trying to implement reforms with inadequate training or support:

> The Ministry of Education, I think they have a very good intention to develop or to reform education but people, people who are supposed to do their job, they don't have any motivation or knowledge to do it. Like when they said write your own material which is relevant to your students' needs, for example, how can they do that? Writing materials is not that easy, it's difficult. They need somebody to come and sit and help, look at their job and then give them advice. And then what the government does, they just bring teachers together and train [them] for one week for example. And some of the knowledge of the speaker is very high like that and the teachers' knowledge is like this low [makes gestures to illustrate the difference]. (Hayes ibid.: 313)

This teacher's experience can be seen as support for Canagrajah's (2002: 140) stance that 'this is perhaps the right moment to empower the local knowledge of teachers deriving from years of accumulated experience, wisdom, and intuitions about what works best for their students'. Yet the empowerment of local pedagogical knowledge runs counter, not just to much of the prescriptive advice on methods found in the ELT literature, which as we have noted influences curriculum and syllabus development worldwide, but is also inimical to the very nature of many educational systems, which are highly centralised. Schools are generally 'rule-steered', which, as Berg (2000: 198) explains,

> ...implies that street-level bureaucrats get directives, instructions, and/or orders from superior political levels within the organisation. In the extreme case, these instructions do not leave any actual scope for the street-level bureaucrats' own independent actions.

In rule-steered systems, school principals feel they have no leeway in implementing ministry directives and they direct their subordinates – teachers – to follow suit, rather than consulting them about the nature of the changes they are being asked to implement and feeding this information back to the central administration. This administrative style may guarantee public adherence to centralised reforms but does nothing to ensure that they are implemented in the more private world of the classroom.

Grass-roots involvement: lessons from experience
To call for the empowerment of local pedagogical knowledge may be swimming against the tide of centralised control of teachers' work, but research shows quite clearly that current centralising trends result in teachers feeling 'that they have little autonomy in their work, that they are constantly overloaded, and that they are not always able to meet the needs of their students as they would wish: in essence, that their sense of a professional self is under threat' (Hayes 2006: 160). This de-skilling of teachers, as Dadds (2001) concludes of experience in the United Kingdom, results in the sacrifice of learning for the teaching of prescribed coverage, which is paradoxical, given the espoused focus on LCE. Thus, if educational administrators and others who are responsible for educational reform are truly concerned about the effectiveness of what they propose and wish to heighten the chances of its being implemented in the classroom, it is essential that they listen to classroom teachers at every stage of the reform process. As Kiely (this volume) puts it, 'the key locus of innovation management [is] that of practice rather than policy'.

Adequate support during the process of implementation
As the teacher in Hayes' (2010) case study in section 3.2 lamented, education officials may have very good intentions but they often fail to appreciate the demands they are placing on teachers, when they ask them to innovate. O'Sullivan (2001: 111) reminds us that:

> The process of implementing change can be very deep, striking at the core of learned skills, philosophy, beliefs, and conceptions of education, and creating doubts about self-purpose, sense of competence, and self-concept.

The full extent of the demands placed upon teachers may not even be apparent until they begin to implement an innovation. This means that, even if teachers are consulted during the design and planning stage of an educational reform, they are still likely to need considerable support during the implementation phase, as they strive to incorporate the innovation into their existing patterns of classroom practice.

For many education systems, the implementation of an innovation is simply a matter of providing in-service courses to teachers to inform them about what they are required to do, often in a cascade model of training. We have known for almost 20 years that research shows investment in in-service teacher development can have an impact in raising the quality of schooling (Pennycuick 1993) but, unfortunately for educational administrators, there is not a simple one-to-one correspondence between an in-service course and improved classroom practice. There are all too many examples over the years of in-service courses having limited or no impact on the teachers involved, particularly in the long term (see, for example, Lamb 1996; Stronkhorst and van den Akker 2006). Cascade systems have also been criticised for offering diluted training the further one progresses down the cascade, though, where this has happened, the lack of take-up at grass-roots level may be as much a function of the lack of consultation with teachers by policy makers in the initial stages of curriculum (re)design as the cascade model itself (Gilpin 1997). Hayes (2000) feels that cascades can be made to work successfully provided, *inter alia*, that they operate with notions of professional development which go beyond top-down, skills-based training. His experience is that the most productive courses are those that adopt a reflexive approach *vis-à-vis* the curriculum innovation. In essence, this means that if, for example, an activity-based, learner-centred curriculum is to be introduced in schools, the training methods used on courses for both trainers and teachers should model this activity-based and learner-centred approach. Without such reflexivity, it is likely that teachers will see a divorce between their own training and the innovative practice they are being asked to implement in the classroom. In such a case, why should teachers have faith in the innovation itself?

Research also favours a cyclical programme of in-service courses for maximum effectiveness in the classroom. O'Sullivan's (2001) study of courses in Namibia revealed that teachers benefited from linked programmes of courses, with data from follow-up visits to appraise teacher behaviour in the classroom after one course then informing a subsequent course.

The Namibian experience is reinforced by qualitative research into in-service programmes from the perspective of teacher trainers. For example, in Hayes' (2004) study in Thailand, the trainers themselves expressed the view that teachers needed a regular programme of courses if there was to be any significant improvement in classroom practice. This kind of approach, with the opportunity to respond to teachers' needs at various points in a programme of courses, has great scope for showing how an innovation may be accommodated to the classroom realities which teachers face on a day-to-day basis as they implement change and which might otherwise militate against the change taking root.

O'Sullivan's (2001) study points to the importance of in-school follow-up for the success of teacher development courses. This is reinforced by a review of teacher professional development in Australia (Ingvarson, Meiers, and Beavis 2005: 9), which noted that many in-service programmes aimed to improve teachers' classroom skills, but it 'found that few participants actually received assistance and evaluation in their classrooms during the critical and difficult implementation phase when they were trying out new practices'. It concluded that:

> One of the most significant findings in this study across the 80 programmes was how rarely designers built in opportunities for feedback and coaching in the workplace, despite research on their centrality to learning new and complex skills.
> (Ingvarson et al. ibid.: 18)

One of the reasons for the lack of this type of coaching (or mentoring) is obviously the cost, both human and financial, but:

> ... money spread thinly, when it comes to professional development, is unlikely to produce significant change. Where significant change is sought, it may be wiser to involve fewer teachers than produce less significant change among many.
> (Ingvarson et al. ibid.: 17)

Whether a school system would want to be seen to promote such an inequitable practice is a moot point, given that, in many contexts, those most in need of the help – teachers in poor, under-resourced schools – would be the least likely to receive it.

Adequate support for implementation: lessons from experience
Developing supportive conditions and establishing professional learning communities amongst teachers in all schools – which can provide the right conditions for fostering opinion and coaching – are vital if innovations are to succeed across an educational system. Muijs and Lindsay (2008: 195) note that the literature 'has confirmed that where teachers are able to reflect, access new ideas, experiment, and share experiences within school cultures and where leaders encourage appropriate levels of challenge and support, there is greater potential for school and classroom improvement'. However, in research by Day, Stobart, Sammons, Kington, Gu, Smees and Mujtaba (2006), teachers commented that the time and opportunities they had to reflect on their own teaching and to share practice with their colleagues were insufficient. This indicates a mismatch between the forms of in-service development which are shown to be most effective and the time available to teachers to pursue them in their own school contexts. As Ingvarson et al. (ibid.: 17) note, it:

> ...is not enough to provide well-designed professional development programmes from outside the school. Policy makers and school administrators need to give equal attention to building the conditions that will enable schools to provide fertile ground for professional learning on an ongoing basis and as a routine part of the job. This study indicates that a substantial level of professional community is vital to significant change. The key ingredients here are time to think, analyse, and talk about the specifics of what is going on in classrooms and what students are doing and learning.

Thus, unless the 'considerable gap between the conditions that research indicates are optimal for professional development and those that are provided' (Ingvarson et al. ibid.) in schools worldwide is lessened, successful innovation is unlikely to occur.

Power and leadership in managing innovation

Innovation in English language education, like any other form of change, should be seen as a process, and one which needs to be managed (Wedell op.cit.). Initially, the power emanating from a Ministry of Education and other relevant authorities at provincial and district levels will secure at least surface acceptance of any innovation. However, much more is needed if an innovation is to persist and particularly if it is to alter classroom teaching and learning behaviours. Support from administrators for change, crucially at local as well as national level, and effective management of change at all levels of the educational system is vital (Wedell op.cit.). In this connection, O'Sullivan (2001: 113) found in her study that 'the least improved teachers worked in schools with ineffective principals who did not support the programme as effectively as principals elsewhere'.

In many countries teachers have expressed a great deal of concern about the nature and dynamics of their relationships with school principals. Typical of this, as noted above, is the experience of teachers in Thailand where 'rule-steered' school directors were heavily criticised for being remote from the classroom and autocratic in their decision-making processes (Hayes 2006). Yet, teachers in Hayes' study did not necessarily wish to see school principals' powers curtailed, perhaps as deference to authority was the norm in the context, but they expressed a specific desire to have them more involved in day-to-day teaching in a supportive fashion. The indications from the teachers' perspectives were that, too often, principals were more concerned with fulfilling administrative requirements than they were with the quality of classroom instruction in their schools and that this was something to be regretted. Moreover, teachers generally felt that their work was not appreciated. In this respect, teachers' experience in Thailand has much in common with the experience of teachers in other countries reported consistently over the years. In Malta, Farrugia (1986) found that teachers wanted to have their efforts appreciated by school principals; while Evans (1998), in a study of teachers in the United Kingdom, found that teachers were strongly motivated by recognition of their efforts and demotivated by lack of recognition. Murray and Christison (this volume) also emphasise the role of school leadership in managing innovation, exploring the skill sets required and noting the importance of building effective interpersonal relationships in support of change.

Power and leadership: lessons from experience

Teachers, as research has long since shown, favour effective leaders of schools who 'focused on active leadership, motivating staff, motivating students, reaching the community, and continually improving the school' (Fullan and Stiegelbauer 1991: 159). And, in contexts of educational reform, 'leadership demands include being responsible for the professional development of staff so that they may cope better with the complexity, dynamism, and unpredictability that are the keystones of change' (Bajunid 2000: 184). If, as we concluded above, the development of professional learning communities is a key factor in successful change, then, given the way in which schools are structured at present, principals have primary responsibility for the establishment of conditions conducive to teacher learning in collegial working environments which will assist in the implementation of educational innovations. We cannot assume, of course, that principals have the skill to do this by virtue of their position, and they too must be provided with effective support as they learn how to foster collegial environments and innovation in their schools.

Conclusion

All education systems must cope with change (Wedell op.cit.) and if innovations are to be successfully implemented, there are important lessons to be learnt from research into international practice. To draw together the conclusions from the discussion above, there are three critical areas which require focused attention.

Policy and resources

Educational innovation is not value- or culture-free but must be considered in relation to the context in which it is to be implemented. Sometimes, there is a failure to recognise how costly innovation can be and the resources needed to implement it successfully are underestimated. Often, too, the impact of an innovation in one area of the system on other areas is not fully thought through or the powerful effect of existing practice on the likelihood of an innovation being adopted is not adequately appreciated, particularly where there is a curriculum – testing mismatch. There are thus three key lessons for policy makers.

1. Innovation in English language education must be contextualised within a specific education system and the impact of an innovation on all other aspects of the system must be considered when it is being planned.

2. Particularly important is that pedagogical innovation must go hand in hand with parallel innovation in high-stakes testing.

3. Sufficient financial, material, and human resources must be available to implement the innovation.

Stakeholder engagement

No matter how sound an innovation might be theoretically, if it does not secure the wholehearted support of the people who have to transfer it from theory to practice in the classroom, the chances of successful implementation are very limited. The process of implementation is also long-term and support must be provided to teachers on a continuing basis and in a variety of ways as they come to terms with an innovation. Policy makers who are responsible for innovation must, therefore, consider three key points.

1. All innovations require the support of those primarily responsible for implementing them: classroom teachers. Teachers must be consulted – and their views respected – at all stages of the innovation process, from initial conception to implementation.

2. Adequate support must be provided at all stages of the innovation process, in the form of effective in-service training and in-school follow-up to training.

3. Developing professional learning communities amongst teachers is critical to school improvement; and time and opportunity for reflection on teaching and sharing practice are central to the development of such communities.

Management

Educational innovation is a process, rather than something which is accomplished simply through policy statements at ministry level, though these official policies are clearly a necessary element in that process. As such, any innovation needs to be managed actively throughout the various stages of its formulation, adoption, and classroom instantiation. What is often neglected in English language educational innovation, as with innovation in other curriculum areas, is that its managers require just as much support as they come to terms with an innovation as do the implementers in the classroom, the teachers. Once again, there are three key learning points for policy makers.

1. Power from ministries may secure surface acceptance of an innovation but is insufficient to guarantee change in classroom practice.

2. Effective management of an innovation at all levels of an education system is vital if it is to succeed; and school leadership is particularly important in a centralised system.

3. Just as teachers need adequate support at all stages of the innovation process, so too do those charged with managing change: educational administrators, in-service trainers, and school principals.

Understanding innovation in English language education: Contexts and issues

Denise E. Murray and MaryAnn Christison

Introduction

The terms 'innovation' and 'change' are mostly used interchangeably. However, as technical terms in educational policy and planning, they represent quite different concepts. In this context, change can be defined as 'predictable and inevitable, resulting in an alteration in the *status quo* but not necessarily in improvements', while innovation 'results from deliberate efforts that are perceived as new, that are intended to bring about improvements, and that have the potential for diffusion' (Stoller 2011: 37). For the purposes of this chapter, we will use the terms innovation and change in accordance with Stoller's definitions, understanding that the introduction of innovation brings about changes that need to be managed.

Innovation is a highly complex process, because different individuals and cultures have different attitudes towards and beliefs about innovation. Therefore, innovations that are successful in one context may have to be adapted (or even rejected) in another. Contexts for English language education vary across the globe and so policy development must be responsive to the local context. This study discusses innovation and change, details the various contexts for English language education around the world, and then examines issues common to all contexts, but whose responses need to be local.

Innovation and change

There has been extensive research done on the nature of innovation (see, for example, Dyer, Gregersen, and Christensen 2011). For innovation both to occur and to continue various local conditions are required. These relate to the organisational cultures that support it, the role of leadership, and the nature of the innovation itself. Each of these conditions is discussed below.

Organisational cultures and structures

Much of the work on organisational cultures and structures has been in relation to the business world, rather than education. However, some groundbreaking research in business has also been found applicable to education. One such piece of fundamental research is that of Kanter (1983), who identified organisational cultures that facilitate change and those that impede it: these are classed as segmental and integrative. Segmentalist cultures suffocate change, because they do not foster interaction across areas or encourage thinking outside the box; instead they view ideas and problems in isolation. In contrast, integrative cultures see issues as part of the whole and experiment with different ways of addressing them. Employees identify with the whole organisation, not just their own section.

Organisational cultures lead to specific organisational structures, so that segmentalist cultures have organisational structures that are *hierarchical or mechanistic* (Gibson, Ivancevich, Donnelly, and Konopaske 2009), with different departments and levels insulated from one another, with no interaction among them, except for reporting and instructions. Employees' tasks and positions are narrowly and strictly defined, so they do not think beyond their assigned tasks. Problems and issues are seen and attended to at a very segmental level. There is little, if any, communication between sections and so there is no exchange of ideas. Not only do segmentalist organisations fail to foster innovation, but their culture and organisational structures are threatened by change. Such organisations try to keep everything on course and to maintain the status quo, looking only to the past for ideas and solutions.

Integrative cultures, on the other hand, have organisational structures that use a team approach to problem solving (also known as organic organisational structures—see Gibson et al. ibid.), with teams consisting of people from different parts of the organisation who are chosen for their range of specialisations. Not only does this type of organisational culture lead to innovative approaches to dealing with issues, but it also allows the organisation to embrace and take charge of change.

In practice, the organisational cultures in English language teaching programmes (ELTPs) are variable and varied and dependent on context. For example, a successful ELTP may promote a segmentalist culture and a mechanistic organisational structure, while a sister programme in the same city may have success with an integrative culture and an organic organisational structure. It is also possible that a programme with a history as a segmentalist organisational culture may adopt characteristics of an integrative culture for the purposes of making specific changes that are perceived as distinguishing the programme from others. In many of those countries which Kachru (1986) has characterised as being in an 'Inner Circle', ELTPs have elements of both mechanistic and organic organisational structures with definite protocols in place for reporting and decision making, as well as considerable freedom among instructors in relation to change and innovation in their courses (for example, programmes that encourage action research projects among their teaching staff).

The role of leadership
Integrative organisations need leaders with a specific set of skills so that they can manage innovations (and change) effectively. 'First are "power skills" (also called *relational skills* (Fullan 2003) or *soft* skills (Christison and Murray 2009a) – skills in persuading others to invest information, support, and resources in new initiatives driven by an "entrepreneur"' (Kanter 1983: 35-36). Success as a leader is not only based on what one knows but also on how one interacts with others. These two components of leadership determine a leader's overall sphere of influence

(Donaldson, Marnik, Mackenzie, and Ackerman 2009). A leader's ability effectively to bring about change and innovation is dependent on the relationships cultivated both inside and outside of the school. 'Second is the ability to manage the problems associated with the greater use of teams and employee participation' (Kanter ibid. 36). Leaders need to be able to facilitate groups and support others as they learn how to facilitate their own teams and groups, as well as to confront conflict and build consensus. 'Third is an understanding of how change is designed and constructed in an organisation – how the microchanges introduced by individual innovators relate to macrochanges or strategic reorientations' (Kanter ibid.).

The skill sets needed for leaders who are managing innovation and change, and at the same time having to work to build school capacity, require forms of learning and experiences with leadership development that are not typical of leadership certification programmes and courses. Most leadership courses involve learning about leadership through lectures, readings, case studies, simulations, and role plays. Although these activities can certainly be valuable for leaders as they hone their skills, they are not sufficient for building leadership capacity for innovation and change. Leading for innovation requires that leaders learn skills for leadership on the job and by participating in real team meetings or in discussions among colleagues with differing points of view, resolving conflicts, or caring for and supporting others in the workplace.

The nature of innovation
Whether an innovation is adopted depends largely on people's perceptions of the innovation, whether or not they fall in what Stoller (2009) calls the 'zone of innovation'. She identifies the following parameters of this zone:

- compatibility: whether the innovation is sufficiently compatible with current practice

- complexity: whether the innovation is neither completely simple nor too complex

- explicitness: whether adopters are clear about exactly what the innovation involves

- flexibility: whether the innovation is sufficiently flexible for some variation in implementation to be possible

- originality: whether the innovation is not so novel that adopters do not understand it

- visibility: whether the innovation will increase the visibility of the organisation positively.

Therefore, policy makers, in trying to implement innovations to educational practice, need to examine their own specific contexts to determine whether the conditions for innovation uptake and diffusion are present. Is the organisation integrative? Does it have leadership with the appropriate skills? Is the innovation within the zone of innovation?

Contexts for ELT innovation

Quirk (1988) posited three types of language spread: demographic, econocultural, and imperial. Demographic spread is the result of the migration of people to new areas, while the econocultural spread results from the language used for high culture (for example, French in previous centuries) or technology (for example, English as the medium of information technology). The imperial model refers to the introduction of a new language through political domination. Although the demographic model requires the movement of large numbers of people, the imperial model does not necessarily. Usually just sufficient people for administration of the colony settle, but the language of administration, education, and law is that of the coloniser.

The spread of English during the British colonial period and, subsequently, the economic and political dominance of the United States, also an English-speaking country, have resulted in English being used across the globe. Kachru (op.cit.) was the first to articulate the linguistic features and consequence of this spread, developing a model of three concentric circles of English use: an Inner Circle, an Outer Circle, and an Expanding Circle. The Inner Circle comprises countries where English is the dominant language, such as Australia, while the Outer Circle includes countries where English is one of several functional languages, such as Singapore. The Expanding Circle comprises countries where English is taught as a foreign language, such as China. The differentiation between Outer and Expanding Circles has been that, in the former, English is used in intranational domains; whereas, in the Expanding Circle, it is used in international domains (Lowenberg 2002).

Since Kachru's seminal work, however, the landscape of English use worldwide has changed considerably. For example, the distinction between 'second language' (L2) and 'foreign language' use has less contemporary relevance than it formerly had. There is much more use of English nowadays in some countries of the Expanding Circle, where it is only a foreign language (as in Scandinavia and the Netherlands), than in some of the Outer Circle, where it has traditionally held a special place (Crystal 1997: 56).

Further, for many Outer Circle users, English is their primary language. For example, in India, many families use English in the home, as well as in education or government. Similarly, the distinction between Outer and Expanding Circles is blurring, because many countries in the Expanding Circle are teaching bilingually or even teach subject areas in English in high school, as is the case in Germany. In addition, the model does not account for the complexities of language use in immigrant countries such as Australia or the United States, or in multilingual countries such as Malaysia or India with their code-switching, pidgins, and creoles.

English now plays a critical role in many domains of international communication, communication in which non-native speakers now outnumber native speakers three to one. In 1997, Graddol listed 12 domains:

■ working language of international organisations and conferences

■ scientific publications

- international banking, economic affairs, and trade

- advertising for global brands

- audio-visual cultural products

- international tourism

- tertiary education

- international safety

- international law

- relay language in interpretation and translation

- technology transfer

- internet communication (Graddol 1997: 8).

Additionally, it plays a major role *intra*nationally, not only in Inner and Outer Circle countries, but in Expanding Circle countries where people listen to popular music, watch TV, or see and hear advertising in English. Thus, we see the move from imperial to econocultural spread. 'It takes military power to establish an international language, but it takes economic power to maintain and expand it' (Yano 2001: 21).

English language education, therefore, has to respond to these different contexts and different uses and varieties of English. For the purposes of this study, we will use Kachru's three circles to describe the overarching different contexts, realising that within each of these circles are different contexts and the circles themselves are permeable and fluid.

Issues in ELT innovation

A number of issues in ELT cross contexts. Here, we identify these issues and describe how they vary across the differing contexts of Kachru's circles. We limit these issues to (1) teacher knowledge and beliefs, (2) the quality and content of teacher education programmes, (3) print, multimedia, and teacher-developed materials, and (4) public and political perceptions of language teaching.

Teacher knowledge and beliefs

Research has shown that teacher knowledge and beliefs are critical to shaping instruction and, therefore, have an impact on student performance (Kennedy 1991; Richards and Lockhart 1994; Freeman and Johnson 1998; Farrell 2004; Borg 2006). The knowledge that teachers have and the beliefs they hold about teaching and learning can affect their abilities to adopt innovative approaches to instruction. Teacher perspectives are crucial in developing policies, because the best policies and practices will only be effective if they are implemented, and teachers are the linchpins in the implementation process. Innovation in fact often requires a reculturing on the part of teachers (Fullan 2007; Wedell this volume).

The Organization for Economic Cooperation and Development (OECD) surveyed more than 70,000 middle-school teachers and leaders in 23 countries, representing a workforce of two million teachers, in order to provide comparative insights on teaching and learning (Schleicher 2009). Although the OECD survey was not specifically focused on English language teaching, the results of state school teacher perceptions in these international contexts can provide important insights into the challenges that teachers face in teaching and learning, and can be instrumental in promoting policies that can make teaching more effective.

The comparative results of teacher perceptions in the OECD study targeted four distinct areas for change: professional development, teacher evaluation and opinion, teaching practice, and school leadership. In each of the targeted areas, teachers' perceptions of how teaching and learning could be improved were consistent with the six parameters outlined in Stoller's zone of innovation. For example, one-half of the respondents reported that the most common obstacle that kept them from participating in professional development was conflict with their work assignment. This suggests that professional development activities are often inflexible, with little or no variation possible in implementation.

Teacher perceptions suggest that if more teachers are to become involved in professional development opportunities aimed at making change, the offerings need to be more flexible. In addition, relatively few teachers participate in collaborative research projects and qualification programmes with a teaching appraisal component, even though teachers acknowledge that both of these professional development activities are among the most beneficial in terms of making changes in their practice. The highest participation rates for professional development are in professional development activities with which teachers are the most familiar, even though teachers consider these activities to be the least effective. In the examples provided from the OECD data, the teachers stated they would select familiar professional development activities over novel ones, even though they believed the familiar ones to be the least effective and the novel ones to be the most effective. Two parameters in Stoller's zone of innovation may provide explanations for these perceptions, namely the parameter of compatibility— whether the innovation is sufficiently compatible with current practice—and that of originality – whether the innovation is so novel that adopters do not understand it. Throughout the OECD data are examples of teacher perceptions that suggest state school education could benefit from considering change within the framework of a zone of innovation.

Teacher language awareness

Knowledge of and about language and about how languages are learnt is necessary to teach language learners effectively in both language and mainstream classes (Fillmore and Snow 2000; Andrews 2003). Knowledge of language can be characterised in terms of level of language proficiency, while knowledge about language refers to understanding language systems, and knowledge about how languages are learnt refers to how to manage language learning in a classroom environment (i.e. pedagogical knowledge) (Edge 1988; Andrews ibid.). Each of these three areas of knowledge plays a critical role in ELT innovation and should be borne in mind by policy makers who are considering introducing innovations in English language education.

Level of English proficiency

The level of teacher proficiency in English is a critical issue around the globe; however, the nature of the issue varies among the three Kachru circles. Often the issue is exacerbated by (or even caused by) government or local policy that attempts an innovation without a full understanding of its implications. In the Expanding Circle, many countries are moving towards beginning English language instruction at earlier and earlier grades of schooling, but primary teachers are trained as instructors in their country's medium of instruction (MOI). These teachers may or may not have acquired communicative skills in English or the specific skills associated with academic English; consequently, they may be unable to provide effective language input for their learners (see Simpson in this volume). In Outer Circle countries, by contrast, teachers may use the local variety of English, whereas the Ministry of Education requires that teachers use Standard British English or Standard American English as the target language. In Inner Circle countries with large immigrant populations, there is often resistance on the part of administrators to employ non-native English speakers as teachers, even if they have advanced proficiency and high levels of pedagogical expertise, despite research having shown that non-native speaking English teachers provide additional strengths to the language classroom – as role models and mentors for their students (Amin 2001; Ellis 2002). These employment practices are based on the naïve assumption that native speakers of a language are automatically better teachers of that language and often on ethnocentric attitudes towards non-native speakers. Additionally, in Inner Circle countries, primary teachers are often native speakers of English with little or no language learning experience. As such, they are usually proficient speakers of English but possess little knowledge about language systems and so are unable to help their non-native English speakers develop their English skills.

Knowledge about language

Teachers need to develop expertise about language in order to understand their roles as teachers of English language learners (Wright 2002). Being a native speaker of a language (i.e. a proficient user of the language) does not inherently qualify someone to be a teacher of that language. This area of teacher language awareness encompasses teachers' knowledge about the forms and functions of language systems with specific focus on syntax, morphology, phonology, pragmatics, and semantics. Teachers need to develop high levels of metalanguage – language that is used to talk about and analyse language – to be conscious of their own linguistics processes, as well as of the linguistic processes of language learners. In many Inner Circle countries, teachers may have high levels of language proficiency but low levels of knowledge about language. This is also the case in Outer and Expanding Circle countries that employ native speakers without training. In countries in the Outer and Expanding Circles, teachers may have knowledge about language but may struggle with high levels of language proficiency.

Pedagogical expertise

In Expanding and Outer Circle countries, individuals who can speak English often fill positions as English teachers, even though these individuals may have no pedagogical expertise or no specific training as English language teachers. Language teaching organisations and institutions often provide in-service training for untrained teachers, with varying degrees of success, believing that it is easier to develop pedagogical expertise, rather than language proficiency. The practice of employing untrained teachers suggests a view of pedagogical expertise that is rooted in learning as a 'discrete set of behaviours, routines, or scripts' (Freeman and Johnson op.cit.: 399) that can be easily acquired, rather than in a view of teaching in which teachers use their knowledge about teaching and classrooms and the processes involved in teaching to develop pedagogical expertise. The latter views the development of pedagogical expertise as a sophisticated and complex endeavour that is cognitive in nature and develops from one's practice.

In Inner Circle countries, mainstream teachers are responsible for educating English language learners (ELLs) at primary and secondary level; however, these mainstream teachers may lack the pedagogical expertise necessary to do so effectively, so that the result is negative student outcomes such as lack of class participation and low scores on measures of academic achievement (Harper and de Jong 2009). Historically, state school systems have not made investing in professional development to improve teacher preparation for ELLs a priority (Fillmore and Snow 2000); consequently, pedagogical expertise among mainstream teachers as it relates to language learners is often quite low. Similarly, at the college level, lecturers have classes that include both international students and immigrants for whom English is not their primary language. Yet discipline staff lack the knowledge of how best to help these students, often resorting to an 'error correction' approach that focuses on surface grammar, rather than on discourse and organisation (Christison 2011).

Subject matter expertise

The integration of language and content in second and foreign language teaching has become an important curricular trend in Inner, Outer, and Expanding Circle countries, and it has created some challenges for teachers as it relates to subject matter expertise. Academic subjects can be taught through the medium of a language that is being learnt. The reverse can also be the case in contexts where English is taught by studying academic content (Graddol op.cit.). Because few English language teachers are experts in both academic content and language, teaching English by studying academic content often proves difficult. When English is taught through academic content, it requires that teachers either develop subject matter expertise in the content area or collaborate with content area teachers. Both of these approaches require changes in schools and in relationships within schools. In Outer and Expanding Circle countries, particularly in institutions of higher education, many lecturers are finding it necessary to deliver all or portions of their lectures in English, because much of the commercially available material and the research is available in English. Although these teachers and lecturers have subject matter expertise in the country's medium of education (MoE), they may struggle with the delivery of subject matter in English.

Attitudes of content teachers to being responsible for language learning

Many mainstream teachers, particularly in primary and secondary school contexts in Inner Circle countries, define their roles as content area experts, not as language teachers (Mitchell and Hooper 1991). The refusal of mainstream teachers to see the dual nature of their roles as content and language teachers is problematic, because language learners in such contexts continue developing academic language skills for anywhere from five to ten years (Thomas and Collier 2002) and mainstream teachers are their main source of language support. In some cases, mainstream teachers may willingly assume the roles of both content and language teacher; however, they are most often underqualified to fulfil the role of language teacher (Short and Fitzsimmons 2007; Escamilla 2009). Integrating content and language in English language instruction has become an important curriculum trend in a number of countries in the Outer and Expanding Circles, particularly in Europe, where it is known as Content and Language Integrated Learning (CLIL). Subject matter and language are taught together; however, learners are not expected to have English language proficiency, so it is different from English-medium education. Because there is no agreement on how content and language integration should be implemented and no specific training or educational programme for teachers, the practice has evolved in many different ways, thereby, creating a situation relative to teacher qualification as exists in Inner Circle country primary and secondary school contexts.

Implications for policy makers

Policy makers, therefore, need to consider the language proficiency of the teachers in their particular context and how they can develop that proficiency to appropriate instructional levels, before they embark on innovations that are dependent on high levels of proficiency. Similarly, policy makers need to focus on the linguistic and pedagogical expertise of their teachers, ensuring that appropriate in-service is provided. Such in-service needs to consider teaching as a complex, continuing, cognitive activity and that teachers learn through reflective practice (Wallace 1994; Edge 2002; Whittaker in this volume). Because language and content areas are often intertwined, policy makers need to consider what organisational structures will best facilitate both language and content instruction. Traditional barriers across subject areas may have to be broken down.

The quality and content of teacher education programmes

In the previous section, we have focused on teachers. However, teacher education programmes play a critical role in the education of current and future teachers. Through their own instruction and attitudes towards instruction, they can model innovative practice and be incubators for innovation. Traditional teacher education programmes are often in organisations that are highly segmentalist, with little or no interaction across disciplinary boundaries. However, for innovation to occur in schools, teacher education programmes need to involve discipline staff in the content areas being taught in schools, as well as linguistics and applied linguistics staff, with their knowledge of language and language learning. This may require retooling and re-culturing (Fullan 2007) education staff so that they can work in new ways. Komorowska, in this volume, provides a case study of a programme designed to achieve this retooling and demonstrates the importance of context in implementing any innovation in ELT.

Pre-service programmes to develop new teachers with appropriate knowledge and understanding

It is incumbent on institutions of higher education to develop teacher education programmes that reflect current research on effective teacher preparation in order to respond to the changing needs of learners and society in the 21st century. In Inner Circle countries, practising primary and secondary school teachers need both academic subject matter expertise and teacher language awareness so that they can assume responsibility for adapting the curriculum. This view of teacher preparation stands in sharp contrast to traditional views of pre-service teacher preparation that focused on differences, rather than similarities, and led to separate teacher education programmes for different academic disciplines.

The development of pre-service teacher education programmes that are collaborative and interrelated is dependent on a complex set of institutional factors that are best addressed from a top-down rather than a bottom-up approach (for example, redesigning an existing pre-service teacher education programme to make it collaborative and interdisciplinary, as opposed to adding courses to already existing pre-service teacher education programmes to create an ESL endorsement). Similarly, in Outer and Expanding Circles, teacher education programmes are traditionally highly segmented. However, as governments insist on English language competence for students exiting their educational systems, all teaching staff become models of English and language instructors.

In-service programmes to develop current teachers' levels of expertise

In Inner Circle countries, the changing demographics have created a situation where most mainstream teachers have language learners in their classes. Many of these teachers have not developed the teacher language awareness needed to work effectively with language learners. For example, the state school ad hoc decision-making process in the US state school system for policy and planning places the focus on how to train in-service teachers quickly to work with language learners by giving them short workshops that are composed of toolbox-type strategies, rather than on an integrated educational programme derived from theory and research and on an understanding of what teachers need to know to provide effective instruction.

Coupled with this demand to train teachers as quickly as possible in ELL education is the misconception that L2 teaching is 'just good teaching' (Harper and de Jong op.cit.), a position that undermines the credibility of English language teacher expertise and contributes to misunderstandings about what teacher language awareness is.

In Outer and Expanding Circle countries, the need for English teachers exceeds the number of teachers available. Consequently, many ELTPs employ individuals with English language proficiency, but with no training or experience as teachers. While some programmes are willing to invest in teacher education, many programmes are not. Creating in-service teacher education programmes can be expensive, and the fear is that if teachers get training and become better qualified, they may end up leaving to work for another school or sector of education. The workshop approach to in-service teacher education in Outer and Expanding Circle countries is also prevalent and results in teachers who may be trained in the use of specific classroom strategies but not educated to make decisions about teaching on their own or to reflect on their practice in order to develop their professional expertise (see, for example, Hayes, in this volume).

Teacher educators' ability to convey innovative approaches

Challenging the *status quo* is often difficult for teacher educators, even in university-based teacher education programmes. This situation is true in Inner, Outer, and Expanding Circle countries. Teacher preparation must often be aligned with local agencies (for example, state standards and core curricula), school procedures, and approved materials. Further, because of the hierarchical nature of many university-based programmes, the *status quo* is preferred, and newer, younger staff with innovative ideas are marginalised. Primary and secondary school teachers are often worried about learners' performance in standardised exams and can be guilty of implementing a 'teaching to the test' curriculum. These constraints often make it difficult for teacher educators to use innovative approaches and to convince teachers to experiment with approaches in their teaching.

Implications for policy makers

Policy makers need to examine their own contexts to determine what changes are needed in their teacher education programmes in order to facilitate innovation in English language teaching. They need to apply the theories about innovation development, implementation, and diffusion to the teacher education programmes, turning them into learning organisations (Duke 2002; Zarins 2002) that are integrative, rather than segmental.

Print, multimedia, and teacher-developed materials

In the classroom teaching-learning enterprise, teachers, learners, and materials all play crucial roles. Materials fall into three categories: print, multimedia, and teacher-developed. The term 'print' refers to commercially available books, pamphlets, workbooks, and other paper-based and printed materials. Multimedia (also referred to as non-print materials) is an umbrella term that is used to refer to images, sound, video, and interactive content that can be accessed by using portable electronic devices such as computers in the classroom. The most common teacher-developed materials are paper-based handouts, overhead transparencies, and PowerPoint presentations.

One of the attractions of using materials in classroom learning is for teachers to be able to convey information quickly and effectively to all students and to keep them interested in learning. Resource-poor contexts occur in all three circles: in inner city and rural schools in Inner Circle countries, in rural and marginal community schools in Outer Circle countries, and throughout state schools in many developing countries in the Outer and Expanding Circles. While access to resources does not in itself improve education, there is evidence that it can have a positive effect on learning. For example, children's ownership of books or access to book lending has been shown to have a positive affect on behavioural, educational, and psychological outcomes (Reading is Fundamental 2011).

Difficulty of getting innovative ideas published

Commercially available English language teaching materials have a huge impact on the way in which English is taught, particularly as these materials are used by untrained teachers or by teachers who have low levels of English proficiency. Despite their influence, commercially available materials are not generally thought to be original or to represent the most recent thinking and research in language teaching methodology; and publishers are often resistant to new and innovative ideas, preferring to publish tried and tested ideas with modest variations. Because textbooks need to be profitable, publishers design their materials so they will have the broadest possible reach. Thus, the materials are often bland, general, and culturally neutral. They do not always provide learners with the models of discourse that they will encounter when interacting with other English speakers, whether they be native speakers or not. Additionally, materials may move too quickly for a particular teaching context or be at an inappropriate language level (see Simpson, in this volume) or the innovative materials are not carefully aligned with the textbook currently in use (see Woodward, in this volume).

Difficulty for teachers in devising supplementary materials

In Inner Circle contexts, teachers have English language learners in their classes with differing levels of language proficiency. Unless teachers are lucky enough to find multilevel texts, they are responsible for creating supplementary materials to support their learners.

In Outer and Expanding Circle countries, in institutions of higher education, many of the books for academic subjects are in English and often too difficult for the language learners; consequently, teachers must create supplementary materials in the form of additional readings, lecture notes, and PowerPoint slides to support their learners. However, teachers may not have the expertise or resources to develop adequate supplementary materials.

The dilemma of multimedia

Many countries are trying to find ways to improve education when they have limited funds and a limited number of trained teachers. Multimedia has therefore been proposed as a panacea by many companies and Ministries of Education. These proposals rest on assumptions that are not accurate. These assumptions are that multimedia can replace teachers, that it is cheaper than teachers, and so more efficient. However, only 30 per cent of the world's population is actually online (Internet World Stats 2011) and these statistics do not tell us the level of usage and understanding of the medium, which vary from negligible to expert. While there is a strong argument for including multimedia in instruction, because students will need it for their future work lives, its implementation in education is still in its infancy. Initial costs are high, and continuing maintenance and upgrading are also high. Therefore, with limited resources, institutions need to consider what is the best use of those resources.

Implications for policy makers

Policy makers have a clear stake in the materials that are used in their classrooms, because they reflect attitudes to and understandings of language and language learning. They need to consider both the external materials that are adopted for use in schools, the expertise teachers have in developing their own materials, and be judicious in their use of multimedia.

Public and political perceptions of language teaching

At the broadest level, language teaching across all three of Kachru's circles is largely misunderstood by the general public, and often by policy makers who are not language experts. All individuals, except for those with severe disabilities, learn a first language, seemingly seamlessly. Therefore, the non-language specialist public's perception of language and language learning is often misguided, and they propose simplistic remedies for the teaching of a second language such as English. For example, many countries have started the teaching of English early in the child's education, assuming that children learn languages easily. However, as we discussed earlier, while this may be the case in natural language settings, it is not the case in instructed settings, where the quality of instruction relies on the expertise of the teacher, as well as the motivation of the learners, a point made by Reilly in this volume when discussing the implementation of bilingual education for young learners in Spain. Other myths include the beliefs that the native English speaker is automatically a better teacher and that the only appropriate variety of English to learn is Standard British or Standard American English. Policy makers in many countries have adopted frameworks, methodologies, and materials developed in a different context but, as we discussed above, while such innovation may be adopted at national government levels, it will often be adapted or even rejected by teachers and local administrators because of local contexts (Rogers 2003; Adamson and Davison 2008).

Conclusion

While responding to change innovatively and also consciously innovating are critical to the improvement of English language teaching worldwide, innovation must be undertaken with a clear understanding of its nature and how the local context impacts the way the innovation will be adopted and diffused, as is illustrated by Zikri in this volume for an innovative project in Egypt. In understanding the nature of the particular innovation, policy makers and administrators need to ask whether the innovation lies within the zone of innovation discussed by Stoller (2009), illustrated in this volume by Simpson's report on the introduction of English-medium education in Rwanda and O'Donahue's project in Tamil Nadu to improve teacher confidence in using English in the classroom:

■ How compatible is the innovation with current practice?

■ Is the innovation too complex or too simple for adoption?

■ Are adopters clear about exactly what the innovation involves?

- Is the innovation sufficiently flexible for some variation in implementation to be possible?

- Is the innovation so novel that adopters do not understand it?

- Will the innovation increase the visibility of the organisation positively (or negatively)?

In examining the local context, policy makers need to consider teacher knowledge and beliefs, the quality and content of teacher education programmes, materials, and local perceptions about language and language learning. If ELT teachers worldwide in all three of Kachru's circles are actively to adopt innovative practices, they need to be supported with appropriate in-service education that develops their English language proficiency and their pedagogical and linguistic knowledge, and addresses their beliefs about language, language learning, and teaching. Further, policy makers need to view teaching as a complex, cognitive activity that teachers adopt and adapt through continuing reflective practice. Teachers need to be supported to adopt a current reflective approach to their practice. Policy makers need to ensure that organisations have permeable structures that allow for cross-disciplinary interaction. They need to invest in teacher education programmes that are integrative, model innovative practice, and promote innovation. They need to consider the external materials that are adopted for use in their schools, the expertise teachers have in developing their own materials, and be judicious in their use of multimedia.

Designing evaluation into change management processes

Richard Kiely

Introduction

The early 1990s were a seminal period for both innovation management and programme evaluation in English language teaching (ELT) projects. The work of two writers in particular captured key strands of changes in thinking: Adrian Holliday and Pauline Rea-Dickins.

Holliday, in a series of publications drawing on his experience of ELT projects and his Ph.D. research into change and innovation processes in ELT, articulated the importance of context, the notion of tissue rejection in projects, and the role of means analysis as an alternative to initial needs analysis in the process of managing change. For Holliday, a key requirement was analysis of the context – human, cultural, and socio-historical – to complement any technical specification of the change to be introduced as part of the project (Holliday 1992; 1994).

Rea-Dickins, like Holliday, an experienced ELT project consultant and evaluator, wrote a state-of-the-art article (1994), where she predicted a shift from evaluation as a management experience to evaluation as a learning and development strategy:

> In addition to focusing on the evaluation of quality processes in language teaching, there will be greater appreciation of the different role(s) of the evaluator(s), both internal and external, and of the relationships that hold between practitioners, sponsors, and other relevant stakeholders. If evaluation in ELT is to be effective, we will see a stronger integration of evaluation within practice, as part of an individual's professionalism, and an increase in collaborative activity where teachers (and other relevant participants) are actively engaged in the monitoring process. (Rea-Dickins ibid.: 84)

The 'stronger integration of evaluation within practice' indicates a key role for stakeholders. This has been developed in work with Dermot Murphy (Murphy and Rea-Dickins 1999) and with me (Kiely and Rea-Dickins 2005). The imperative here is to involve all participants, to analyse their stake, and to extend their capacity to determine the steps required for effective change and to take action to improve practice.

Together, these changes in orientation in the management of innovation in ELT signalled an engagement with process and complexity which established a pivotal role for programme evaluation processes. This article maps these changes over the subsequent two decades. The second section examines the challenges of outcomes-focused evaluations in ELT and discusses new quantitative strategies which hold promise for ELT projects. The third and fourth sections explore the ways in which the focus on context and the involvement of project stakeholders have changed evaluation designs and strategies. Their impact is linked to a range of other factors which have come to shape educational processes, such as engagement, investment, and culture change through intense experiences, where participants can envisage a different future for themselves. The fifth section considers different constructions of innovation in ELT and the sixth examines the changing interface between research and evaluation. The seventh section explores the implications of this discussion and outlines roles for three characterisations of evaluation which contribute to stakeholder involvement and the effective management of change. These, evaluation as project support, as quality assurance, and as practitioner research provide for a rigorous, context-sensitive strategy for designing evaluation into change management processes in ELT projects.

Evaluation and the measurement of impact

An ELT project is constructed around goals. The investment of resources is justified in terms of desired outcomes, and project activities are designed to achieve these goals. It seems reasonable, then, to consider project evaluation as a means of measuring these outcomes and assessing the impact of project activities. However, the realisation of this logic has proved problematic in our sector. Six factors in particular make the measurement of outcomes as a focus of project evaluation challenging.

1. In the evaluation of alternatives in social practice generally, the gold standard has long been comparative studies using rigorous experimental designs (Kiely and Rea-Dickins op.cit.). In foreign language education and ELT, the problem has always been the specification and control of the alternatives. In the Bangalore Project evaluation (Beretta and Davies 1985), for example, it was not clear how the task-based classrooms differed from the 'traditional' oral-situational classrooms; in the Hong Kong EELTS (Expatriate English Language Teacher Scheme) evaluation (Kiely and Rea-Dickins op.cit..), it was not clear how the teaching of the expatriate English teachers differed from the teaching of local English teachers. In the ELT field, the complexity of the activity, especially in the tangled mix of orthodoxy and context-driven diversity of teaching practices in the post-method age, defies easy resolution of the comparison problem.

2. The timing of measurement of outcomes is always problematic. In measuring increased language proficiency from a new English curriculum, a new teacher education initiative, or a new course book, it is reasonable to expect that this will not be evident in the short term. There may even be a reduction in learning gains as the innovative practice beds in. A measurement of attitudes may be achievable before outcomes in terms of practices or learning, but here too there

is likely to be a delay in achieving the full impact of the project. Many projects are funded for periods of one to five years. The case studies in this volume which reflect positive outcomes are those which look at impact over decades: the Polish Teacher Training Colleges project (see Komorowska, this volume) and the PROSPER (Project for Special Purpose English in Romania) project in Romania (see Bardi, this volume) show positive outcomes of English language teacher education and University English projects initiated two decades ago. Resources cannot be allocated, however, on the basis of positive outcomes a decade later: propriety in such spending quite reasonably expects evidence of value for money (VFM) at funding renewal points. Such outcomes-based, short-term evidence is not easy to access when the focus is on short-term outcomes (see, for example, the Egyptian CDP and the Paraná ELT case studies, Zikri and Palmer, this volume).

3. The actual measures to be used may be problematic. Where the project goal is improved language proficiency, the default measure is test results. This raises the question of which test type to use, an issue profiled in accounts of the Bangalore project (Prabhu 1987). In the Paraná ELT project, (see Palmer, this volume) the initial focus was on increasing the language proficiency of English teachers, to be measured by a Cambridge ESOL (English for speakers of other languages) test. Further engagement with the teachers showed that confidence and self-esteem, in relation to English language skills, were the key issues requiring change. These aspects of language use, however, may not be developed by test processes or evidenced by test results. Identifying measures for improved teaching is equally challenging: using features of the communicative orientation of language teaching (COLT) construct (Spada 1987) or measures of teacher talk and student talk is problematic, as these practices have value in qualitative rather than quantitative terms (Walsh 2002; 2006). The situation can be even more difficult: in situations such as the CBB (Council for Business with Britain) ELT project in Sri Lanka (see Dick, this volume), the focus of the project was more communicative teaching in schools and classrooms, but the course books and examinations remained unchanged, so that teachers were placed in a situation where they were expected both to innovate and to continue with existing practices. Our understanding of how English language classrooms work is still insufficiently theorised to facilitate the use of valid, convincing measures of success in learning or improved teaching practices in the evaluation of ELT projects.

4. ELT, as an activity, is subject to change from many directions. Therefore, a project designed and implemented to improve changes in teaching and learning is likely to coexist with other factors which constitute drivers for these changes. For example, in the last two decades, increased awareness of English language proficiency as an economic good and the growth of English language use in electronic contexts (media and communication) may be substantial contributors to increased English language proficiency among schoolchildren and students, independently of any project activities or inputs (Kennedy 2011). In the Spanish EBEP (Early Bilingual Education Project) project (see Reilly, this volume) and Azerbaijani ELTA (English Language Teachers' Association) project (see Leather,

this volume), the key successes of the projects may well be influenced by these factors from outside ELT. Of course, such convergence does not detract from the success of the project: it just creates a challenge for the effective measurement of the specific contribution of project activities and resources.

5. A significant challenge for the measurement of project success in terms of quantified outcomes is 'soft' impact, such as culture change, ownership of innovative pedagogies, and acceptance of learner-centring of the curriculum. Many ELT project case studies (for example, O'Donahue, Leather, Solly and Woodward, Whittaker, and Popovici in this volume) reference such phenomena as achievements. While such accounts may be valuable as indicators of project success before the 'harder' results are evident, they are challenging to incorporate into valid quantitative evaluation designs. The Egyptian CDP (curriculum development project) project (see Zikri, this volume) emphasises the centrality of such soft impact. This project was set up in the 1970s, when a focus on rational, technical measures was dominant. The problems of communication and local ownership limited the chances of success from the outset.

6. Finally, an evaluation which measured project outcomes and addressed challenges 1–5 above would be very expensive. It would require a specialist team, oriented to collection and construction of attitude, classroom interaction, and test data, possibly with involvement of an external assessment body. There would be limited contribution to management and development of project activities. There is a risk of practitioners – teachers, teacher educators, materials writers – feeling that the evaluation is focusing on issues and using terminology which is alienating, which was an issue in the Tunisian PRINCE (Projects in Controlled Environments) project (see McIlwraith, this volume). The question of whether project resources for evaluation should be used for external testing emerges as an issue in the CBB ELTP (English Language Teaching Programme) project in Sri Lanka (see Dick, this volume).

These are enduring challenges for traditional positivist experimental evaluations and explain why they have not had a major profile in ELT project evaluation since the 1980s. Two more recent approaches to the measurement of impact may present opportunities in our field. First, the realist approach to evaluation (Pawson and Tilley 1997), which takes a theoretical rather than probabilistic approach to understanding outcomes data, offers the possibility of determining the impact of specific interventions in complex contexts. The realist orientation is theoretical: through analysis of the chains of reasoning and volition which characterise the social world, measures of impact can be predicted and operationalised in terms of quantifiable data. Pawson and Tilley focus on mechanisms (M) and contexts (C), which generate outcomes (O), a framework which could, for example, be used to design a learning materials evaluation which theorised links between classroom processes and learning outcomes (Kiely and Rea-Dickins op.cit.: 46).

Secondly, multilevel modelling (MLM) (Thomas and Goldstein 2008; Rasbash, Steele, Browne, and Goldstein 2009) is a statistical process which allows for drilling down in statistical data on whole systems (national examination results, for example) to identify the factors which cause or contribute to success in certain school types and classroom contexts, and in relation to individual teacher and student characteristics. The Student Performance in National Examinations (SPINE) project, funded by DfID (Department for International Development) and ESRC (Economic and Social Research Council), and directed by Pauline Rea-Dickins (see Rea-Dickins, Khamis, and Olivero 2009; Rea-Dickins, Yu, and Afitska 2009), illustrates the potential of this strategy for project evaluations.

I am not aware of evaluation studies in ELT which used these approaches. A key factor here is the level of resource involved: realist and MLM designs are expensive, and the resource involved is a specific commitment to knowledge building and accountability, without any early or significant contribution to the development of the project. Both orient towards research, rather than the tradition of project evaluation which comments on impact (or early indicators of impact), while at the same time offering consultancy, professional development, and communication opportunities to the range of people brought together by a given project. It is this set of concerns and opportunities which have characterised developments in ELT project activity in the last two decades, notably in the work of Adrian Holliday and Pauline Rea-Dickins.

Tissue rejection and means analysis

The notion of 'tissue rejection' in Holliday's seminal article (1992) is based on the organ transplant metaphor, which sees systems as organic and coherent and with a capacity to reject any alien element which does not fit in with the ecology of the situation. Thus, innovations introduced by an ELT project risk being rejected either straight away or when special measures to maintain them are lessened or withdrawn, experiences well documented in the ELT project literature, for example, Holliday (1994), Hayes (1995), Bolitho (2005), and Kiely and Rea-Dickins (op.cit.). The case studies in this volume, for example Wedell on the Oman project, illustrate the reality of rejection when a project seeks to change the culture of schooling and teaching.

The metaphor is important in two ways. First, the existing system, though not functioning well, does not see itself as deficient in the way an external perspective might (see Zikri, this volume, as an example of such a perspective). Rather it sees itself as coherent and self-sustaining, and through a range of processes which Holliday labels 'informal orders', it achieves stability and a capacity to meet the diverse interests of people working in the system. Secondly, because the system has this form of operational stability, a change, in order to be effective, has to be implemented in a way which acknowledges the key features of the existing system and negotiates a way forward on this basis. Thus, the key process is not so much needs analysis (an objective perspective on what a context needs, based on available technologies and experience elsewhere and carried out at an early stage in a project) as a means analysis (a continuing process of negotiation which adapts both the specification of the innovation and the timeframe in which it is introduced).

The Holliday analysis draws on an explicitly sociological account of the nature of communities and organisations, and their inherent capacity to meet their members' social and material needs. It also addresses a range of perspectives on project evaluation in language education which portray the difficulties in implementing and evaluating a project as initially conceived. Tomlinson (1990), Coleman (1992) and Hayes (1995), for example, illustrate the forces of resistance which may be encountered by a project management perspective which seeks to implement faithfully the activities of the project as originally designed. More recently, Widin (2010), writing about ELT projects supported by the Australian government, describes the same process of 'tissue rejection' which Holliday analysed. The key issues on the surface are resistance and limited impact of changes introduced. Underlying these are issues of cultural appropriateness and ecological validity, that is, what can be made to work and sustained through ownership by professionals in the project context.

A stakeholder perspective

Rea-Dickins sees such project contexts as peopled spaces and identifies a key role for these people at all levels in the activities of the project. Her call for greater involvement of professional constituencies in such project evaluations reflects a stakeholder approach. This approach sees innovations as primarily changes in practices and holds that practitioners should have a voice in how practices operate and how changes in practice might be achieved. Her work draws on the characterisation of teacher-led curriculum evaluation of Stenhouse (1975), democratic evaluation set out by Macdonald (1976) and the CARE (Centre for Applied Research in Education) group of educational evaluators at UEA (University of East Anglia) (Kushner 1996; Norris 1998), as well as evaluators in the US context such as Weiss (1986) and Patton (2008).

The stakeholder approach has two key features. First, it establishes the key locus of innovation management and project evaluation as that of practice, rather than policy: the practicalities and possibilities of practice should inform policy development and lead the change process, rather than an exclusively top-down policy development process, where teachers and other practitioners are required to implement curriculum changes in which they have had no design role. The task in stakeholder evaluation is to document and extend practitioners' understanding of their work, a role clearly evidenced in all the case studies in this volume. Secondly, it acknowledges the power and authority ecology within project contexts. While senior policy makers may have the authority to determine what should be done, it is the practitioners who have the power either to make this happen or to subvert it. The PROSPER and SSA (Sharva Shiksha Abhiyan) case studies illustrate the benefits of building on the agency of teachers and trainers (see Bardi and O'Donahue, this volume). The Oman BA (bachelor of arts) and Korean INSET (in-service education and training) case studies provide insights into project contexts where there is a gap between policy maker and practitioner perspectives (see Wedell and Hayes, this volume).

The importance of people and their social relations in change management has been an important theme in the literature on ELT. Arnold and Sarhan (1994) emphasise such relationships in their analysis of how counterparting can be more effective in ELT projects. Bax (1995) emphasises 'content-negotiability' as a principle for managing change in teachers' work, thus highlighting the need for them personally to adapt innovative practices. Kiely and Rea-Dickins (op.cit.) and Kiely (2009) illustrate how important the social dimension of teachers' work is and how evaluation can be a context for structuring collaborative activity within programmes and schools. Palmer (this volume) emphasises the importance of 'emotional intelligence' in developing the Paraná ELT project, illustrating the need to build confidence and self-esteem as part of the development of project activities.

Stakeholder roles within projects are complex. A conventional view (for example Alderson and Scott 1992) divides stakeholders into project insiders and outsiders. Insiders can participate in project activities (including evaluation) in three ways: in planning, implementing, or benefiting. DfID defines stakeholders as 'intended beneficiaries and intermediaries, winners and losers, and those involved or excluded from decision-making processes' (DfID undated). These are further classified as primary and secondary stakeholders. The former are typically those closely involved with, and affected by, project activities. The latter are more remote stakeholders, for example, public sector authorities, bodies such as trade unions, professional associations, and businesses, and DfID. A further classification is 'key' stakeholders, who are those, either primary or secondary, who have the power to shape projects and determine the likelihood of success. This 'power' factor, which varies from context to context and may be difficult to predict at the outset, is a key element in discourses of stakeholding (Weiss op.cit.; Guba and Lincoln 1989; Murphy and Rea-Dickins op.cit.). In the Polish TTC (Teacher Training Colleges) project, for example, local authority figures who had been members of the Communist Party, and as such might not have supported the change in language teacher education, proved instead to be key enablers, by ensuring that educational institutes in their towns participated constructively in the project, and setting up and staffing colleges (see Komorowska, this volume). In the ELTA (English Language Teachers' Association) project, a teachers' association became a key stakeholder and contributed to the goals of the project through local ownership of curricular innovations and teaching resources. Where powerful local stakeholders engage with the project, the chances of success are enhanced (see Reilly, this volume, on the involvement of local inspectors in the EBP (Early Years Bilingual Project) in Spain; where they distance themselves or are excluded, achieving project goals is more difficult (see Zikri, this volume, on the limited involvement of university teachers in the Egyptian curriculum development project).

The Rea-Dickins and Holliday positions come together in focusing projects on the actual, rather than the ideal. They posit a theoretical answer to the problems encountered in designing and carrying out programme evaluations and in using these to understand key issues in project development and promoting change. They establish a coherence across the different levels in ELT project activity, in particular through linking the characteristics of the communicative classroom with the wider policy development process. Thus, as in the classroom, where effective learning results from engagement, agency, ownership, and investment of the students, which is supported by teachers, projects which aim to innovate in the contexts of teaching, teacher education, assessment, and materials development need to act to secure engagement, agency, ownership, and investment by the key stakeholders in these processes. Processes which are particularly important here are the evaluation activities such as listening, debating, negotiating, and building in ownership and use of evaluation findings as part of projects. These processes not only communicate an understanding of the changes proposed by the project, but also open up spaces for discussing these changes and their impact.

The nature of change and innovation

Our understanding of change processes has also developed over recent decades. As set out in Rogers (1983), Kennedy (1988) and Stoller (1994), an established approach to change management has been an analysis of the change-context relationship according to five parameters:

- net relative advantage over superceded policy/practice

- compatibility with existing values

- complexity [inversely related]

- trialability

- observability (Kennedy ibid.).

These constitute a basis for a needs analysis undertaken from a rational, external perspective. They provide a perspective on the likely success of the change and, thus, guidance as to the change management processes which might be beneficial. This assumes a top-down, somewhat industrial process, such as the research and development model outlined by White (1988), and locates processes of analysis at the planning stages, undertaken at the policy level by experts, rather than practitioners (see Hayes, Wedell, and Zikri, this volume). An additional perspective on this is provided by Kennedy (1999b) and Lamie (2004; 2005), who draw on the work of social psychologist Ajzen (1988) to examine the gaps between attitudes and behaviours (of teachers in particular) as the locus of problems in the management of change in ELT. Their analysis is based on the phenomenon that teachers on training courses commit to the new practices introduced but then on return to the workplace fail to implement these (see Wedell, this volume for a telling illustration of this). While this phenomenon can be labelled resistance, or lack of effort or commitment, a better explanation comes from understanding the complexity of such changed practice by teachers: they can only do what is possible for them, and as classroom practice is shaped by many factors, a new instructional technique introduced in isolation will not seem possible or useful.

Waters and Vilches (2001) provide a valuable overview of the complexity of change management processes in ELT. They identify eight areas at two levels where change is necessary. The foundation-building level is a starting point, and 'potential-realising level' represents what the project should achieve. Project activity is in four areas:

PROJECT ACTIVITY	1. Curriculum development	2. Teacher learning	3. Trainer training	4. ELT manager learning
POTENTIAL-REALISING LEVEL	MODERN	SCHOOL-BASED	METHODOLOGY	DEVOLUTION
FOUNDATION-BUILDING LEVEL	TRADITIONAL	COURSE-BASED	CONTENT	ORIENTATION

Table 1: Four areas of project activity (Adapted from Waters and Vilches 2001:140)

Waters and Vilches observe that conventional activity focuses on two of the eight cells: the 'modern' in curriculum development and 'course-based' activity in teacher learning. This is due in part to a belief in the superiority of communicative language teaching over traditional pedagogies and, in part, to a judgement of how widest impact might be achieved. The lack of attention to the other cells constitutes a persuasive analysis of why effective change within ELT projects has been less successful than anticipated and indicates ways in which an continuing means analysis might be structured for teachers and project leaders.

The weaknesses of established approaches to change management within ELT projects are the limited engagement with practitioners at the planning stage (see Zikri and Palmer, this volume), the assumption that experts' reasoning and strategies will address the challenges practitioners face in their work in classrooms and training rooms (see Wedell and Mathews, this volume), and the reliance on making teachers aware of new approaches through training courses (see Donahue, and Solly and Woodward, this volume). Where the project focus does not connect with teachers' perspectives, there may be perceived resistance or lack of investment by teachers, which may lead to limited impact in classrooms and on English language learning (Holliday 1992; 1994; Palmer 1993; Hayes 1995; Wedell 2011a).

More recently, change is seen as affecting all stakeholders and impacting differentially on them, according to their tasks and their understanding of these tasks and the resources they draw on in undertaking these tasks. This is particularly important in the key activity in ELT: classroom teaching. This is a social activity, where teachers perform their social identity (Block 2003; Richards 2006; Kiely 2008) in organising and managing learning activities for their students. They take into account:

1. the expectations and needs of the students

2. the assessment processes involved

3. the materials available

4. the experience and insights of the teacher which inform a view of what can work in that situation

5. and the training and guidelines provided for the teachers which frame a view of what should work.

Any proposed change must have what Prabhu (1990) labels 'a sense of plausibility' for teachers: it must be seen as possible, relevant, and likely to resolve the problems they experience and consider are important for them. Each teacher manages change in their own context, not so much in terms of implementation of the policy, but rather in terms of what is possible, appropriate, and desirable for them as individual professionals, and what is valued in the context. The notion of innovation at this level of practice is more complex than characterisations at policy levels. The change management process must reflect this, and project evaluation, as a set of enquiry and communication activities, can structure and guide the process. In Holliday's term, it is 'means analysis' which is particularly important. This cannot be undertaken at the planning stage, but rather it has to be carried out as the project is implemented and led by professional stakeholders such as teachers and teacher educators. This has implications for evaluation design.

Innovation, evaluation, and research

While there is an increasing literature on ELT innovation and programme evaluation, much activity is not documented or in the public domain. There are good reasons for this: ELT project activity (including evaluation) is a domain of practice, rather than research; many project reports to sponsors remain unpublished, and what is published is likely to represent bodies of practice which are successful and which participants are proud to document and disseminate. What is published tends to fall into four categories:

1. Books on management of change and programme evaluation in ELT which either draw on studies in one context (such as Lynch 1996; Markee 1997; Lamie 2005) or guidance for practice drawing on studies in a range of contexts (Rea-Dickins and Germaine 1992; Alderson and Beretta 1992; Kiely and Rea-Dickins 2005).

2. Research studies which provide focused, theoretically-informed accounts of project impact, drawing on extensive (and expensive) data sets and focusing on theoretical issues such as language learning interventions. The most celebrated programme evaluation of this kind is the Bangalore evaluation (Beretta and Davies 1985; Prabhu 1987), with the studies in Alderson and Beretta (1992) and Norris (2009) also reflecting this research focus.

3. Reflective articles by experienced professionals which draw on a range of experiences to analyse recurrent problems in managing innovation and carrying out programme evaluation, and identify solutions which might be taken up in new contexts and projects. The case studies in this volume are examples of such accounts.

4. Articles in the ELT Journal and professional newsletters in which ELT professionals describe innovative practices which they and colleagues have developed. A survey of such articles in the ELT Journal: Volumes 57 and 60 (2003 and 2006) (Kiely 2008) found such studies constituted programme evaluations which described both process and impact.

It is not the purpose of this paper to review all the strands of relevant knowledge building in these publications and the wider education, management, and development theories and frameworks on which they are based. Rather, it is to note that they constitute an account of the complexity of the activity we are focusing on and to recognise the plurality in knowledge building in our field. Four decades ago, it seemed that theoretical work in Applied Linguistics and Second Language Acquisition would lead policy and practice development in ELT. Now, most would agree these play a role, but as Ellis puts it, 'like any other body of technical knowledge, [SLA] can feed only indirectly into the practical knowledge that informs acts of teaching' (2009: 141-2). The themes set out by Holliday and Rea-Dickins constitute gateways to engaging with this 'practical knowledge'. Language programme evaluation as a varied basket of activity types provides a framework for articulating it, sharing it, and extending it. The next section outlines two ways in which evaluation can play this knowledge-brokering role in ELT programmes and projects.

Implications for evaluation design

The key theme in the discussion of ELT project evaluation so far is 'complexity'. Projects are themselves complex, often having pedagogic, managerial, cultural, political, and social dimensions which do not sit easily together or which do not all contribute towards project goals in a period of two or three years. To manage this complexity, the messages of Holliday and Rea-Dickins are fundamental:

1. understand the context and the informal orders, and complement any needs analyses or baselines with continuing means analysis

2. understand and involve stakeholders, and base strategies and activities on an analysis of their stakes.

The discussion in the preceding sections shows that there is a richness of possible designs for project evaluation. Three approaches to project evaluation are outlined here: evaluation as project support, evaluation as quality assurance, and evaluation as practitioner research. These contribute respectively to project management and development; project embedding in local systems and structures; and the building of knowledge relevant to project success, both local and in the wider field of ELT. In a given project, the best design is a situated, customised one, providing both guidance and opportunities for creativity, and autonomy for project leaders and participants.

Evaluation as project development support

The shortcomings of the one-off project evaluation study carried out as a consultancy or research study have been well-documented in the field: Bowers (1983); Greenwood (1985); Alderson (1992); Markee (1993); Tribble (2000); Elder (2009). The case studies in this volume all observe that continuity and continuing partnership are beneficial in achieving the desired impact of ELT projects. An alternative model is the building-in of a continuing developmental strand, so that the external contribution is part of the project, advocating for the success of the project activities, but also constitutes an analytic, critical voice which identifies both problems and solutions.

An example of this is the British Council Project Development and Support Scheme (PRODESS), which was established to provide such support for a range of initiatives in Eastern and Central Europe in the 1992–98 period. The context was the post-Soviet era, when a range of countries were looking west and rewiring their education systems. A major shift in policy was the establishing of English, instead of Russian, as the first foreign language. Projects included the development of pre-service language teacher education institutions and curricula, in-service programmes, including retraining of Russian teachers as English teachers, English language programmes for the university and primary school sectors, and materials and assessment renewal initiatives. The aims of PRODESS were the development of project evaluation skills and the capacity of project personnel, both local and expatriate, so that they could carry out a range of review activities for the effectiveness of the various activities (Kiely and Rea-Dickins 2005). A key theme was continuity, developed through visits, formative evaluation reports, continuing communication, colloquia and seminars, a newsletter which was published from 1993–98, and participation in regional seminars and conferences. The impact of the PRODESS initiative is evidenced by major evaluation studies such as that of PRINCE in Poland (a collaborative evaluation) (Rea-Dickins, Reid, and Karavas-Doukas 1996) (see Komorowska, this volume); and PROSPER in Romania (carried out solely by the project team) (Bardi, Chefneux, Comanetchi, and Magureanu 1999) (see Bardi, this volume); a range of studies published as conference proceedings, such as Melia (1998); and the English Language Teaching Contacts Scheme (ELTECS) set up by the British Council to maintain the project evaluation community of practice in the region and extend it further east, where educational reform and extension of English language teaching was taking place in the 2000s.

One driver of the PRODESS scheme was the perceived need to counter the negative impact of a perceived accountability focus in project evaluation. The perception of many in the sector, for example Alderson (1992), Coleman (1992), and Jacobson (1995), was that the need to be accountable in terms of the original outcomes and time frames involved exaggeration of successes and minimising of problems. This can lead to a lack of openness, which in turn limits dialogue, sharing of project concepts and values, and critical debates on what is possible and desirable, and why.

A core concept in PRODESS was the wide dissemination of core concepts of quality in ELT activities and use of such understandings by stakeholders at all levels in programmes and projects. Thus, the development of a pre-service English Language Teacher programme involved a construct of teacher education which was developed locally, rather than transplanted from outside, and built an understanding of this construct by programme leaders, teacher educators, mentors in schools, and teacher trainees themselves (see Komorowska, this volume). This feature of PRODESS demonstrates the transformative potential of evaluation activity, achieved through the dialogue initiated when stakeholders carry out evaluations and reflect on what they find.

Within a project support approach to evaluation, the audience for an evaluation report is primarily the local project team: it is a working document, a stimulus to debate and discussion in meetings where periodic reviews and planning are undertaken. This notion of externality in programme evaluation as the voice of a critical friend has continued in recent years. In contexts such as the evaluation programmes to introduce foreign language learning in primary schools in Ireland (Harris and Conway 2002) and year abroad studies in higher education language learning (Byram 2000; Saunders 2000), the role of the evaluator was an continuing one, participating in programme meetings and contributing as both advocate and sceptic. Tribble (2000), drawing in part on one of the projects supported by PRODESS, outlines one specific way in which professionals within the ELT context might play a stronger role in projects and project evaluation: they might manage baseline studies, so that it is this insider account which has an ecological validity and is a basis for project activity.

Evaluation as quality assurance (QA)

Project and programme evaluations have always had a quality enhancement and assurance function: their *raison d'être* is the improvement of learning experiences in language education. To this end, they have focused on what are generally acknowledged as the drivers of quality: the education and training of teachers, the development of effective assessment formats, learning materials and uses of technology, and classroom activities which promote and sustain English language learning. In the past, the focus has often been on quality control: adherence to some externally conceived and validated process, determined through a rigorous inspection process. Measures of learning outcomes – tests – still have an important role in quality assurance. In the case studies in this volume, internal and external tests are used to understand patterns of student and teacher learning (see, for example, Palmer, Dick, Bardi). Such data on learning outcomes should be related to data on quality enhancement: accounts of positive learning experiences, growing professional confidence, and a sense of ownership and agency. The quality is located in implementation: materials are used by teachers in classrooms in ways they consider possible and appropriate, regardless of the constructs course book writers worked with; schemes and instruments for lesson planning and reports on classroom practice in language teacher education are interpreted and used by teaching practice supervisors according to their understanding and values.

This view of quality embeds an important role for programme evaluation. In documenting the experience of students, trainee teachers and those supporting their learning, we can capture both how successful the learning experience is, the factors which contribute to this, and how these might be further enhanced. Where this evaluation process is part of a wider dialogue linking comment to enhanced understanding and action, there is a reasonable expectation that evaluation activity leads to learning and to quality enhancement. Weir and Roberts (1994) and Kiely and Rea-Dickins (2005) examine how this activity, typically carried out by questionnaire or focus group study at the end of courses, contributes to change in both teacher and student behaviour.

Establishing a quality assurance system in the project context or integrating local QA practices are important strategies for external accountability and sustainability. The Polish TTC project illustrates how involvement of local universities in supporting QA in the new colleges was a strategy which contributed to the success of the project (see Komorowska, this volume). The EBEP project in Spain benefited from the QA role played by local school inspectors (see Reilly, this volume). In contrast, the positioning of the CDP project in Egypt as separate from and independent of local universities proved a major factor in the limited success of that project (see Zikri, this volume). An evaluation as QA approach works both ways in terms of capacity building: integration with local practices can establish credibility and sustainability, and the expertise of professionals in the project context can be extended through working with project activities and resources.

Evaluation as practitioner research

Kiely (2008) analyses the scope and focus of articles in two volumes of the ELT Journal which are carried out by teacher researchers in their own programme contexts. These are evaluation studies of innovations these teachers have developed, sometimes as part of a wider curriculum development and research project, sometimes in the context of study for a higher degree, and sometimes as part of an individual professionalism (Leung 2009) which motivates a career-long search for better practice.

Such studies meet three important goals in the nexus of innovation and project evaluation. First, they document practice in detail and show how it connects with policy and models of good pedagogy elsewhere. The articles surveyed examined practices such as the use of poetry and drama in the English language curriculum and the development of process writing and peer review in classrooms. Such practices and accounts of innovation and detail are the lifeblood of effective ELT, but are unlikely to be documented in detail in conventional evaluations or other reports. Secondly, these studies reflect the stakes of practitioners in a valuable way: their work achieves recognition, and the achievement of a publication such as this can be a form of career capital. Thirdly, such accounts can be examples of how innovations achieve socio-historical and cultural fit, and constitute means analyses of how innovations can be introduced, teacher by teacher, classroom by classroom, and made to work. In this way they show how a single coherent policy is not so much one recommended practice, but rather a framework, encompassing a range of possible practices, which can only be understood when implemented, documented, and accounted for by the teacher.

These three forms of programme evaluation represent three separate dialogues. Programme support captures a dialogue between programme insiders and an external who is both an advocate and a sceptic. Quality assurance processes structure a dialogue within programmes between students and teachers, and teachers and managers. Practitioner research studies frame interactions between the local and the global, between specific parts of programmes and theories, trends, and issues in the ELT sector as a whole. These are dialogues which can be structured as part of project design, planned for and resourced at the outset, or engaged in during a project as a context for project personnel to consider how the evaluation resource might be used.

Conclusion

This chapter has reviewed key trends in programme evaluation over recent decades. While, overall, the picture has become more complex, two strands in the discourse are particularly salient: the need to engage with the socio-historical and cultural context of projects and the need to involve stakeholders. By working with these principles, the processes of change can be understood and managed more effectively, and the project personnel can be engaged in debates about what is possible as well as desirable, and in what time frame. The range of approaches to designing evaluation into change management processes is rich and varied. What has become clear is that evaluation is not one thing, one research type-study. Rather, it is a multifaceted dialogue, as complex as a conversation, with structure and distributed agency contributing to its development. The three approaches to evaluation set out in this chapter – evaluation as project support, evaluation as quality assurance, and evaluation as practitioner research – are different ways of taking forward the themes outlined by Holliday and Rea-Dickins nearly 20 years ago.

The cases:
Policy and design

Case 1:
Peacekeeping English in Poland

Mark Crossey

The project

Background

The programme which became known as Peacekeeping English Project (PEP) commenced in the Baltic States of Estonia, Latvia, and Lithuania under the name of the 'Baltic Battalion ELT Project' and in a further five Central and Eastern Europe states, among them Poland, in late 1994. It was funded by the UK Foreign and Commonwealth Office and Ministry of Defence, and was consciously moulded as a high-level ELT change project acting with and within the reforming Ministries of Defence of Central and Eastern Europe. It was also closely, although not exclusively, associated with NATO's Partnership for Peace programme, which also commenced in 1994 (Green and Wall 2005: 379).

The PEP was a pioneering initiative on a number of fronts: developing new projects in partnership with Ministries of Defence was something new for the British Council. PEP also operated in arguably one of the most politically sensitive project contexts in the modern history of language training. The programme was designed and established as primarily an English for Special Purposes (ESP) reform programme, featuring consultancy on curriculum design, language training policy, and the design of centralised testing mechanisms. All of these were normally conducted employing the existing teaching structures of the host countries.

In this brief case study, I look back at my own experience as project manager of the Polish PEP from its inception point and throughout its early development.

Design and aims of PEP Poland

The PEP Poland was funded by the British Government originally in order to meet the perceived English language needs of the militaries of the NATO accession states of Central and Eastern Europe (CEE). This was at a time when there was still considerable interest from NATO in these states ensuring that their militaries adapt to civilian management and move away from the Soviet-style counter-insurgency model to a lighter defence structure. PEP, therefore, inevitably had a political character, with its managing body, the British Council, openly regarding the project (by means of its representation of values such as transparent governance) as a key aspect of UK Defence Diplomacy (Meixner 2005).

Further analysis of the goals of the programme are unclear from what early documentation survives, as there were no standardised reporting mechanisms for the programme until 1999 and scoping study documentation for PEPs varies in terms of methodology and approach from country to country. However, it is fair to state that the programme's UK government sponsors consistently looked for, on an annual basis, evidence of numbers of military personnel trained, as well as evidence of high-level English language training policy change from each country project. It was made clear to British Council London that such evidence was needed by the UK Government on an annual basis to secure further funding. In 1999, London PEP Steering Group was formed, with representation of the British Council, the Ministry of Defence, the Foreign and Commonwealth Office, and, eventually, the Department for International Development. This body was key to defining and agreeing goals of the programme as well as geopolitical priorities.

Key indicators related to, for example, involvement in high-level change, such as examination reform, were now included and standardised in programme reporting and became integral to its work and goals. The work of the Steering Group was vital for the programme. Only at this point was agreement between the UK and host Ministries of Defence on co-operation in many areas of key policy reform agreed and stipulated. It is likely that this added to the political prestige of PEP, as work on high-stakes areas such as ministry-administered language testing were then formalised and built into the programme[1].

At this point it is worth comparing the UK approach to military ELT with that of US counterparts (Woods 2006), the latter preferring a direct input of US-designed and taught courses, as well as a number of attractive placements in the United States of America. PEP Poland, specifically, was soon engaged in high-level consultation on curriculum reform, selection policy, and achievement testing. In a way, this was an inevitable course of action, as the size, history, and nature of the Polish forces at this time meant that they lacked the selection mechanisms for well-targeted ESP inputs.

Stage – design

This study looks at the inception stage of PEP Poland, in particular focusing on how design translates to early implementation and how features of the local political context, as well as project management structures, can shape and characterise a given country project for years to come.

Story

Key factors for success in the design and engagement stage

The Polish project developed or shared with other Central and Eastern Europe PEPs several key characteristics which helped ensure its deep, long-term impact. First, its working model of three to four UK ELT consultants working directly within the

---

[1] It has been claimed that examination reform, for instance, is seen as a necessary agent in any overall ELT reform project and that it is simultaneously 'the most powerful area of influence in educational reform', albeit 'probably the most difficult to penetrate and influence from an outside perspective' (Bolitho 2005:190).

Polish Ministry of Defence and its most influential military language wings offered it unique leverage and access to key decision makers, ensuring that the UK voice on ELT reform was heard. This was a key factor in securing follow-up UK government funding for the PEP in future years. More than that, the direct day-to-day work with relevant Polish Ministry of Defence staff on remoulding a national ELT programme[2] was a unique, trust-building experience which directly enhanced bilateral relations in a comparatively sensitive field (there being at the time a dozen foreign nationals at most directly engaged within Polish Ministry of Defence structures).

Another key driver for project impact was that the PEP Poland was comparatively well resourced at a time of significant financial constraint within the Polish Armed Forces and was able to 'encourage' more reform-minded ELT centres with high-profile resources such as self-access centres. The project also had a light, non-institutionalised character: its UK PEP staff were employed by the British Council on a fixed-term contractual basis and were based within Polish Ministry of Defence structures – which again reduced overall programme costs; level of project activity and costs could, therefore, be easily adapted by agreement with the Polish partners. This flexibility in planning was also, once again, a key factor in ensuring continued UK government support.

Another factor making the context favourable for the British intervention in Poland, at least in terms of its political impact and profile, was that (unlike most other countries in the region) there were initially no analogue organisations, such as the US Defense Language Institute, working *in situ* in Poland. This left the British project with the high profile and impact afforded by a highly desired commodity: communicative ELT know-how and resources.

A final important factor was that a context of flux, brought about by huge and traumatic structural change within the Polish armed forces, created power vacuums in education and training polices. While it was a sensitive and high-risk environment, this in some ways made change easier to effect, at least in terms of centralised policies and legislation. This meant that the British Council PEP consultants, comparatively unconstrained by institutional policies and priorities, but also working to high levels within the Polish Ministry of Defence and with the support of the British Embassy Defence Section, were able to act with an enviable degree of professional flexibility.

Key weaknesses in the PEP Poland design and engagement stages
A number of factors in the setting up of this, at the time, unique programme represent useful learning points for similar high-level ELT interventions.

The initial scoping visit for what was to become the PEP Poland was actually conducted by the UK Defence School of Languages, which held the contract for the project in several Central and Eastern European states for one year (1995/6). This Ministry of Defence body was, at the time, seen as the traditional provider of

---

[2] At the time the Polish military ELT programme was possibly the largest such in the world, as a previous Defence Minister had made the study of English compulsory for all serving officers.

specialised foreign-language services for UK military personnel, as well as military English courses, normally funded by the British government, for selected foreign delegations. It also delivered highly regarded methodology courses for military English teachers from all over the world. However, its capacity to scope new international programmes was limited and arguably hindered by its military and perceived political associations.

These limitations were reflected in the scoping process for PEP Poland in several key ways. First, recommendations for UK inputs focused heavily on the need to introduce 'NATO-standard' testing mechanisms, supporting curricula and INSETT (in-service teacher training) programmes, but were not backed by evidenced support from Polish Ministry of Defence practitioners, who mostly seemed to value the input of 'native-speaker teachers' and 'genuine representatives of UK life and culture' – evidence of any Polish support for the a priori goals of overall reform (as desired by the UK side) could be found in the statements of ministry officials only.

This mismatch in perceptions led to delays in commencing the higher-level inputs desired by the UK, as after the opening of the project each consultant was initially placed by the Polish Ministry of Defence within a leading language training wing, each with its own agenda, and direct communications with the Ministry of Defence training department suffered accordingly.

Perhaps more importantly though, no conclusions of the scoping study, either in its full or any abbreviated form, were shared by the United Kingdom with the Polish Ministry of Defence, which was simply informed of the UK's decision to proceed with a project by the UK Defence Attaché. This apparent lack of openness was noted by the Polish side, which assumed it to be the result of post-Cold War suspicion on the part of the UK Ministry of Defence. This had the unintended effect of further politicising the project in its opening stages.

Most significantly though, there was a lack of investigation of and reference to the key role which English language learning and certification was then playing in the traumatic change context of the post-Warsaw Pact Polish forces. In particular, as certification in English language proficiency had become essential to most forms of career progression (and retention of key positions), ELT had become a potent political tool in shaping the future of the Polish forces. The British Council team soon found that this potent issue became a fundamental consideration when making any key policy and activity decisions.

Overall, it arguably took at least two to three years for the Council-managed PEP Poland to overcome the shortcomings of the initial scoping process. PEP Poland's eventual success resulted, in part, from its unexpectedly long duration: from an initial plan to operate for three to four years, the PEP Poland actually completed in 2006, 11 years after opening.

Other factors that had a negative impact on project goals related to the difficulty of aligning Whitehall planning and realities with sound project design principles. Funding for the PEP was decided on an annual basis, was very often confirmed at the last minute (as it was largely secured from an increasingly marginalised source: the Global Conflict Prevention Pool), and despite plans to do so, UK stakeholders were never able to commit to a three-year project cycle. This insecurity was central to the PEP and affected most of its operations for its project life.

Lessons

PEP was a groundbreaking programme which delivered impressive results in terms of numbers trained and a demonstrable improvement of vital communicative English skills on the part of military personnel, often used in dangerous peacekeeping contexts. In the specific case of PEP Poland, initial problems relating to engagement with stakeholders and project design resulted from lack of experience on the part of both sides in co-operation in the field. It is an indication of how important both sides regarded the input to be that these initial misunderstandings were overcome to deliver a programme which shaped communicative ELT in the Polish military for years to come.

However, there were some valuable learning points for the profession. First and foremost, a project scoped without significant buy-in from local stakeholders on the development of its goals and input (or with buy-in from the 'wrong' local stakeholders) will be seen as having a political provenance which will, in turn, impact on project outcomes, however effective the project may be in terms of content. Secondly, overall central programme management needs to be sufficiently resourced in order for individual country projects to remain on track and avoid becoming to a larger degree the creation of the local context. With regard to programme funding channels, projects dependent entirely on politically low-priority funding pots which are decided on an annual basis cannot develop an effective or credible project plan and will experience a highly political character to their activities and presence.

Conversely, the significant political weight of a foreign intervention such as the PEP (offering a high-demand end product), when managed with sensitivity, can ease implementation of project objectives in difficult and traumatic change contexts, as well as bring significant multiplication effects throughout large national training structures.

Case 2:
Mismatched perspectives: In-service teacher education policy and practice in South Korea

David Hayes

The project

This case study discusses in-service teacher education (INSET) policy and practice for teachers of English in South Korea. In common with many other countries, educational policy makers in South Korea have been extremely concerned to enhance the quality of teaching and learning of English in schools, seeing proficiency in English as a key constituent in strengthening national economic competitiveness in response to increasing globalisation. In late 2006, the Ministry of Education, Science, and Technology (MEST) announced a major programme of continuous professional development (CPD) initiatives for teachers, as part of a package of reforms in primary and secondary schools to help to realise this goal. These initiatives included both short-term and long-term residential INSET courses. The courses involve considerable financial commitment on the part of MEST, with, for example, the cost per teacher of the six-month 'Intensive English Teacher Training Program' (IETTP) running at 13 million Korean won or £7,500 per participant, £4,122 of which was spent on a five-month course in Korea and £3,378 on a one-month overseas course in North America or Australia. However, in spite of the opportunities available, take-up of courses is not as high as it could be, with, for example, less than half of the 1,000 available places on residential INSET courses being taken up in recent years. Official concerns about the quality of English teaching and learning in government schools remain.

Stage – design

In this case study, I shall focus on factors relevant to the design of effective INSET programmes. One reason for the low take-up of courses in South Korea may reside in the divergent perspectives amongst teacher development providers and school teachers about the most productive forms of INSET, and about teachers' capabilities and their classroom needs. Another factor is also an absence of the kind of in-school follow-up which research indicates is crucial to maximising the impact of INSET. The mismatch in perspectives between teachers and trainers regarding INSET, and between research and practice with respect to follow-up, has implications for the design and organisation of INSET courses, with a consequent influence on their impact on teacher classroom behaviour.

Story

Key goals for MEST's programme of INSET courses in South Korea are:

- *to improve English teachers' communicative competence as well as to reinforce pedagogical skills*

- *to involve English teachers in long-term professional development while in service.*

(Chang, Yeon, Kim, Jung, and Hayes 2008: 13)

There is thus a view amongst educational administrators that (a) teachers' English language proficiency is somehow deficient; while (b) their pedagogical skills do not need improvement as such, but only some kind of modification; and (c) that INSET is conceived of as a long-term process which continues throughout a teacher's career. The administrators' view of the priority of language improvement over classroom teaching skills is epitomised in the design and evaluation of the IETTP courses, which MEST sees as the key element of its CPD initiatives. The medium of instruction for the course is English, trainers are predominantly native speakers of English from other countries, training centres have an 'English Only Zone', and one month (rising to two months in 2011) is spent in an English-speaking country. Pre- and post-course language tests are administered to teachers and improvement is measured statistically. In contrast to this formalised, external testing of language competence, classroom teaching skills are evaluated simply by means of a 'self-assessment checklist', i.e. the determiners of teachers' initial efficacy in the classroom and how their skills might have changed in response to the course input are the teachers themselves. (I highlight this, not to question the teachers' ability to self-assess, but to point out the contrast between the two modes of evaluation and the weight given to formal language testing.) Figure 1 outlines the evaluation process for an IETTP course.

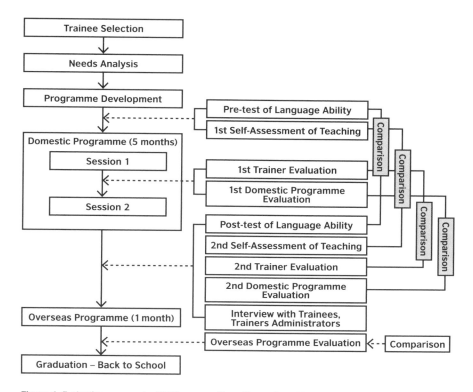

Figure 1: Evaluation process for IETTP courses (from Chang, Jung, Hayes, Yeon, Kim, and Lee 2010: 138)

Summative evaluation of INSET at the very end of short courses and at selected points in longer courses like the IETTP is typical in South Korea, as elsewhere. This kind of evaluation is generally formulaic and rarely goes beyond participant satisfaction surveys which are clearly unable to assess long-term impact. As we can see from Figure 1, the exit point is 'Graduation – Back to School'. There is no sustained follow-up to courses which examines how teachers take the knowledge they have gained and the skills they have practised on a course and integrate them into their regular classroom practice. This is as true for short INSET courses as it is for the longest IETTP course.

Perceptions of South Korean teachers and course providers regarding in-service courses were examined as part of research into INSET in South Korea, Indonesia, Japan, and Thailand for the British Council Primary Innovations Project (PIP). Data was collected by local researchers using standard research instruments which were developed for use across the countries, but which were open to modification to suit particular contexts. All data was collected in participants' first language and then translated into English. Questionnaires on INSET experience were distributed to 100 teachers and 50 INSET providers in each country. The 100 Korean teachers (100 per cent response rate) who completed questionnaires came from 18 different areas of the country, from the capital, provincial cities, and rural areas; the 42 INSET providers (84 per cent response rate) who completed questionnaires came from

16 different areas. Two hour-long focus group meetings, one in the capital and one in a semi-rural area, with six teachers, took place once questionnaires had been returned. There were also two online discussions with six INSET providers from the capital and six from the provinces. The focus groups were intended to illuminate, through in-depth discussion, topics and themes central to INSET policy and practice in South Korea.

The PIP teacher focus groups further explored the issue of observation in relation to INSET courses and revealed that, where teachers are observed in schools, such observation is considered unhelpful, because 'it is just for showing what we prepared for them', i.e., as advance notice is given of observations, teachers generally prepare and often rehearse lessons which are then obviously staged for the audience. Observation is not, then, linked to an INSET course in such a way that it could be regarded as a follow-up to the course to assist the teacher in implementation of what he or she has learnt on the course. This is in spite of the fact that:

> Follow-up support to teachers during the implementation phase of change has long been identified as an important feature of more effective [INSET] programmes. (Ingvarson, Meiers, and Beavis 2005: 9)

South Korean experience is not uncommon in this respect. In their survey of INSET programmes in Australia, Ingvarson, Meiers, and Beavis concluded that:

> ...one of the most significant findings in this study across the 80 [INSET] programmes was how rarely designers built in opportunities for comment and coaching in the workplace, despite research on their centrality to learning new and complex skills. (Ingvarson et al. ibid.: 18)

Nor do teachers have any opportunity to share their experience of INSET courses with other teachers. The predominant pattern in South Korean schools is of teachers working alone in their classrooms and only collaborating with each other when it came to schemes of work or other administrative requirements. When asked about working with other teachers in the PIP survey, 50 per cent of respondents said that they did not do so; and those who did reported that they collaborated on such things as required schemes of work rather than on reflection on practice or on mentoring schemes with other teachers. There literally did not seem to be any time for effective collaboration. In the focus group discussions, teachers reported that they 'do not have any chance to collaborate with other teachers for their work or improvement of teaching methods'. The situation was the same for the INSET providers who were 'pressed with lots of paperwork and administrative work' and thus not in a position to visit schools to assist teachers with integrating knowledge and skills gained on their courses into existing patterns of classroom teaching.

With respect to the prioritisation of English proficiency, teachers' own views of their language skills seem to be contradictory. In the PIP survey, teachers reported that they felt confident in using English to manage the class and promote interaction. For example, on a scale of 1 (no skill) to 4 (highly skilled), in response to the statement 'Using English I can manage the general learning environment effectively', 51 per cent said they had 'good skill' and 20 per cent that they were 'highly skilled'. Yet, in spite of their confidence in using English in the classroom, only 7 per cent of teachers thought their English language level was 'excellent', with the majority saying it was either 'good' (32 per cent) or 'adequate' (43 per cent), and 18 per cent reporting that it was 'not very good'.

These contradictions perhaps have connections to the official view expressed both in MEST's goals for INSET and in the views of INSET providers whose ratings of teachers' English language competence were not high. In the PIP survey, 21 INSET providers rated teachers' English as 'adequate', nine as 'not very good', and 12 as 'good'. None rated teachers' English as 'excellent'. From the PIP focus group discussions, INSET providers felt that teachers focused too much on receptive skills when teaching, while productive language skills were in dire need of improvement. So, though teachers might feel confident in their use of English in the classroom, if they are told often enough that their language skills are deficient, they may well come to believe it. Further, placing primary emphasis on language proficiency inevitably contributes to pedagogic skills being seen as of less consequence for English teachers.

Lessons

Teachers in South Korea are not generally consulted on the development of courses beyond a needs or wants analysis asking them to say what topics they would like covered. This is not unusual in INSET practice worldwide, though experience (see, for example, Scholey, this volume, for a discussion of change processes in Turkey) does show the value of a bottom-up approach to change 'in a way that teachers could see and understand'. Perhaps as a result of this lack of effective consultation, too much INSET is grounded in a deficit theory of teachers' knowledge and skills, with educational administrators deciding that teachers are lacking in some way that impedes their professional efficacy. Moreover, in South Korea, this may contribute to the lack of positive attitudes towards INSET expressed in PIP focus group meetings, with teachers complaining that courses are 'made up of theoretical and formal lectures which are not applicable to class teaching'. It is no exaggeration to say that, at present in South Korea, INSET seems to be largely something done to inferiors (teachers) by superior others (education officials, inspectors, university professors), rather than a shared enterprise amongst equals collaborating for the improvement of education for students in school.

Given the vision of INSET as a long-term process for South Korean teachers, a corollary is that the school system should offer scope – time and resources, both human and material – for this process to occur. Research across a range of countries strongly suggests that INSET is much more likely to contribute to school improvement if it provides teachers, both alone and in collaboration with colleagues, with the space to reflect upon their prior experience and any new knowledge and skills introduced (Day, Stobart, Sammons, Kington, Gu, Smees, and Mujtaba 2006). However, if the institutional context fails to provide either group with the time to collaborate – teachers to work with each other on issues more substantive than records of work; teachers to work with INSET providers as follow-up to courses – then a basic condition for effective INSET programmes is not being met and thus the huge sums of money expended by MEST are likely to be wasted.

This is a significant issue for educational systems in and beyond South Korea, as 'creating a collaborative professional learning environment for teachers is the 'single most important factor' for successful school improvement and 'the first order of business' for those seeking to enhance the effectiveness of teaching and learning' (Muijs and Lindsay 2008: 208). The South Korean teachers' reports of their INSET experiences allied to the lessons from international research provide a clear message regarding the impact of professional development activities on school improvement and student learning outcomes which transcends national boundaries. This is that educational policy makers and administrators must work to remove those constraints which research has identified as inhibiting successful development, most notably teachers' lack of time and opportunities to reflect on their own teaching and to share practice with their colleagues (Day et al. ibid.).

A concern with what actually happens in classrooms as a result of INSET must also be reflected in a more sophisticated conceptualisation of INSET evaluation. This must go beyond the teacher, the trainer, and the course itself. Muijs and Lindsay (ibid.) put forward 'a hierarchy of levels of impact' which acknowledges the importance of the institutional context in fostering change, as well whether/ how teachers implement what they learn during in-service development and – something which is much more contested – whether this all results in enhanced learning outcomes for students in schools. The levels of impact are:

■ Level 1: participants' reactions

■ Level 2: participants' learning from CPD

■ Level 3: organisational change and support

■ Level 4: participants' use of new knowledge and skills

■ Level 5: student outcomes

(Muijs and Lindsay op.cit.: 198-99)

If a major reason for the lack of impact of much professional development activity is the absence of follow-up to INSET in school, where Levels 3-5 are realised, supportive school contexts and the establishment of professional learning communities – which can provide the right conditions for fostering opinion and coaching during in-school follow-up – are critical ingredients of successful INSET and CPD in the longer term. If Ministries of Education throughout the world are to realise their goals for successful English teaching-learning as a contributory factor in national economic competitiveness, they would do well to devote more time and resources to re-imagining how teachers and schools operate, rather than simply assuming that the mere provision of INSET courses for teachers will yield the changes in teacher behaviour and thus student learning outcomes that they seek.

Case 3:
Designing a 'Language-in-Education' planning strategy in Tunisia

Hamish McIlwraith

The project

The English Language Reform Project (ELRP) in Tunisia began in 2007 and has been developed jointly by the Tunisian government and the British Council. It will result in wholesale restructuring of Primary and Secondary English language teaching and learning nationwide. The aim is to help enable young Tunisians to acquire and use the language competences described in Tunisian Ministry of Education (MoE) documents. It is based on an assumed need for Tunisians to be able to use English in an increasingly interconnected world in order to achieve the best chances for Tunisia's economic transformation. The intended outcomes are:

- students who can use English for study needs

- school leavers who can use English proficiently at work

- school leavers who can use English effectively for international communication or dialogue.

It took three years to negotiate and develop a ten-year implementation plan. In 2007, I led a three-person team on a scoping study. The scoping report set out the business case and project brief for a reform project. Then, in February 2009, I wrote a Framework Plan that served as a Project Initiation Document (PID). The purpose of this document was to help enable the MoE and the British Council to agree on the project's scope, aims, and objectives. I advised on the time frame, created new management structures from ministerial/executive level down to day-to-day management (with job descriptions for the lower levels), and suggested the principal stages and phases of development. I specified the main risks and options for controlling them. Later, in June 2010, I submitted a revised and updated Implementation Plan to the MoE and British Council that took into account their comments and suggestions on the Framework Plan.

Stage – design

This study examines the design stage of the ELRP and focuses primarily on the extended negotiations on the terms of reference for the plan. The main players in this process were officials from the MoE, a team of three senior English language teaching inspectors attached to the Ministry, British Council senior management and project staff, and the author of this paper. The main lesson to be learnt for those designing an English language reform project is to be acutely aware of the potential for misunderstanding and conflict which can arise from using terminology which is interpreted in vastly different ways depending on the perspective of the people or agencies using it.

Story

The ELRP took three years to plan. Three years might seem a lot of time to devote to planning, but it was probably a safe minimum considering the historical (and current) importance of French as the main first foreign language and also the huge scale of change required by the MoE. Much of the negotiation revolved around notions of language policy, a perceived threat of English to culture and (Arabic) language, and the extent to which language change can be 'planned' at all[1] or, specifically, in education. Eventually we agreed to use categories derived from Baldauf's 'Framework for Language Planning Goals' (Baldauf: 2004). These were: Access; Personnel; Curriculum [i.e. syllabus]; Methods and Materials; Resources; Community; Evaluation. We used them to form the ELRP's thematic structure.

The categories emerged from a broader discussion we had on how to develop the existing Tunisian Language Policy (LP). LP is a multi-layered concept operating at macro and micro levels. An example of a micro LP would be choosing the language for a sign in a shop's window or a newsagent deciding which foreign language newspapers to stock (Kaplan and Baldauf 1997: 4). At macro (state) level, LP is the principal mechanism for organising, planning, and manipulating the use of language in society (Shohamy 2006: 45). Baldauf (ibid.) reduces these to four main reasons to reform a language:

1. for status, for example, reversing the decline of a language considered culturally significant

2. for standardisation, for example, the simplification of standard Chinese in the 1970s[2]

3. the promotion of prestige forms, for example, the language of high culture or diplomacy

4. strategies for language learning, viz. 'language-in-education' planning, i.e. the ELRP context.

---

[1] NB: The few attempts by governments to plan for the use of English (and keep it out) have largely been unsuccessful. This includes the attempts by France, Brazil, and Russia, which have, for the most part, failed. The Académie Française, for example, did not prevent the Académie des Sciences making a decision in 2002 to give preference to articles in English in its *Comptes Rendus*. (Spolsky 2004:.63 and 90).

[2] http://www.sacu.org/pinyinissues.html (accessed 14 June 2011).

We extracted the categories for the ELRP's themes from this final reason to reform, i.e. 'language-in-education' planning. At the same time, we looked at practical ways of ensuring the ELRP's successful implementation. Initially, I was given two models of project management to use. The first was a British Council model, which draws heavily on the Association of Project Management (APM) terminology. This approach makes a distinction between 'deliverables' and 'benefits', which, in education projects, are usually described in terms of positive changes in behaviour or capacity. In British Council projects, 'deliverables' are (generally) 'products' and 'outputs'. 'Benefits' are 'outcomes'.

The second model was the PRINCE2 (PRojects IN Controlled Environments) approach, which was presented to me in my consultancy terms of reference. PRINCE2 is a management method endorsed by the UK government for projects funded from the public purse[3]. It is often described as an uncomplicated way of organising, managing, and controlling projects to give them the best chance of being delivered on time, on budget, and to an appropriate standard. It is not a prescription; it is generic and can be modified and applied to work in any planning context (Bentley 2005). The main focus of PRINCE2 is 'products'. In contrast to a British Council approach, PRINCE2 'products' can be all-embracing. They can be things like course books, teachers' books, CDs, tests, assessments, teacher/trainer training courses, and lists of intended learner outcomes. Even a trained teacher (in PRINCE2 planning terms) is a product. Product-based planning is fundamental to PRINCE2.

The three inspectors who, along with me, comprised the planning team looked at both planning models. The APM-derived terminology in the British Council model troubled my Tunisian colleagues for two reasons. First, they reported that the terminology was potentially confusing to non-experts. Secondly, they were concerned that the British Council model, while of good quality, was not an internationally recognised standard. (One team member went so far to suggest that a 'British Council' model would be an external 'imposition'.) It was for these two reasons that they felt that the less complex and internationally recognised PRINCE2 model was more appropriate for the Tunisian context.

This resulted in a dilemma for my British Council colleagues in Tunisia. Their initial reaction was that they needed to have the same reform plan, but in two planning formats. The first would be written in an APM-derived British Council format. This would be used as an internal British Council document and sent to London for 'concept checking', i.e. to determine whether the plan was viable (or not) according to British Council criteria. The second plan would be written using PRINCE2 terminology and used as the primary document by the MoE and British Council when implementing reform on the ground in Tunisia. The MoE would not have access to the APM/British Council plan.

---

[3] http://www.ogc.gov.uk/methods_prince_2.asp (accessed 20 January 2010).

After some reflection, British Council colleagues concluded that, rather than help, the two plans would not necessarily be wholly compatible and thus could result in mix-ups at a later date. They therefore decided to use one model – the PRINCE2 model. One factor in their reflection was the practical question as to who was to implement the plan on a day-to-day basis.

Choosing the right person was the single most divisive issue we faced. Members of the British Council team were convinced a job so complex and vast (and, by implication, demanding someone with the experience and competence to explain project management terminology to a wider audience) meant that it was one for a UK consultant. The Tunisian team was convinced that a need for long-term sustainability and project ownership meant that only someone already fully immersed in the Tunisian system should be employed.

The quality of the day-to-day project manager, in particular, is crucial to overall success. He or she needs to have the experience, understanding, and strength of character to be able to stand up to, say, a powerful civil servant or a knowledgeable and well-respected school inspector in order to push through necessary change. The overall profile for the ELRP Project manager post stated that he or she should have experience in successfully tackling complex tasks and finding solutions to unanticipated problems. In addition, he or she must be collegial and collaborative in nature, be able to communicate clearly, and actively involve colleagues in making decisions, where appropriate. The specific duties included a requirement to manage the production of English Language Reform products (in PRINCE2 terms) in the three main project strands, i.e. Teacher Training; Syllabus and Materials; Testing and Assessment to prescribed quality standards. This entailed managing team leaders, liaising with the MoE, planning and monitoring project progress, managing risk, and engaging with a Steering Committee and external evaluators to assure overall direction and quality of the project.

In the end, the British Council and the MoE decided on a compromise: The Tunisian project manager, after a successful six-month probationary period, will be shadowed and mentored by an external consultant for up to three years. (Whether this turns out to be the right strategy will have to wait. At the time of writing, the unrest across the Middle East and North Africa, which started in Tunisia, has put everything on hold.)

Lessons

There were two main lessons that surfaced during the design stage of the ELRP. The first is that while project management terminology may be generally accepted and uncontroversial in one context, this does not necessarily mean that it will not be challenged in another context; the terms may be open to subjective interpretation.

The second lesson follows on from the first, i.e. to recognise that technical terms (i.e. terminology) are a means to an end, but that they can be (and in some cases should be) refined and altered to suit the unique setting of every planning context.

Case 4:
The ETeMS project in Malaysia: English for the Teaching of Mathematics and Science

Mina Patel

The project

Malaysia is culturally and linguistically an extremely rich and diverse country. 'Malaysia, due to the exigencies of history, is a post-colonial nation with a diverse ethnic population possessing great social and cultural complexity. Malaysia has not just one but many significant languages, largely as a result of the immigrant ancestry of its multi-ethnic population' (Gill 2007). Malays form over half of the population, the Chinese are the second largest ethnic group, and the Indians make up the smallest of the three main ethnic groups. There are many more indigenous ethnic groups in East Malaysia and an increase in minority groups throughout the country made up of migrant workers coming to Malaysia.

The official language of Malaysia is Bahasa Melayu. In 1970, the language of instruction in schools was changed from English to Bahasa Melayu. As well as national schools where Bahasa Melayu is the medium of instruction, there are also vernacular schools in the primary sector, where the medium of instruction is either Chinese or Tamil. This has led to the labelling of schools as Chinese, Tamil, or Malay schools (Tan 2005: 49). In the last decade, there has been growing concern that the levels of English language among Malaysians have dropped quite significantly and that this is due to English no longer being the language of instruction in schools (Nor, Aziz, and Jusoff 2011: 36).

In 1991, the Government developed its Vision 2020 strategy, the essence of which is that by 2020, Malaysia will be a fully-developed country. In order to achieve the aims of this strategy, Malaysia has to 'overcome nine central strategic challenges' (Prime Minister's Office 2011: 2). Two of these challenges are:

> The sixth is the challenge of establishing a scientific and progressive society, a society that is innovative and forward-looking, one that is not only a consumer of technology but also a contributor to the scientific and technological civilisation of the future.

The ninth challenge is the challenge of establishing a prosperous society, with an economy that is fully competitive, dynamic, robust, and resilient. (Prime Minister's Office ibid.)

Many believe that it was with these challenges in mind that on 6 June 2002, the Government announced the decision that Mathematics and Science should be taught through the medium of English:

*Mathematics and science represent the gateway to a world of creativity, innovations, and discoveries. The MoE [Ministry of Education] is striving to emphasize the learning of mathematics and science because the future of the world rests upon new breakthroughs and cutting-edge technologies ...
The decision to switch to English language as the medium of instruction was based on the rationale that a good command of English would enable students to access the internet, read articles and research papers and other materials published in English.* (Ministry of Education 2004: 10)

The implementation of this policy was to begin in January 2003.

The role of English, therefore, changed significantly from being a subject that was compulsory to take, but not pass, to the medium of instruction for two core subjects.

The change in policy received varied reactions from professionals in the education system as well as the general public (Pillay and Thomas 2003: 27; Mukundan, Hajimohammadi, and Nimehchisalem 2011: 82).

Stage – design

This case study will focus on the design and implementation stages of the project. They are obviously very closely linked, and this case study will aim to show that, if a large scale programme is not designed thoughtfully and potential risks considered carefully, projects with the most noble of intentions will not have the desired impact.

Story

The decision to teach mathematics and science through English in Malaysia was an extremely bold one. Bilingual education in any form is very complex, not only from an educational point of view, but from a cultural and societal point of view as well. There are many factors and risks to consider, for example, 'a) the difficulty of providing an adequate supply of teachers who are both proficient in the language and competent in teaching through the medium of the language and b) the many anxieties and misconceptions which exist in the minds of various parents, teachers, high officials, school managers, and the media' (Johnstone 2010: 132).

July 2002 to January 2003 was a period of intense activity. Every available resource in the Ministry of Education was dedicated to realising the policy. This period 'heralded a flurry of chain actions and reactions that did not spare any strata of the education system. From the primary to the tertiary level, the affected agencies and institutions had to quickly put their plans in place and into action to achieve the stated goals' (Tan and Chan 2003: 3).

Teacher training

The Ministry of Education set up 14 working committees to plan and implement the strategy. One major working committee was that of Teacher Training. The English Language Teaching Centre Malaysia, an in-service teacher development centre which is part of the Teacher Training Division, was assigned to develop a programme to help improve the English language proficiency of mathematics and science teachers (Pillay and Thomas op.cit.: 28). The training package was made up of five complementary elements:

1. two interactive phases (weekend training and full immersion)

2. self-instructional study pack (with self-monitoring and differentiation in levels of access)

3. dictionaries with CD-ROMs and grammar books (as reference points for meaning and pronunciation)

4. internet-based learning through freeware (for pedagogical approach and activities)

5. the buddy system (for teacher in-situ support) (Choong 2004: 4).

The two interactive phases were developed as cascade programmes with master trainers from each state being trained initially and then training other teachers.

The teaching and learning of mathematics and science through English happened on a national scale and simultaneously at primary and secondary levels. Implementation began in 2003 with Year 1 of primary, Form 1 of secondary and Lower Sixth, and this was followed in 2004 by Year 2 of primary, Form 2 of secondary and Upper Sixth, and so on until all years and levels were covered by 2008.

By July 2004, 'more than 50,000 science and mathematics teachers have gone through curriculum induction training and language proficiency training' (Ministry of Education 2004: 39). However, teachers struggled to get to grips with becoming learners themselves while still on full timetables. Motivation varied enormously. Very experienced teachers, who had been teaching their subject in Bahasa Melayu for over 20 years and were close to retirement, were now being asked to go on English courses. At the other end of the continuum, younger teachers, who had been taught through the medium of Bahasa Melayu at school themselves, struggled with the concept of having to suddenly teach through another language.

In 2003, the national examinations in the final year of primary school, the third year of secondary school, and the final year of secondary school were bilingual. Students could choose to take them in Bahasa Melayu or in English. By 2008, it was envisaged that all examinations would be solely in English.

ICT

Part of the transformation of the teaching of mathematics and science was an investment in ICT. Computer rooms appeared in schools all over the country, mathematics and science teachers were given laptops, and courseware in the form of CDs was translated into English and in some cases developed especially. The CDs contained complete mathematics and science lessons in English and were provided to complement and supplement existing classroom teaching and resources. This ICT thrust received mixed reviews. Some teachers welcomed it, others feared it, simply because they had had no experience of using technology in the classroom before this, and others relied on it heavily to make up for their own lack of language and pedagogy to teach their subjects in English (Yassin, Mars, Ong, and Lai 2009: 56).

School-based oral assessment

The third main initiative of 2003 was school-based oral assessment. This form of continuous assessment was first implemented in the first year of secondary school in 2002 and then included the second year of secondary in 2003. It was also offered to students in all years at primary school. The aim of this form of assessment was to encourage students to use English and Malay in authentic situations, and offer them increased and varied opportunities to be assessed and hence build their confidence (Ministry of Education 2004: 14).

In July 2009, six years after the policy of teaching mathematics and science through English had been announced, it was officially reversed with the Government stating that since the policy had been implemented, the improvement in English among students was only 'moderate' (Chapman 2011).

In November 2011, after considerable public pressure, 'the government has allowed an option to students who are already learning Science and Mathematics in English (PPSMI) to continue in the language in the wake of protests from a number of parents' groups... However, this solution does not mean the Government is reversing its stand to scrap the English language policy, which was decided in 2009' (Pathmawathy 2011).

Lessons

Pilot study

Large scale projects are immensely complicated and work on numerous levels. Therefore, it is worth considering undertaking a smaller pilot study first. A small-scale pilot study that is closely monitored and properly evaluated can often highlight areas of strength and concern in a project and bring to light elements that may have been overlooked. All of these are learning points that can then inform the project at national level. It is much easier and more effective in the long term to modify planning documents, rather than a large-scale project that is up and running.

Johnstone takes this idea one step further by suggesting that a feasibility study should come before a pilot study, which should then inform national project design (Johnstone 2010: 133).

Time

Large national projects need time for planning, preparation, and implementation. ELTCM (English Language Teaching Centre, Malaysia) is to be commended for developing a comprehensive training package in a very short time frame. However, by the time the training was ready to roll out, the new term in January 2003 had begun, and so trainers and teachers spent considerable periods of time absent from the classroom, which was unsettling for both teachers and students alike (Pillay and Thomas op.cit.).

Stakeholder involvement

Johnstone (2010) describes significant factors that emerge from a study of five East Asian countries that have had experience of bilingual-type programmes. Among these factors are provision for parents and consultation, negotiations, and discussion, within and among schools and departments of the Ministry of Education (ibid.: 127, 129). The inclusion of key stakeholders in initial discussions and continuing planning will create a sense of investment and ownership for those concerned, and these individuals and/or groups are more likely to help towards achieving goals and outcomes.

Learner readiness

In educational change programmes such as the one described in this paper, teachers are the main change agents, but we often forget those at the heart of the change process, those at the very core of the change we want to bring about: the students. We must ensure as much as we can that students are considered as active participants in the process and not just passive recipients, and that the change is implemented at a level and pace that will build their confidence and motivate them to want to learn.

One initiative at a time

Change takes effort, energy, time, and sometimes courage. One big change can be substantial, two daunting, but three can be completely overwhelming, and teachers can find it difficult to integrate or even prioritise practices or initiatives. There is a strong argument for implementing one initiative first, laying its foundations, and then building on it with other initiatives over time, rather than implementing too many initiatives at once.

Case 5:
Materials design and development in English for the world of work in Turkey: Policy, strategies and processes

Mike Scholey

The project

The tourism sector is a key area of the Turkish economy and in 2006 the Turkish Ministry of National Education (MoNE) and the British Council instigated a textbook and INSET (in-service education and training) project to transform the language skills of 22,000 students studying in Turkey's 106 Hotel Management and Tourism (HMT) vocational high schools. One of the major findings of a small baseline study carried out by the author (the UK consultant to the project) was that the HMT schools appeared to be considerably underperforming in terms of the vocational English language knowledge and communication skills which their students could realistically be expected to acquire during Grades 11 and 12, before leaving to work in the hotel and tourism sector. The most important initial aims for the MoNE, the British Council, and the author were to decide on remedial alternatives for the project intervention and develop a 'consensus of accountability' (Bray and Luxon 1999: 38).

Stage – policy, strategy, and design

This case study focuses on the initial stages of the ELT reform project: policy, strategy, and design.

Story

Project policy

A crucial question to ask in initiating educational innovation according to Kennedy (1999c: 4-5) is whether we want radical, continuous, or incremental change. The author (in his role as consultant) proposed that only radical measures were going to ensure a new fit between practice and context. Consequently, the first tasks were to:

- convince the MoNE of the changes in vocational English pedagogy deemed necessary to bring about the desired changes in ELT practice

- persuade the MoNE that it was possible for radical change to the ELT culture in Grade 11 to be effected quickly

- overcome pockets of resistance to change within the system

- solicit the support of the tourism industry for the intervention

- formulate specific project objectives, such as improvement in vocational content and skills, and training model(s) and procedures.

Throughout the three-year project, all the parties were aware of the need to keep communication channels open in all directions – either formally or on an organised/ informal social basis – so that any dissatisfaction, doubts, or difficulties could be dealt with promptly and any problems nipped in the bud. In this way, unpredictable delays in the three-phase process would be minimised and, most importantly, the consultant's target of producing three draft textbooks in the intensive writing phase would not be compromised. Implicit trust in each other's commitment and preparedness to change plans and processes to accommodate new realisations – in so far as this was possible or feasible –was expected and displayed from the outset.

The management of the project was thus both organic and flexible, and at the same time well-organised – a process which worked within a strong project framework and also according to the local contingencies and developing needs generated by the different stakeholders during the three years.

Project strategy
Kennedy (citing Bray and Luxon op.cit.) enumerates three sets of expertise required if the above vested interests (the project stakeholders) are to be managed successfully:

- *knowledge of subject content:* selected vocational school subject teachers of HMT and selected English language teachers (ELTs)-cum-materials writers

- *control skills (e.g. project strategy and design, and materials writing/design expertise):* MoNE officials, British Council manager, Teaching Knowledge Test (TKT) trainer (the British Council trainer brought in to give the two-week pre-writer selection TKT course), UK consultant

- *process skills (dealing with people, working in teams):* MoNE; vocational and regional education administrators; head teachers involved in piloting schools; vocational school ELTs; selected vocational HMT subject teachers; British Council; TKT trainer; UK consultant.

Smith (1999: 45) suggests that good practice in project innovation lies in, *inter alia*, 'achieving agreement between all the different stakeholders on the way the project is implemented'. Although this may seem obvious, it is far more easily said than done, and making use of the different sets of expertise enumerated above through genuine collaboration – and linked to the concepts of ownership and consensus building – was a key and conscious element of the *English for Work* innovation process. What was both significant and crucial in this project was the teamwork between the British Council, MoNE officials assigned to the project, the writing team, and the UK consultant: the very time-consuming and constant to-and-fro consultation process was a sound investment, ensuring shared ownership of decision making to maximise the chances of success of the project.

According to Holliday (1999), our own professional discourses can prevent us from seeing the real worlds of the people we work with, so that cultural continuity (adjusting an innovation to enable the best possible fit with a host environment) may not be achieved. The author was also constantly aware of the dangers of interfering, in this curriculum innovation, with the established Turkish socio-educational context. As Holliday (ibid: 31) also notes, the unrealised, unconsciously constructed logic of many of the management and project concepts we propound or subscribe to may be a product only of our own discourse, making us 'see others in our own terms, and not in theirs'.

It was recommended in the baseline study report and later agreed by all parties that the best way to change the system was to do it from within the classroom, using a bottom-up approach and in a way that teachers could see and understand – i.e. what was changing and why. New materials have an immediate impact on classroom teaching, pushing teachers to reflect on the innovation and encouraging them to change their methodology and content. Brewster (1999: 90) notes how the development of teacher-made materials 'acts as a catalyst, encouraging teachers to combine theory with practice while providing a highly motivating course outcome'; acknowledged, too, is the important benefit of a boost to teachers' professional confidence and competence through the acquisition of transferable curriculum development and training skills.

The model of innovation adopted, then, had the potential major advantage of a widespread and sustained impact. A second advantage was that the selected writers could themselves act as INSET trainers later on in their schools and school clusters. The model of intervention also tied in with the MoNE's desire for a high-impact, long-term solution, rather than a series of short-term, stopgap measures.

Specialist vocational teacher training in methodology, whereby the trained teacher would cascade-train in an INSET framework in the regions, had been discounted at the project proposal stage. Cascade training can be an unreliable training model, as rarely are sufficient time, commitment, or motivation either available or sustainable for effective INSET after the initial stimulus event has taken place. Instead, the project strategy was for the new materials, in combination with the core group of properly trained and committed HMT ELTs-cum-materials writers, to be the key agents of change.

The real curricular and methodological innovation would be done via the production and piloting of (hopefully) high-quality vocational language learning materials, written by Turkish teachers in Turkey, about Turkey, for Turkey. After an initial two-week TKT course, the writing group was given training in methodology, materials writing, and tightly focused INSET, with the author acting as trainer, INSETT (in-service teacher training) materials developer and observer. Later, the team would first do initial INSET themselves, training between 80 and 100 teachers, under the guidance of the author, with, later still, INSET work with ELT colleagues – as opposed to an anonymous mass of regional participants – in their own local school clusters. Many HMT ELTs were ripe for training, having had none for several years, and the innovation would soon, hopefully, result in a rapid improvement in the effectiveness and quality of vocational language learning in their schools.

Project design

The project model comprised three main phases: preparation and selection; writer training, materials writing, and piloting; INSET and dissemination. In Phase 1, the MoNE identified participating schools and 40 teachers, and the writing team was selected from this group by the UK consultant. In Phase 2, the author took a huge risk (which necessitated a correspondingly high level of trust on the British Council's part and a similar degree of faith on the MoNE's) by proposing that all of the textbooks could be written in six weeks. The writing team would be 'good' teachers representing schools in different regions of Turkey. They would be released by their schools to attend the TKT training, which would be followed by the six-week residential materials development and writing programme on the principles and processes of materials writing, and they would concurrently produce and draft three textbooks for piloting.

The MoNE arranged the intensive materials writing programme away from the commitments and distractions of home, in a comfortable MoNE-owned hotel/ vocational school on the Aegean coast (with three MoNE-nominated HMT subject specialists), where the pleasant residential working environment could support and enhance the intensive training programme and the production of the new materials.

The viability of the whole project was predicated on the successful outcome of this six-week programme, which would be followed by editing, piloting of the materials, and a short post-writing INSETT methodology course for the writers elsewhere. Immediately after that, there would be INSET and dissemination activities.

The materials, once written, would be edited by the writers under the guidance of the author, piloted, re-edited, and later published by the MoNE through the regular Ministry textbook publishing processes and procedures. Finally, there would be a national conference in Istanbul to disseminate the rationale for and the objectives of the new teaching approach and materials from three different perspectives: the MoNE's, the British Council's and the consultant's.

All of the intended project outcomes listed below were achieved:

- A small cadre of vocational HMT ELTs was trained in contemporary teaching methodology, materials development, and short INSETT course design and methodology for INSET work.

- A large number of other HMT ELTs from the regions were apprised of the new materials and the rationale underpinning them, and trained in their use.

- A handbook/rationale for the use of the new materials in the classroom was produced (in Turkish) for both MoNE use and for head teachers of HMT vocational schools.

- Pilot school head teachers and ELTs understood and appeared to be committed to changes in the classroom teaching and learning of English for HMT.

- The rationale for and content of the new materials was disseminated at a national conference for all Turkish ELT/HMT stakeholders.

Stakeholder experience

A brief characterisation of a Turkish writer-participant's viewpoint should give the foregoing outline of the project policy, strategy, and design a clearer perspective. When Özlem Keskin, a young teacher from an HMT vocational high school in Istanbul, expressed an interest in the project, she was unaware of its real aim and the lengthy training it would involve. She was expecting to improve her teaching skills and interact with colleagues from other HMT high schools, but little else. A much greater challenge awaited her, however. Overcrowded classes, unmotivated students, and a lack of effective classroom materials were some of the difficulties she regularly faced. 'It was really motivating to realise that this materials gap was going to be filled.' During the six-week workshop in which she was trained in the CLIL (Content and Language Integrated Learning) textbook writing process, her excitement and self-confidence grew, as her participation in the sessions came to be appreciated by both trainers and colleagues. However, she worried about the difficulty of both learning to write and creating the books at the same time, and doubted the group's ability to perform within such a limited time frame. This aside, the most inspiring aspect of the process, she explains, was that she always got the encouragement she needed from the trainer/consultant, who constantly motivated the team to think positively, outside the box. She feels that creativity was the most important element in the process, combined with her own knowledge and previous experience. 'It was amazing to discover that, as teammates, we stimulated each other's creative thinking and the ideas flowed astonishingly freely. This made me believe in the power of teamwork, despite occasional serious disagreements.' Özlem began to observe and enjoy the professional progress she was making, with the piloting stage being another turning point, when she was able to observe how well task-based teaching worked in the classroom. Later, she had the opportunity to present the project and share her experiences with colleagues at a national dissemination conference. 'I now feel confident enough to take part in similar projects and even to work on my own textbook someday. The best part for me,' Özlem concludes, 'was realising I was capable of designing my own activities to meet the needs of my own students, and I feel privileged to have left my signature on a project which was the first of its kind in my country.'

Lessons

1. Any major change in curriculum, methodology, materials, or teacher training requires several kinds of systemic adjustment in school systems. Such adjustments invariably involve the head teachers having to reconsider their own perspectives on teaching/learning; being prepared to accept some degree of disruption – possibly major changes to the syllabus, materials, timetabling, learning and assessment processes; and modifying their notions of what constitutes worthwhile and effective INSET for their teaching staff. In order to minimise any resistance from this direction, it was appreciated at the baseline study stage that any systemic change in the HMT schools necessitated by the innovation would require some INSET for head teachers themselves, preferably via efficient dissemination of the nature of, rationale for, and means of the proposed curriculum change. This was done during Phase 3, with an explanatory handbook on the new materials being translated into the mother tongue for MoNE and school administrative use. The consensus among the heads involved was that if change were materials-driven, then it would largely take care of itself and lead to minimum disruption in their schools.

2. There was a need to consider both how the national stakeholders – in traditional project-speak, the 'recipients' of the curriculum innovation – were 'perceived, accommodated, and managed' (Holliday op.cit.: 25). Technical project documents such as the logframe and timelines for resource input – often incomprehensible to stakeholders – were largely avoided during Phases 2 and 3, and were not a concern for the author, who had his hands full with practical training. Also avoided were 'naïve notions of mutuality' and 'appearance of agreement ... with regard to project documentation' (Holliday: ibid), although there was an acceptance – with good grace – of the inevitable and necessary initial going through the motions of agreement, as there invariably is on such projects some unfamiliarity on both sides' parts with each other's administrative *modus operandi*.

3. For the UK consultant to be involved with the same personnel from different levels of the administration for the duration of the project and get to know and trust the same people over innumerable professional meetings *and* social gatherings was a crucial ingredient of the project and contributed enormously to the successful achievement of the planned outcomes. Whenever a problem arose, large or small (such as whether the authors should be thinking about a follow-up textbook for Grade 12; or whether the same authors' names would be allowed to appear on the textbooks – contrary to MoNE regulations; or how many ELTs would attend the INSET course, etc.), it was dealt with rapidly and effectively, so that any dissatisfaction among the team was addressed and had a largely satisfactory outcome. In this way, project team motivation and morale were maintained, worries and problems were minimised, and a cohesive and largely satisfied and happy team was moulded.

Conclusion

The project reached a successful conclusion within the planned time frame and with all stakeholders seemingly satisfied with project productivity and outcomes. According to the Minister of National Education, Dr Huseyn Celik (British Council 2008), the project 'brought into focus for the Ministry many of the issues related to English language teaching and learning', and the findings and recommendations of the project formed the possible 'basis for reform of ELT throughout the vocational education sector'. What is required now is an impact study to evaluate how and to what extent the project intervention has affected the classroom teaching and learning in the HMT vocational schools.

Case 6:
Mind the gap: Language policy reform in Rwanda

John Simpson

The project

Context and rationale

Rwanda, one of the smallest and most densely populated countries in Africa, is a current locus of English language teaching reform: as in other developing country contexts, the reform relates to wider issues of economic development and poverty reduction. In dealing with these issues, the Government of Rwanda (GoR) places a high premium on the growth of human capital with the necessary knowledge and skills as a vehicle for socio-economic development.

GoR views the creation of a knowledge-based economy as central to its Vision 2020 (Government of Rwanda Ministry of Finance and Economic Planning 2000) and Economic Development and Poverty Reduction Strategy (Government of Rwanda Ministry of Finance and Economic Planning 2007), and sees English as the gateway to global knowledge. The 2010-2015 Education Sector Strategic Plan (Government of Rwanda Ministry of Education 2010) identifies the sector-wide establishment of English-medium education as a cross-cutting priority and states that a major challenge will be the enabling of all teachers and learners to become proficient in English.

Within this context and in line with the constitution, which stipulates that Kinyarwanda, French, and English are official languages, these three languages are taught in schools so that Rwanda can have regional and international advantages associated with trade and foreign relations. Ensuring fluency in these languages is considered important to national development and the self-actualisation of citizens.

The East African Community

Rwanda is a relatively new and active member of the East African Community, where the use of English has become more prominent and the need for literacy in English greater. In order to compete effectively in East African Community markets and become a regional IT (information technology) hub, Rwanda wishes to expand its use of English. The sector-wide shift to English-medium education is thus a bold and ambitious plan to help meet GoR's goals of East African Community integration, including harmonising its education system with other East African Community member states.

Science, technology, and ICT (Information and Computing Technology)

As a further means of stimulating economic development, GoR is investing heavily in science, technology, and ICT, and has made these priority areas in education, with English playing a key role in this process.

Language policy

Previously, a trilingual language policy offered a choice of medium of instruction based on the linguistic background and experience of the pupils. However, the high cost of learning materials and teacher training made it expensive to maintain three languages of instruction. Against this background, GoR revised language policy in 2008 to prioritise English as the medium of education. This has led to a new configuration of roles and relations amongst the three languages, with Kinyarwanda the foundation for initial literacy, English the main language of learning, and French an additional language. Sector-wide English-medium education is thus enshrined in the mandate of the Ministry of Education (MINEDUC) through cabinet policy decision.

English language teaching challenges

Since English has a relatively short history and small footprint in Rwanda, the decision to adopt it as Language of Instruction is recognised as neither a small nor a short-term undertaking. Some of the main challenges in implementing the revised policy in classrooms are: the need for teachers to develop their language skills and ability to teach effectively in English; increasing pupils' exposure to English, particularly in rural areas; a shortage of learning materials in English; and the language level of some textbooks being above the pupils' existing competence.

Project description

Across the sector and in key parts of the system – curriculum, textbooks, examinations, and inspection – lack of English proficiency is a constraint on quality education. The situation is exacerbated by there being few opportunities for teachers and students to use the language outside the classroom. As the main planned intervention to facilitate the transition to English-medium education, the Rwanda English in Action Programme (REAP) sets out to address these challenges by providing support to teachers and learners developing English language proficiency. MINEDUC's preferred option has been decentralised face-to-face training for around 50,000 teachers, supported by self-directed study, school-based mentoring, and an assessment tool to help ensure all teachers perform in English to the level required. Students will benefit from the provision of English language support in core curriculum subjects, including audio-visual materials.

Project goal and purpose

The goal of REAP is to contribute to the sector-wide establishment of English-medium education, the purpose being to enable all teachers and learners to become proficient in English by providing them with appropriate learning opportunities and school-based support. The beneficiaries are both teachers and students – male and female – in urban and rural schools. The programme will operate in two three-year phases to help meet the demand for English proficiency amongst teachers, teacher educators, and students,[1] as well as amongst the staff of GoR education agencies.

Stage – policy

This case study focuses on the first stage of English language teaching reform: language policy formation. In the Rwandan English language teaching reform cycle, the policy formation stage, which is critical to the success of other stages in the cycle, offers a number of lessons for policy makers: language policy not only shapes the project framework, but issues arising in the policy design process can have a knock-on effect – with potentially serious implications – for other stages downstream.

Story

Introduction

This narrative of the first stage of English language teaching reform in Rwanda revolves around both the strengths and weaknesses in the policy formation process, in particular an observed gap – or series of gaps – in this process.

Vision and urgency of GoR's development agenda

On the plus side, GoR has a clear vision and sense of urgency for national development. This imperative includes strong investment in the education sector, as 'one of the main pillars of development'[2]. Education policy, including English language teaching reform, is linked to its perceived ability to contribute to the achievement of GoR's broader agenda of economic development and poverty reduction.

The education context of English language teaching reform

English language teaching reform takes place amidst a number of other key initiatives in the sector: the roll-out of Education for All and Nine Years Basic Education, the strengthening of science education, new policies on girls' education and special needs education, curriculum and textbook renewal, reform of national examinations, introduction of early childhood studies, etc. In such a context, it is perhaps not surprising that English language teaching reform competes for time, attention, and resources with other major education developments; or that the risk arises of there being more change-in-the-making than the system and its personnel can comfortably cope with. Understandable as it is that GoR wishes to address a range of issues in the sector, there is the added risk that the quality of individual reforms may be jeopardised by their number and – in a skills-deficit, resource-constrained context – lack of capacity and funds to implement numerous large-scale changes concurrently.

Reform drivers and dynamics

A corollary to the combination of powerful systems drivers (national goals of regional integration and economic development) and GoR's desire to propel forward contributory activities (evident in the fast-tracking of reforms to expedite

---

[1] In a 2009 baseline survey, 85 per cent of primary teachers and 66 per cent of secondary teachers presented at lower levels of English - beginner, elementary, or pre-intermediate.

[2] Extract from President Kagame's address to staff and students at the National University of Rwanda, reported in The New Times on 17 May 2011.

goal achievement) is that it may be necessary for stakeholders and development partners to work harder so as to create time and space for dialogue between decision makers and language policy experts, before key policy decisions are taken. Should this not happen, an information gap may be created in which decisions made by government officials may not be as well informed or taken in the round, were language policy experts to provide input and advice on issues pertinent to language in education.

Policy process and streams

Language policy formation may be conceived as essentially a process coalescing around three broad streams which may be understood as follows:

1. personal/professional desires – encompassing aspirations to English, fluency in which is perceived to facilitate access to socio-economic benefits such as a wider range of jobs, enhanced remuneration, and increased mobility

2. pedagogic issues – based on research findings and understandings of best practice regarding choice of Language of Instruction and learning outcomes in formal education

3. political drivers – such as the government's national vision and desire for English as a gateway to global knowledge, science, and IT.

Gaps in the policy process

In reviewing the early stages of the English language teaching reform in Rwanda, some important questions arise. The first is: might the drive to reform as a means of helping achieve the government's goal of fostering regional integration – including harmonisation of education systems – and economic development, have eclipsed the desirability of giving due weight to pedagogic considerations in policy formation, particularly an understanding of the role of the first language in promoting early literacy and learning? The second is: might the enthusiasm for English language teaching reform have contributed to a policy dialogue gap between decision takers and language experts which may, in turn, have influenced the cabinet's decision in February 2009 to adopt a 'straight-for-English' policy in the sector-wide reform, by substituting it for Kinyarwanda as Language of Instruction from P1 (Primary One)?

Benefit of hindsight

In terms of how language policy makers can best be supported in the decision-making process, one wonders whether, had expert advice on pedagogic issues been available at the time, the cabinet would still have taken the decision to go 'straight for English' in its policy reform? Had such advice been available at the time, would it have led to a moderation of policy? If so, it would then have obviated the need for cabinet to reverse its decision two years later, in February 2011, when Kinyarwanda was reinstated as Language of Instruction from P1 – P3 (Primary One – Primary Three), partly, it seems, on the basis of a new appreciation of the role of the mother tongue in supporting early years' learning[3].

Lessons

Although REAP is a work in progress, with the first implementation phase now under way, there are a number of lessons to be learnt from the initial stage of language policy formation:

1. The need for greater awareness of the dynamics at work in policy formation, in particular the various streams that coalesce in the process; and improved understanding of the link between options and streams – for example, privileging the mother tongue, as a consequence of foregrounding the pedagogic stream, or English (or another world language), by way of emphasising political or personal/professional considerations. Arguably, adopting this wider frame of analysis enables a richer discussion of MoI (medium of instruction) issues; and taking into account the personal/professional, pedagogic, and political strands of the debate yields a more balanced view of some of the key challenges in shaping language policy.

2. The need for an inclusive or holistic approach to policy formation which brings together politicians, pedagogues, and practitioners in dialogue which helps to better inform and enhance the quality of English language teaching reform, rather than create what some observers may perceive as a top-down process, whereby key policy decisions appear to be taken in relative isolation by government.

3. The need to find earlier and better ways of resolving tensions within and between the policy streams referred to, in particular between political or socio-economic drivers of English language teaching reform – in the case of Rwanda, regional integration and economic development through access to global knowledge – and pedagogic principles, informed by international research and best practice on Language of Instruction and learning outcomes. If such could have been achieved at the outset of English language teaching reform in Rwanda, it might possibly have led to a different GoR decision from that made in 2009 to go 'straight for English' as Language of Instruction from P1, and thereby done away with any misunderstanding or confusion arising from the reversal of this policy decision two years later.

4. The need for a co-ordinated approach to major changes in education, including English language teaching reform, that leads to better integration of policies, rather than a tendency to deal with large-scale initiatives separately and thereby risk gaps occurring between the various policies, besides a loss of efficiency in implementation.

---

[3] A New Times article of 16 February 2011 attributed the motivation for the policy change to recognition of the positive relationship between mother tongue and learning in lower primary, as stated by the Minister of State for Primary and Secondary Education.

Case 7:
Textbooks, teams and sustainability in Russia

Catherine Walter

The project

In the first decade of the 21st century, the British Council, in co-operation with the Russian Ministry of Education and numerous regional and local education authorities, carried out a project to develop English language textbooks for primary and secondary schools in Russia. The project was based on a previous successful British Council project in Romania; however, there were several ways in which this project differed from the Romanian project. First of all, the scale of the Russian project and Russia's vast geographical area presented much greater challenges for communication during the project and for dissemination. Secondly, the textbook project was only one (albeit a major one) of a nexus of projects designed to have innovatory systemic effects on the teaching of English in Russia. Thirdly, in addition to tangible products and services, the textbook project, like the others in the nexus, had as a specific goal the development of a team which would learn to work together effectively and creatively, and would become a continuing educational resource for the country. There are many ways in which this project was exemplary; the current case study will focus on the extent to which those design elements of the project which aimed to contribute to sustainability actually achieved that purpose.

Stage – design

This case study will focus on the design stage of the Russian textbook project, where choices were based on national and local priorities, where publication was shared between a Russian and a British publisher, and where project participants were recruited very widely and taught to work in teams. Discussion of the lessons learnt from this will inevitably include reporting of outcomes, dissemination, and embedding.

Story

Designing for sustainability

In 1998, the British Council in Russia, in partnership with the Ministry of Education, began the development of textbook series for primary and secondary school learners of English. The original impetus for the project came from the Ministry of Education and from the English teaching community in Russia. The project was structured so that the books should be published jointly by a Russian publisher and a British publisher, who would share origination costs with the British Council. The national and local demand was for textbooks that were innovative in being output-oriented, i.e. incorporating continuing evaluation of student progress; that used the best of modern language teaching methodology; and that responded to the needs of Russian learners.

The textbook project was part of a nexus of British Council English language projects in Russia which were designed to be mutually supportive. The other projects in the nexus addressed in-service teacher training for primary and secondary teachers, pre-service training for secondary teachers, a national post-secondary English language examination, resources and professional development for university teachers, and mentor training. The synergistic approach adopted for this nexus of projects was a key feature of the design of the projects, and *inter alia* was intended to ensure the sustainability of project outcomes. For example, in-service and pre-service training project members helped organise piloting of the textbook materials nationwide, in collaboration with regional and local education authorities. Piloting was intended not only as an integral part of the development of a quality product, but also in order further to embed the materials in local and regional educational communities. In-service and pre-service training project teams were well placed to seek co-operation in piloting from regional and local education authorities, school administrators, regional teacher trainers and methodologists, teachers, students, and parents. A key principle in the design of the project was that, at all stages, it should be, and should be seen as, a partnership between British and Russian participants, with the Russian participants taking the preponderant role.

In accordance with the Romanian model, teams of potential authors for the books were selected from among practising schoolteachers via a national competition. In addition to a good standard of written and spoken English, and an understanding of modern English language teaching methodology, the candidates were chosen for their aptitude for materials writing, their openness to new ways of working, and their ability to work well in a team. A team of 16 teachers from eight Russian regions was selected to write the secondary materials (*New Millennium English*, henceforth *NME*), and when English language teaching was extended to the primary level, a new team of 14 teachers from six regions was selected to write the primary series, *Millie*. Selection of potential authors was carried out jointly by the British Council, a team of UK consultants from University College Plymouth St Mark and St John, the Ministry of Education, and for *Millie*, the National Training Foundation, an independent body financed by the World Bank, which part-funded *Millie*. There was an eight-to-ten-week residential training course and probationary period led by the consultants who would continue to work on the project before the course teams began their work. Each team had a British Council project manager and an academic manager with experience in the Russian educational system, in materials development, and in project management. The care taken in the selection and development of the author teams and their management derived from a concern for the quality of the books that would be produced, but also for the development of a team of authors/teacher educators who would become a national educational resource after the end of the project. This was specified as one of the key outcomes in the original project frameworks.

Another key principle was to avoid the projects being confined to the privileged Moscow and St Petersburg regions. The author teams were deliberately chosen from across 10 regions of Russia. Although it was clear that this would pose challenges in terms of communication within the teams, the intention was to avoid a product that could be seen as the property of one locality and to ensure that individuals with skills in materials writing, presentation, and teacher education would be available to the educational community across the country at the end of the project.

In summary, then, this ambitious project sought to ensure the sustainability of its outcomes by:

■ embedding the project in a nexus of mutually supportive projects

■ constructing the project at all stages as a Russian-British partnership, with Russian partners taking the major role in initiation of the project and the publication of the materials

■ taking great care in the selection, development, and management of the authors

■ ensuring that the author teams were well distributed across the country and not just in the two major cities; and engaging regional and local educational communities.

Lessons

Were the outcomes achieved and sustained?

In 2006, Richard West, Radislav Milrood, and I undertook a review of the nexus of British Council English language teaching projects that included the textbook project. We studied project documentation and carried out 47 semi-structured interviews and three focus groups, for a total of 71 respondents from 17 towns and cities. Respondents were from all groups with an interest in the project: the Russian Ministry of Education, the British Council, the publishers of the textbooks, the Russian Federal Department for Quality Assurance and Quality Enhancement, the National Training Foundation (an independent body financed by the World Bank), university pedagogical research departments in three cities, regional education authorities, teachers piloting or using the books, and project participants at all levels.

In 2010, I returned to Russia at a time when, on the one hand, the project outcomes were clear: the two textbook series had been published and were being commercialised; and on the other, there had been a period when British-Russian relations had not been at their most cordial. Notably for the present narrative, the British Council's presence in Russia had shrunk from 13 regions to Moscow alone. I interviewed a sample of 12 of the respondents from the earlier review, both in

Moscow and in a major provincial city; the sample included British Council staff, publishers, university pedagogical researchers, regional educational authority officials, and former project participants.

In this section I will use the data from the 2006 and 2010 reviews to make brief comments on each of the design elements discussed above and their impact on the success and sustainability of the project outcomes.

It was felt overwhelmingly by project participants in 2006 that the synergy between the different projects in the nexus was vital both for their development as authors and for their relations with local educational communities in the piloting process and, later, in local adoption of books. In 2010 it was reported that alumni of the pre- and in-service training courses were often key sources of pedagogical innovation for other teachers in their schools and supporters of the textbooks, and that working with the textbooks was recognised as a good preparation for the unified university entrance examination. It is clear that designing a nexus of complementary English language projects can magnify the effects of individual projects.

There were some problems in finding appropriate publisher partners, and lengthy discussions with one British publisher had to be terminated, when it became obvious that they wished to control the project and to use it mainly as a means of promoting their other English language teaching products. This points to the importance of thinking through partnership arrangements in advance, in ways that confer benefit on all partners. However, when appropriate partners were finally found, the publishing process went fairly smoothly, and the Russian publisher reported learning valuable professional knowledge and skills from the UK publisher, and vice versa. The books are being successfully distributed country-wide. There have been some problems with Ministry of Education approval of the books (always a lengthy process in Russia and susceptible to various pressures), but there is no doubt that the clear Russian ownership of the materials and the experience of the Russian publisher will have helped in the process. This output of the project, the textbook series, can be said to be both successful and sustained; sales continue to grow; the Russian publisher is now said to be the largest publisher of English language teaching materials in the country and has expanded its range of textbooks in other disciplines. The binational publishing partnership is a powerful model, if carefully handled.

There was some concern among author team members that funding, equipment, and staff support were sometimes barely sufficient and that this had some impact on stress levels. However, that aside, the development of the author team is perhaps the biggest success story of the project. Over 30 classroom English language teachers from 10 regions of Russia have developed knowledge and skills in syllabus and textbook design and development, principles of assessment and testing, language awareness, principles of teacher training, public presentations, and creative activity in teams. Their expertise is in demand throughout Russia and beyond. A National Training Foundation (NTF) pedagogical expert judged the *NME/Millie* team one of the most advanced materials development teams in Russia, across all educational disciplines. Former members of the team have since been recruited to co-author books in other disciplines than English language. They have been recruited for consultancies in other countries in the region. They are innovators in pedagogy in their regions. The sustainability of this outcome is in no doubt and, given this, future projects might consider more substantial initial resourcing of teams.

The NTF expert also singled out for praise the innovatory model of team-based materials writing distributed across regions, not only for offering opportunities to teachers outside the main cities and for the pioneering model of team authorship, but also because a dissemination network is built in from the beginning of the project. The Russian publisher also commented on this way of working and noted how it shortened the development time for a book. A regional educational authority director interviewed in 2010 contends that his region's consistently superior results in English over the past few years, as compared with neighbouring regions, can be directly linked to the *Millie* and *NME* series and the pedagogy they promote. It is clear that the regional strategy has been successful and has had sustained effects. If this works in the largest country in the world, it is certainly a lesson worth applying elsewhere.

Case 8:
Redesigning a blended learning course in Bosnia and Herzegovina: Introducing new technologies for ELT

Claire Whittaker

The project

This case study will provide an overview of the redesign process of a range of blended learning English language courses in the Armed Forces of Bosnia and Herzegovina (AFBiH). In this context blended learning is defined as a combination of face-to-face, computer, and self-study modes in a single teaching and learning environment. The redesign process was led by the Military English Support Project (MESP) that was established and centrally managed from the United Kingdom by the British Council's Peacekeeping English Project, along with a number of other military English projects across the globe. The courses ranged in level from elementary to upper-intermediate and were taught in 13 centres across the country to accommodate the geographical spread of the AFBiH personnel. The low-level courses were taught by unqualified officer instructors who had received pre-service training from MESP and the higher-level courses by qualified English language teachers employed by MESP.

The redesign process was undertaken in response to the findings from a study which investigated the design of the blended learning courses in the language centres across Bosnia and Herzegovina (BiH). The study revealed numerous and significant inconsistencies between the centres in the duration and intensity of the courses, and the syllabi. This was possibly the consequence of each centre independently developing its own courses. In light of the findings, it became apparent that MESP needed to standardise English language delivery across the centres, primarily to provide learners with comparable learning opportunities. This resulted in what became a three-year iterative redesign process.

Stage – design

This case study principally addresses the design stage of the blended learning courses or, more accurately, the redesign stage, since blended learning courses were in place when the design process commenced. In considering this redesign stage, this case study will stress the importance of identifying the contextual drivers for change at the start of the process and highlight the iterative and therefore potentially lengthy nature of course design. It will also outline one of the challenges to the redesign process that arose from the lack of literature on blended learning course design in ELT settings.

Story

Drivers for change

Once it had been determined that the courses needed to be redesigned, the context was carefully considered, and two drivers for change that would shape and, to a degree, constrain the redesign process were identified. The first was the need to ensure long-term post-project sustainability. The reason for this was that the UK-funded MESP had a fixed end date, after which the management of the centres would be handed over to the AFBiH. Sustainability was, therefore, paramount in terms of cost (i.e. the centres should be inexpensive to run and maintain), content stability (i.e. the course content and materials should be valid for a significant period of time), and instructor fit (i.e. the courses should be relatively straightforward for the unqualified officer instructors to teach, as after the project they would have to teach all the levels). The second was the opening, during the redesign process, of an internationally funded Peace Support Operations Training Centre (PSOTC) that provided education and training for junior officers in the region through the medium of English. This, for the first time, gave the English language centres a clear goal, i.e. to prepare students linguistically for the PSOTC through the provision of General English and English for Specific Purposes courses.

In addition to the contextual drivers for change, two other 'personal' drivers for change were identified. First, opinion from users (who, unless it is otherwise stated, were the officer instructors and teachers) regarding the shortcomings of the original blend was taken into consideration. Furthermore the users were consulted at every stage of the redesign process and essentially formed the design team. The second was my views, as the lead designer, supported by my knowledge and previous experience of course design, on how best to redesign the blend for our context.

By working closely with the users, I was able to make sure that very few aspects of the evolving blend were overlooked. I was also able to widen the knowledge and experience base in relation to the three modes in the blend, in this instance face-to-face, computer, and self-study. (Interestingly this third mode is seemingly uncommon in most blended learning courses and is only referred to in passing in the literature). The self-study mode was championed by two members of the team. One was a qualified teacher of many years standing with an interest in learner autonomy and the other a highly reflective officer instructor with an interest in designing self-study materials. Their advice resulted in the mode being redesigned and integrated in such a way that it became a fundamental component of the blend, rather than playing a peripheral role, as I believe it had in the original blends.

At times the contextual drivers acted as a constraint on the choices that the design team could make with regard to the blend. This simplified the decision-making process by removing some of the challenges. One example was when the design team was divided over the removal and replacement of the language-learning software that had been used in the original blend. However, as cost had been identified as one of the key components of post-project sustainability, the software, which came with a substantial annual licence fee, had to be replaced with software that required a one-off payment.

All four drivers for change played an important role in tailoring the courses throughout the redesign process and led to ensuring the success of the resultant blend. (The success was measured through a summative evaluation using the Delphi Technique[1] that asked the users which aspects of the resultant blend were an improvement on the original blends. The results indicated that a consensus of opinion was reached in favour of numerous features of the resultant blend, although there were areas that required further development, such as testing). The success could be the result of the users' close involvement throughout the redesign process, and indeed such teamwork has been identified in various studies as being vital to the ultimate success of a design. In addition to ensuring the success of the resultant blend, close co-operation during the redesign process also, I believe, fostered a sense of ownership, which was vital, as after the project the officer instructors would be the ultimate users and owners of the blend.

An iterative approach

The English language courses continued to run during the redesign process and, in order to minimise the impact on the users (officer instructors, teachers, and learners) and to allow time for reflection and comment, they were approached in stages over a three-year period. This resulted in an iterative approach to the redesign process, which, according to the literature, is fairly typical, as 'effective designs will only evolve through cycles of practice, evaluation, and reflection' (Beetham and Sharpe 2007a: 8). In fact 'as many as three of four iterations of course design, development, and implementation may be needed to complete the transition from traditional to blended e-learning course' (Sharpe and Oliver 2007: 48). For this redesign project, this would have been a conservative estimate, as the number could almost be doubled for the transition from the original to the resultant blend. This was largely context-dependent, in view of the number of users involved in the process, their widespread geographical distribution, the number of courses that had to be redesigned (ranging from elementary to upper-intermediate), and my relative inexperience, at the time, as a blended learning course designer.

Approaching the redesign process in iterative stages, although time-consuming, was essential to allow time to implement the changes, trial them, collect response from the users (officer instructors, teachers, and learners), reflect on the findings,

---

[1] The Delphi Technique 'is a method for the systematic solicitation and collection of judgements on a particular topic through a set of carefully designed sequential questionnaires interspersed with summarised information and feedback of opinions derived from earlier responses' (Delbecq, Van de Ven, and Gustafson (1975), quoted in Lindqvist and Nordanger 2007: 2).

meet as a group to discuss them, and plan and prepare for the next iteration. This approach was intended to reduce the impact of the redesign process on the users, by minimising the number and size of the changes that were being implemented at any one time. Moreover, the repetitive process demanded a high degree of user involvement, which, as was previously stated, was believed to have led to the ultimate success and acceptance of the resultant blend.

The theory behind the practice
At the time of the redesign process, little had been written on the practicalities of blended learning design in ELT settings above lesson level. However, at this level, the literature advocated that the face-to-face and computer modes should be linked grammatically or thematically. It also stressed that the 'effective implementation of technology is not accomplished just as an 'add-on' to existing tools: it must be synergised into the language learning environment with the support of surrounding educational systems' (Yang 2001: 92). No references to the inclusion of a third mode, self-study, were found in the literature. Therefore, with little theoretical support or practical advice at course level, the concept of agreement between the modes, which, as the literature advocated, could be realised either grammatically or thematically, was adopted as one of the guiding principles in the redesign process.

The absence of information on blended learning course design meant that development of the blend was practice-led and context-dependent. This lack of theoretical support or practical advice could have been viewed as a challenge and certainly at times was frustrating, but ultimately it gave the design team freedom to design without restrictions and to learn by experience. Nevertheless, research is still needed on blended learning in ELT settings to enhance the quality of the blends, because there is a 'huge deficit in terms of research on using blended learning by individuals or small language schools' (Westbrook 2008: 14).

Lessons

Two key learning points emerged from this redesign project. The first was the importance of identifying the contextual drivers for change before undertaking any design or redesign process, as ultimately they will shape the direction that the design takes. This supports the view that, when designing a blended learning course, there is '...no single optimal mix. What configuration is best can only be determined relative to whatever goals and constraints are presented in a given situation' (Shaw and Igneri 2006: 3). In addition to the contextual drivers, the personal drivers for change also need to be recognised, and in this instance the success of the resultant blend was to a large extent due to the involvement of the end users in the redesign process.

The second learning point is not to underestimate the length of time required to design or redesign a course effectively, if an iterative approach is adopted. The redesign process in this case study was conducted over an arguably long three-year period and, although the reasons for this were largely contextual, it does illustrate the potentially lengthy nature of such an undertaking.

Lastly, in the course of the redesign project, a lack of literature on blended learning course design specifically related to ELT settings was identified. This needs to be addressed in order to enhance the quality of blended learning environments in these contexts and to redress the balance of studies on the matter that are emerging from the tertiary sector.

The cases: Implementation

Case 9:
Making it work: A case study of a teacher training programme in China

Lin Hong

The project

For quite a long time English was not a required subject in the national curriculum in China, although it was offered at primary level from the early 1990s at grade 4 or 5 (ages 9–11). Schools could choose to offer English to students, if they felt it necessary and if they had the teachers. However, in 2001, as a result of the global expansion of programmes in English Teaching to Young Learners, as well as of China's rapid social and economic change, the Ministry of Education of China initiated a curriculum innovation: the promotion of English as a foreign language in primary schools, from grade 3 (ages 8–9).

The overall goals of primary English in China are to 'develop students' comprehensive language competence by making learning a process during which students can develop language proficiency, form positive attitudes, improve thinking skills, increase cross-cultural awareness, and learn to use learning strategies so as to gradually become independent learners' (Ministry of Education 2001: 7). The framework of strands in the English curriculum for the primary phase is designed with specific can-do statements for each strand. The performance descriptors indicate a change in methodology which encourages an activity-based approach designed to involve students in the learning and make it an enjoyable experience. Thus, the training of primary English teachers was seen as crucial to the success of this nationwide English teaching reform.

The Primary English Teacher Training Project (PETT) was launched in Guangdong province in 2001 against this background. The aim was to train as many primary English teachers as possible to adapt to learner-centred communicative activities. PETT was co-ordinated by the British Council and Guangdong Department of Education, and was conducted by the University of Leeds and Guangdong Teachers College of Foreign Languages and Arts (GTCFLA). In three years, a total of 102 local trainers were trained, first at GTCFLA and then at the University of Leeds. These in turn cascaded to 4,800 primary English teachers in the province. Although the British Council's involvement ended in 2005, the cascade training is still taking place at the time of writing (2011).

PETT has been regarded as the most successful in-service primary English teacher training programme ever in Guangdong and has earned a good reputation across the country. At about the same time, similar projects sponsored by the British Council were also carried out in Shanghai and Chongqing, but none of them perhaps had such a significant effect as PETT.

Stage – implementation

Localisation is the priority for a foreign training project. Usually, at least in China, it is foreign trainers who design the whats and hows of a programme on the basis of their understanding of the local situation and context, after a brief survey. However, such an approach has been shown to be problematic, in terms of gaining the full appreciation and engagement of local stakeholders. Thus, instead of concentrating its efforts on localising foreign trainers, PETT shifted its approach to training local trainers, using a cascade approach.

In PETT, there were three levels of trainers: the first level covered trainers who had attended the University of Leeds training; the second level, local teachers who received both GTCFLA and University of Leeds training; and the third level, those local teachers who underwent GTCFLA training only. The first level participated mainly in training the second level, and in supervising and evaluating the cascade training. The second level was responsible for designing the whole training package and training the third level. The third level acted as assistants, organisers, or trainers in the cascade training.

What is especially noteworthy about PETT is that it produced a large number of beneficiaries and had a high level of sustainability. The credit for this must go to the cascade training. However, if both the Shanghai and the Chongqing projects also used this model, why was it that PETT in Guangdong stood out, in terms of its impact? Let us look into the implementation of the Guangdong project.

Story

How to select the second-level trainers?

The plan was that four cohorts of trainers would receive training at GTCFLA for two weeks and then some of them, having been recommended by their local governments, would go to the University of Leeds for an additional three months' training. Previously, it had been very rare for a primary school teacher in China to get the chance to study abroad. Thus, the issue of who would be on the trainer list was tricky and complicated. The list of recommended candidates initially appeared anomalous, in that it included some teachers who had not attended the early training at GTCFLA and some who had very poor English. In order to ensure that the later cascade training was implemented to a high standard, GTCFLA consulted with the Guangdong Department of Education and was granted the final say on the choice of candidates for the programme in Leeds. Those who could not pass the special test in teaching methodology and English proficiency set by the University of Leeds and those whose candidature was clearly irrelevant were removed from the trainer list. Thus, a high-level team of trainers was built up. These 102 trainers went on to play a very important role in PETT. They have been referred to as the 'seeds' of PETT and many of them are now well known in the field of teacher training in China.

How to improve the project's coverage with a limited budget?

There are 21 prefecture-level cities in Guangdong province. Except for the six Pearl River Delta cities, the rest, 15 cities, mostly in remote or mountainous areas, are underdeveloped. The provincial government subsidised PETT, contributing 10,000,000 yuan, which covered training fees, but not travelling and accommodation costs. A provincial programme is usually expected to run in the provincial capital, and GTCFLA is located in Guangzhou, the capital of Guangdong province. For the sake of training quality and convenience, in the early days of PETT the cascade training sessions were always based at GTCFLA. Teachers outside the Pearl River Delta are usually of a relatively low professional level and require a good deal of training. As the project went on, however, quite a number of them were to give up what was for them a rare chance for training. It was found that teachers were hesitant to commit if their local government or schools could not pay for their travel costs and their accommodation expenses in Guangzhou.

The question of how to enable more teachers, especially those in remote and mountainous areas, to benefit from PETT was raised. As a result, a major change was made: in order to ease the financial burden on a municipal government, the cascade training would be held locally. Instead of having trainees travel to Guangzhou, the trainers moved from city to city. Afterwards, the provincial training held at GTCFLA was mainly focused on preparing qualified trainers to implement more training. In order to ensure a city had enough trainers, a provincial quota was assigned to each city. In addition, all teachers from underdeveloped areas were given full financial support from the provincial government for their training at GTCFLA or the University of Leeds. As a result, PETT was able to achieve the widest possible coverage of all primary English teacher training projects in Guangdong.

How to sustain the project?

The answer was to make full use of *JIAOYANYUAN*. There is no exact English translation for this. They are teaching and research fellows, and are key people for the success of education reform. They have three roles to play: as teachers, researchers, and administrators. One of their duties is to organise and provide training for teachers in their districts. If they are not involved in a project or take no interest in it, the project is likely to fail. In PETT, all *JIAOYANYUAN* were given priority when it came to attending the provincial training at GTCFLA or going to the University of Leeds for further training. In this way, they automatically became PETT trainers and were under an obligation to help in organising cascade training. For example, Ms Ling, a researcher in Guangzhou city, was among the first cohort of trainers to go to the University of Leeds. She became an advocate of PETT. After she returned from the United Kingdom, she participated as a trainer in six PETT cascade trainings for three consecutive years. When PETT officially stopped in 2005, she continued to organise similar training herself in her district and actively participated in those organised by her counterparts around the province. Statistics show that more than 3,000 primary English teachers received post-PETT training from their district researchers.

Lessons

1. The commitment of all participants in a project should be clearly established before the project starts. For example, if a trainer cannot take part in cascade training, he or she should not be trained as a trainer in the first place. In PETT, all of the trainers joined in the cascade training held at GTCFLA immediately after their return from the training in Leeds. But for some of them, this was the only time they carried out their duty as trainers. Perhaps the trainers should be asked to sign a contract to make their duty clear and ensure their participation.

2. Consider adapting a training package for cascade training according to the local context. China is a huge country and, even within a province, there are great differences from city to city. For example, in a developed area, like Dongguan city, where local teachers had better English and were more open to new ideas, our module *Using drama in language teaching in primary schools* was appropriate and the training courses could be given in English. However, in a less developed area, like Meixian city, where many teachers were not English specialists and held qualifications in other disciplines such as Chinese language, maths, or physical education, the *TPR* (Total Physical Response) module seemed to be a better choice, and the course was given mostly in Chinese. Similarly, the period of training was not fixed and could be varied according to the budget available.

3. Leave the hard nuts to your Chinese counterpart to crack. In PETT, the British Council and Guangdong Department of Education were funding providers and policy makers, while the University of Leeds and GTCFLA were supervisors and executives. So, in dealing with a local government, it was wise for the British Council to act as a funding provider and Guangdong Department of Education as a policy maker. For the same reason, in coping with a tough situation in training, it was advisable for the University of Leeds to act as a supervisor, rather than as an executive.

4. Group trainers operated in a combination that consisted of one trainer from a teacher training college, one from an education bureau, and one from a primary school. This tripartite structure has been proved to work best, because each of them plays an irreplaceable role in the training. In PETT, those from teacher training colleges (teacher trainers) had a superior command of English and knowledge of ELT theory. They took the lead in the cascade training. Those from education bureaux *(JIAOYANYUAN)* had a great impact on classroom teaching and were in charge of local teacher training. Those from primary schools (known as 'backbone' English teachers) were experienced in teaching primary English and practised the teaching ideas promoted in PETT in their classes, as examples for fellow teachers.

5. The lesson is: make sure you get support from local governments at all levels and do not take it for granted that a provincial project can be carried out smoothly in smaller cities or town without the right conditions.

6. It is true that even with sound policy and a well-designed plan, a project may not work successfully if the implementation is flawed or goes wrong. PETT, a successful Sino-British teacher training project, has provided us with valuable experience.

Case 10:
The Teacher Training Colleges Project in Poland

Hanna Komorowska

The project

A new national project, undertaken as part of the 1990 reform, aimed to establish a dense network of three-year colleges which would, in a relatively short time, offer teaching qualifications to secondary school students with intermediate language skills. The training programme focused on language proficiency, teaching skills, and skills that would enable students to function as agents of change in the process of democratising Polish education. The length of study was decided on the basis of research data showing that the language skills of students in Polish language departments plateaued after the third year of studies (Wysocka 1989). The six-term course (around 2,000 hours) consisted of four basic components designed to develop practical language skills, pedagogical competences, and language teaching skills, and to prepare graduates for follow-up MA courses through background studies in literature and linguistics. The course also included a period of teaching practice.

The project was a response to an urgent need to promote foreign languages in Poland after the fall of communism. Before this, Russian was mandatory in schools of all levels from grade IV of primary onwards, but was taught as a political message of dependence, rather than an instrument of communication. A second foreign language was part of the curriculum only in lycée-type schools. As only 14 per cent of learners aged 15–19 attended this type of school, and English and German enjoyed equal status in mass education, English was available to no more than seven per cent of Polish school learners, in spite of the huge demand that could be seen in the large market for private lessons.

The main educational reform introduced by the first democratic government abolished the mandatory status of Russian, introduced equal status of foreign languages taught in the school system, and encouraged the earlier start for the teaching of two foreign languages in schools.

With 18,000 Russian teachers and only 2,400 teachers of English and German, Poland quickly had to train around 20,000 teachers of Western languages, mostly English – an impossible task for the very few language departments offering five-year theoretical courses at universities. Moreover, university graduates educated in big cities were unwilling to work in the provinces. Retraining Russian teachers was unrealistic, because of their lack of skills in other languages, but also because of their lack of communicative teaching skills. Teacher Training Colleges were a chance to solve the problem. The project was implemented in October 1990, in spite of resistance on the part of universities which feared a loss of their monopoly in the field of languages, but with the support of the democratically elected local decision makers and, paradoxically, former communists who – especially in small towns – were eager to show their usefulness in a new situation. To supervise implementation, take care of dissemination and, above all, solve the problems which were sure to emerge, the National Council for Teacher Education was set up by the Ministry of Education.

Although the original plan was to open 30 colleges, pressure from local communities and their guarantee of premises and staff led to the opening of 50 colleges with 1,500 places for students of English (41 language programmes in total in the colleges), 400 for students of French (19 language programmes), and 450 for students of German (13 language programmes) (Komorowska 1991). A few years later, several colleges opened language programmes for future teachers of Spanish and Italian.

Dissemination and sustainability proved more than satisfactory. In 2005, the number of foreign language (FL) teacher training colleges reached 82 (Country Report. Poland 2006). The fact that, in the first years, graduates tended to look for employment outside mass education, because of low salaries in state schools, was not considered a failure of the system, as their appearance on the market raised the quality of education in newly established private schools of all levels, as well as in language schools (Fisiak 1992, Komorowska 2007). Today, i.e. in 2011, the number of colleges is still as high as 66. The college system is supposed to function until 2014 – which will give it a life span of 25 years – and, by that date, colleges are supposed to become fully integrated with the university system. Some colleges will close down as a result of a downward trend in population figures, but most of the programmes taught by today's staff will survive, albeit within different formal structures.

Stage – implementation

The stage which seems to be most useful to describe in the present case study is implementation. This is because most of the decisions worth discussing here were related to difficulties which arose during the implementation of the new system. It is relatively difficult, however, to separate the design stage and the early phase of implementation of the college network because of the speed with which all the Polish reforms were planned and implemented after the fall of communism.

Story

In analysing what led to successful implementation, which in turn ensured the dissemination and sustainability of the system, let us first look at those organisational decisions which proved to be constructive and then at those related to curricular issues which had to be taken to meet some challenges encountered in the early phase of the functioning of the system.

Initial impetus through early organisational decisions

Decisions made in the initial phase of implementation of the project gave initial impetus and proved significant for the future of the system. The overview of difficulties is here presented from the point of view of the designer of the whole system and the first director of the flagship college set up at Warsaw University.

Crucial *organisational decisions* which led to success included:

- the decision to focus the college curriculum on language skills, as this made colleges attractive to students and helped the dissemination process

- the decision to go for a three-year course of studies, which turned out to be a lucky one, as when the Bologna process started in 1999 resulting in the introduction of three-year BA and two-year MA studies at universities, the fact of having the same length of study at colleges and for university BA courses facilitated smooth integration and ensured sustainability; a decision in favour of two- or four-year programmes would have meant the death of the colleges after the first decade of their life

- the decision to create a dense network of colleges, in spite of the lack of the legal uniformity of the system, as this helped to increase the number of graduates and thus to reduce teacher shortages quickly. (University colleges were subject to the Higher Education Act and Local Educational Authority (LEA) colleges to the Schools Act. University students would, therefore, obtain teaching qualifications with a BA diploma and be able to continue their studies towards an MA, while – in spite of having covered the same programme – LEA college students would only get a certificate of teaching qualifications and would thus have to start a BA course at a university in order to enter an MA course three years later)

- the decision to require university supervision and quality control in order to ensure academic recognition of coursework completed at the colleges run by LEAs, and permission for LEA college graduates to sit BA exams and start follow-up MA studies, as this helped to avoid blind alleys in education and to enable all college graduates to obtain a university degree at BA level

- the decision to encourage agreements between LEAs financing colleges and presidents of supervising universities, on the basis of which the university would ensure its staff's participation in the admission process, staff recruitment, language examinations, and final college-leaving exams, while the local educational board would provide the budget for all those activities, as it gave more power and status, as well as extra finance, to the universities, which then took a much more favourable view of the new system.

Facing unexpected challenges – some crucial curricular decisions

Future sustainability of the system strongly depended on *curricular decisions* taken in response to challenges emerging at the implementation stage.

An early difficulty in this area consisted in the fact that a fairly general curriculum framework and differences in the way supervision was conducted by universities brought about huge differentiation in the curriculum structure of individual colleges. Differences in local staff availability were also a factor here. Moreover, teacher trainers jumped at the chance of giving status to their subject areas by increasing their curricular time at the expense of others, to the point where excessive changes undermined the comparability of study programmes. In response, a more precise curriculum framework was laid out by the National Council of Teacher Education, with a centrally decided ratio between curricular components. Individual decisions about the required minimum of contact hours were to be taken by Pedagogical Councils at colleges and approved by the supervising university. Subject-area co-ordinators were also appointed in all the larger colleges. Moreover, conferences for teacher trainers were organised to develop team spirit and a sense of participation in a national teacher education programme. This proved sufficient in terms of diploma and qualifications recognition, and at the same time left enough space for flexibility. A degree of curricular variety proved beneficial for the sustainability of the college system, as, on the one hand, it strengthened the supervising university's link with its own fields of research and, on the other, it helped the local educational authorities maintain the college in their district using human resources available there.

Yet more problems were to arise, some involving the students, and some the teachers. In the first years of the life of the colleges, a high dropout rate was noticed after the first two terms which could not be ascribed to study problems. It became apparent that some students treated colleges as free language schools. The first year gave them up to 700 language hours, after which they chose other study programmes or sought employment for which their newly acquired skills qualified them. To solve the problem, the National Council for Teacher Education decided to spread practical language teaching more evenly throughout the three years of study and to increase dramatically the participation of subjects directly connected with teacher education in the first two terms of study. This helped to attract students who were genuinely interested in obtaining teaching qualifications. The college staff also experienced difficulties as a result of their lack of syllabus design skills. The solution was almost immediately found in international co-operation. Colleges were encouraged to enter international programmes of the European Union such as TEMPUS (Trans-European Mobility Scheme for University Studies) and JEN (Joint European Network) to build contacts and benefit from the sharing of expertise. A special programme, PRINCE (Projects in Controlled Environments), was also set up by the British Council to help link Polish colleges with British universities so that they could benefit from British curriculum construction expertise. As a result of teacher education conferences, special interest groups were formed to work on particular subject methodologies.

It also became apparent that students did not have enough opportunities to observe good practice, although they seemed to have spent sufficient time observing language classes at various schools. This was due in part to the shortage of highly qualified language teachers who could function as mentors. Consequently, students lacked skills to analyse classes they watched critically, and were unable to gain perspective on their own teaching. This marked a difficult moment in the life of the colleges – there were calls for some colleges to be closed down. The solution to the problem was found in collaboration with in-service teacher training centres. Highly qualified teachers were located and their lessons were recorded. Series of recordings illustrating methodology were then distributed among the colleges to enable students to get acquainted with as much good practice as possible during in-college video sessions. Special mentor training programmes were also initiated and a new methodology slot was introduced in the final year of studies during which college teacher educators individually consulted trainees and helped them develop autonomy and self-reflection.

Lessons

The main learning points from the implementation phase can be summarised in the following dos and don'ts:

- Respond quickly not just to burning needs, but also to every difficulty! Immediate reaction to seemingly minor curricular challenges and not just to major problems related to legal issues proved crucial for further success.

- Do not wait for ideal solutions. Forget the 'all or nothing' philosophy! The decision to establish a dense network of small colleges was by no means ideal and created lots of problems, but was worth all the problems which came in the initial period, as the network helped to provide qualified staff for small schools in distant regions of the country.

- Co-operate with everybody, your former enemies included! Friendly co-operation with major universities which initially opposed the college idea resulted in the creation of follow-up opportunities for college graduates and at the same time opened a new source of finance for the universities.

- Do not get carried away by success. Look for critical feedback! Complaints from the teaching staff helped to produce a new curriculum framework which preserved the autonomy of the colleges and the supervising universities, while at the same time ensuring comparability of education and recognition of college diplomas.

- Do not try to salvage a bad situation by fighting undesired behaviour: create rewards for desired behaviour! Instead of trying to block the activity of teachers who wanted to give more status to their own subject area at the expense of other subjects, the work of subject area co-ordinators was rewarded and conference participation was sponsored for teachers who decided to present their ideas at inter-college staff meetings where proposed innovations were to be discussed.

- Think globally, act locally, and always look for good local solutions to share with others! Local changes in the syllabus, teaching practice, and mentor training were successfully communicated to other colleges and made their way into a generalised curricular framework recommended for the whole country.

Case 11:
Change in Tamil Nadu, India

Clare O'Donahue

The project

In 2009 UNICEF (United Nations Children's Fund), Sharva Shiksha Abhiyan (SSA), the Indian government's flagship programme for Universalisation of Elementary Education, and the British Council's regional initiative *Project English* began working together on a large-scale teacher development programme aiming to improve English language teaching and learning for over 6,000,000 children in 37,000 government primary schools in Tamil Nadu, South India.

From 2003-07, Activity Based Learning (ABL) was introduced into primary classrooms in Tamil Nadu. An extensive training and development programme which significantly challenged existing teaching and learning practices in Tamil Nadu was rolled out to teachers. As a result of this ambitious programme, the seeds for change were sown, and teachers began to question their beliefs and practice as they became part of the changing learning environment.

Because of the demand for English in India, many parents are making uninformed choices to remove their children from local-medium government provision and send them to the growing number of low-cost private English-medium schools. It was against this developing background that UNICEF, the SSA, and the British Council's *Project English* set about facilitating change in English language teaching and learning for children in government schools, as they progressed through and beyond the ABL system. A large-scale development programme was initiated which would select and directly train 900 master trainers, who, in turn, would cascade the training to 120,000 teachers of one year group.

Extensive dialogue about the expected outcomes took place between the three partners throughout the initiation stage, during which clear communication channels were established. Following a needs analysis, it was agreed and communicated that the overall aims would be to improve teacher confidence when using English in the classroom and to increase opportunities for learner interaction, while keeping within the existing curriculum and textbooks.

Stage – implementation

This case study aims to explore strategies and reflect on their effectiveness during the implementation stage. Limitations of the cascade model are fully recognised but, because of the large numbers involved and the vast geographical reach in India, direct teacher training was not an option. The cascade model is used extensively in India and mitigating risk was a shared concern. On the basis of the previous experience of the partner organisations, strategies for minimising transition loss were embedded into the implementation plan.

Story

There were many factors which impacted on the effective implementation of this programme. These can be categorised into three key areas: collaboration, communication, and engagement.

Collaboration

Agreeing partners' specific roles (see Table 1 below) at the outset of the programme laid the foundation for a plan which recognised each organisation's expertise and set the scene for reciprocal learning. An environment of mutual respect and trust was created by holding consultations and meetings which involved key stakeholders working at different levels within their organisations. Listening to, acknowledging, and acting on suggestions discussed in these consultations led to buy-in from the key players.

SSA	UNICEF	British Council
• overall action plan • monitoring and field-level support • support residential training programme for master trainers • all logistical arrangements for cascade/planning meetings • funds for monitoring master trainers and cascade training ensuring similar standards in training sessions at cascade levels throughout.	• technical and financial assistance • monitoring both master trainers and cascade training • professional knowledge and expertise relating to context • ongoing advice and support.	• needs analysis and design of training modules for master trainers and teachers • direct training and monitoring of master trainers • monitoring cascade training • providing follow-up support and advice.

Table 1: The partners' roles and responsibilities

Table 1 shows the clearly defined roles and responsibilities related to organisation expertise agreed during the initiation phase.

The co-operation of local implementers was achieved by undertaking pre-programme visits to venues out in the districts to identify and mitigate potential risks. These visits included meeting local administrative staff, teachers, and teacher educators, which enabled a rapport to be built, and assessing the venue and accommodation, inspecting the restrooms, and, perhaps most importantly, sampling the food the participants were expected to eat!

Comprehensive monitoring and evaluation were undertaken throughout the programme by all partners at all levels. Monitoring visits made by representatives from the three partner organisations often coincided with each other, where we made ourselves highly visible and accessible while we shared key findings and agreed on subsequent action. Good relationships with each other, the participants, and the administrators were built up by this close, on-the-ground monitoring schedule. Supporting each other to work towards a common goal meant that there was no place for egos, only reciprocation.

Communication

Establishing clear and transparent two-way communication channels helped to build an atmosphere of trust and ownership, where all stakeholders and interested parties were equally valued. The SSA had already set up a 1,500 strong closed user group mobile network for staff working at all levels across the state. This allowed free access to anyone at any level at any time in an environment where access to the internet and e-mails is extremely restricted. This mobile network proved an invaluable means of communicating, not only from head office to district, but also district to district and organisation to organisation. Text messaging became the *modus operandi*. Many logistical glitches were cleared up swiftly and efficiently on the spot, because of the instant accessibility of the relevant team members located across the state.

In each delivery district, a local media officer was assigned to document the participants' experience and to alert the local press and television networks. A press release was prepared and widely circulated through the extensive networks of the three organisations, and newspaper articles were often released in both English and local language versions to widen the reach.

Engagement

When initiating, planning, implementing, or evaluating the programme, we kept in mind the following mantra: 'It is people who make the change possible, not the policies' (Wedell 2009). Master trainers are the direct communication with teachers and, similarly, teachers are the direct communication with learners. Both layers need to be convinced that the proposed 'change' will have beneficial effects. Not only do they need to know 'What's in it for me?', but it also helps if they know what the intended change in classroom practice might look like.

Several strategies to ensure participant buy-in have already been mentioned, such as meaningful consultation leading to shared expectations and the importance of building a relationship of mutual respect and trust.

In Tamil Nadu all the training courses for the master trainers were residential. This meant that the programme was different, special, and allowed the participants to be fully engaged for the whole 10 days. Much reflection and sharing of ideas took place in the evenings, as well as the forming of new friendships and bonding as a teaching community. Provision for those who had home responsibilities that could not be neglected was also made; for example, one participant brought her mother to look after her small baby while she attended the sessions.

Trainers and teachers of class 5 had already been a party to a certain amount of reculturing (Fullan 2007) brought about by the implementation of ABL in classes 1–4. They had seen and heard the change in the ABL classrooms in their schools; their curiosity had been aroused. Therefore, from the start of the English programme, there was generally a willingness to learn and an openness to change. This pre-acclimatisation had a positive impact on the uptake of new ideas and methodologies presented in the course.

New ideas may challenge existing beliefs and practice, so time must be allocated for adequate sharing and trying out of new ideas. Immediately after the master training and before the cascade to teachers, master trainers attended a three-day planning workshop. They gathered in groups from different batches and districts in order to facilitate cross-fertilisation of ideas, share their experiences, and group-plan their cascade to teachers. It also gave the master trainers time to reflect on their own learning.

Another principle we held in our minds throughout was: 'One size does not fit all.' Bringing the master trainers together enabled them to plan and adapt the materials to make them suitable for teachers in their local context. Master trainers were also strategically paired up to deliver the programme. It was recognised that the benefits of co-delivery outweighed the extra cost implications. Delivering in pairs meant that there was less lost in transmission, strengths of individuals were recognised, and those less confident were supported by their peers; in addition, risks of absenteeism through sickness were minimised.

Lessons

So what lessons did we learn from working on the Tamil Nadu project and what advice would we pass on to others when implementing educational change programmes?

- First and foremost, we learnt to go with the flow. In most instances, it is advisable and significantly less stressful than trying to impose alien procedures which may match your own preconceptions or plan, but may not be acceptable or appropriate for the local context. This is particularly important to remember when partnering with local organisations that have invariably had experience in their own environment. Collaboration, to us, meant recognising each other's expertise, listening to each other, valuing each other's input, and moving forward together towards a shared goal.

- Take considerable care and attention when building up a working relationship and opening effective communication channels with those you are relying on for smooth implementation. It is well worth the time and effort. Identify the most effective mode of communication and adapt and use modes most effective in and acceptable to the given environment, whether this means using cloud computing or carrier pigeons!

- Ensure the overall aims of the programme are agreed and that the partners have a shared understanding of what these aims look like in the classroom. Meeting participant expectations is a crucial factor for success.

- Clearly set out and communicate the agreed roles and responsibilities of all those involved and, when action is demanded, do it quickly and effectively and expect all others involved in the programme to do the same.

- Recognise that state policy cannot take each specific locality into account. Adaptations which do not interfere with the broad aims of the programme should be made by the people who work within the local context. Build in time for participants to share ideas, reflect, and empower them to adapt the programme, if necessary.

- Change takes time and effort, so do not expect to see results overnight. If the outcome of the programme involves a change in beliefs or attitudes, it will very much depend on where the teachers are at the beginning of a programme and how far they may need to travel. Local implementers are key players in communicating change: build a good rapport with them and value their contributions.

- Remember that it is the people and not the policies that effect change. Listen to and value individual expertise. Give due importance to the physical comfort of trainers and trainees; their perception that they are being treated with all due care and respect will minimise the risk of disengagement. Do not underestimate the importance of selecting venues which offer the best possible facilities! One disgruntled participant can cause a negative ripple effect across a whole programme.

- Observations and opinion from comprehensive monitoring and evaluation throughout the programme by all partners at all levels of the cascade are essential, as this allows information sharing both horizontally and vertically within and across the partner organisations.

- Finally, celebrate and communicate success and provide continuing support for trainers and teachers to enable them to continue growing after the initial programme has concluded.

Case 12:
The Romanian Textbook Project: Learning together, driving reform

Ruxandra Popovici

The project

English emerged in the last decade of the 20th century as the dominant foreign language in Romania. In the wake of the 1989 revolution and the overthrow of the totalitarian communist regime, the demand for English kept growing. In the increasingly open world of the end of the 20th century, the English language was seen as a key tool for providing access to European and international communication, information, and the labour market. Therefore, Romania's national education authority placed English language education at the forefront of its reforms. The British Council was quick to partner the Romanian Ministry of Education in its effort to set up the reform process. This partnership placed English language teaching and teachers of English at the forefront of educational change. The British Council's joined-up thinking on ELT in 1991 provided the foundation for the first coherent reform framework in Romanian education, covering new curricula and textbooks, in-service and pre-service teacher training, inspector training, cultural studies, and language for specific purposes.

In 1991, the Ministry of Education, in partnership with the British Council Romania, launched a textbook project, with the aim of producing a new series of eight textbooks of English, one for each of the secondary school grades in Romania (grades 5–12), and creating local expertise in materials writing. The need to replace instructional materials that were outdated in content and methodology was urgent and was recognised by the teaching community and the education policy decision makers as a key part of the overall education reform agenda. Textbooks have been constantly perceived in Romanian education as one of the 'genres of power' (Wells 1999: 145) that construes reality in a form that can influence people's values and attitudes. This perception contributed to the decision to put significant resources into a project that could have far-reaching impact. It became clear in the following years that the English textbook component was, to a large extent, the driving and unifying factor behind the whole area of pre-university EFL (English as a foreign language) education.

The fact that the Romanian textbook project was written locally has been central to its success. As Bolitho comments:

> Locally produced materials can best reflect the values and cultural norms of the society in which they are used and can view the culture of the target language from a position of security. (Bolitho 2002: 44)

Stage – implementation

The novelty of the project and the long and winding road to educational change within the transition context of the early 1990s in Romania made detailed initial planning of the project difficult. Those involved in the project had to exercise critical thinking and flexibility in order to deal efficiently with innumerable setbacks, moving goalposts, and even changes of educational policies. Therefore, I consider that the dynamics of the implementation phase, which I am going to focus on in this paper, are particularly important for those involved in the conceptual planning and development of educational projects.

Story

Acting on recommendations made following a scoping visit by a UK ELT expert in 1991, the British Council and the Ministry of Education agreed on a project outline, and University College Plymouth St Mark and St John was selected as the UK partner institution through an open tender. In late 1991, the British Council in Bucharest advertised nationally for writers. The applicants, all teachers, mostly from secondary schools, were required to submit a sample teaching unit, and the shortlisted candidates were called for an interview. For the first time in Romania, a textbook series was going to be authored by a large team made up of experienced and less experienced secondary teachers from the five regions of the country, who were going to work under the guidance of UK consultants. The selection of at least two teachers from the same city in each case was seen as a means of ensuring that no writer would work in isolation.

For everyone in the team, the sense of responsibility for the great task that lay ahead went hand in hand with excitement at spending 10 weeks in the United Kingdom doing a course commissioned for the group and getting first-hand exposure to British culture. During this initial course, the teachers were given an update on ELT methodology and were trained in syllabus and materials writing design. The Romanian textbook team was one of the first professional groups in the country which started to work in organised teams, thereby proving that the individualist attitudes of the past could be replaced by a collaborative culture. By the end of the course, Rod Bolitho, one of the college tutors, had agreed to take on the role of consultant to the project. His perspective demonstrates the two-way learning process that the textbook project involved from the beginning:

> For the tutors in Plymouth, work with their Romanian colleagues had added a dimension to their thinking about English language teaching ... and had begun to overturn some of their own deep-rooted prejudices about life in a one-time communist country. (Popovici and Bolitho 2003: 506)

Looking back on it, all the writers considered that the initial course was undoubtedly the most important formative experience for them.

In accordance with the working pattern that was initially agreed, that of dividing into two writing teams at lower and upper secondary levels, the writers were allocated units and encouraged to work in teams on a city basis. All writers would then come to the regular workshops, with their units in draft form, for peer-reading and team discussion. These were intense working sessions that soon became points of reference for the writers. Without exception, all those involved in the project saw the writing workshops as a key context for learning, by writing together.

The path of project implementation was not a smooth or straight one. There were highlights and achievements, but also setbacks and moments of crisis. One turning point in the life of the project was the decision to invite one of the writers to take on the manager's role, following the resignation of a newly appointed UK manager. She would become the first Romanian manager of a British Council ELT project. At the same time, the consultancy structure changed when Rod Bolitho was joined by a British consultant, Sue Mohamed, who took responsibility for working with the lower secondary team. This decision made working on two levels of the textbook in parallel possible and ensured that publishers' deadlines and the Ministry's textbook competition schedules were met. Eventually all pieces of the management, consultancy, and team structures fell into place and ensured the project's progress and stability in times of change.

Another turning point was the change in the Ministry textbook provision policy. The 'unique textbook' system was replaced by the 'alternative textbook' system. With this, the state monopoly over educational publishing came to an end. This represented a major change for textbook writers, who now had to face intense competition from other publishers. For our project, it was a time for a rethink of strategies, plans, and attitudes. The writers and the management team needed to overcome feelings of uncertainty and disappointment, adapt rapidly to the new conditions, and make quick revisions to the draft materials in order to comply with the new official curricula and textbook evaluation criteria, which were not always clear and transparent. Publishers in Romania and in the United Kingdom were invited to tender for the production of the remaining six textbooks in the series and a top UK publisher was chosen according to strict criteria. This was a huge boost to the writers' motivation to continue and offered unique professional development.

The ELT methodology that the books represented was a case of innovation that challenged some of the deep-rooted traditional values in Romanian ELT. To make the textbooks a durable educational innovation, an important task of the project was to convince teachers to adapt to new, almost revolutionary methodologies and approaches. The link between textbooks and teacher training was strengthened with the setting up of a complex training project that involved the training of teachers, trainers, inspectors, and university methodologists throughout the country. From the beginning, it was planned that the new textbooks would be closely integrated with all these projects. The materials written by the team were used in training courses alongside other materials mainly drawn from global course books. Universities started including the new textbooks in bibliographies for teacher education courses. For the first time in Romania, extensive piloting was organised for all books in the series in order to keep the dialogue with peers and students open. The team took every opportunity to attend professional events in Romania and abroad in order to speak about the textbooks and present the principles behind them. Appreciation of the new materials was generally very high, but there were times when the team had to face criticism of the results of their work and learn to overcome frustration and defensiveness.

The first tangible achievement of the project was the *Pathway to English* course book series itself. The lower secondary books in the series (Achim, Capota, Comişel, Dinu, Mastacan, Popovici, and Teodorescu: 1995–1999) were published in parallel with the upper secondary ones (Bălan, Carianopol, Colibaba, Coşer, Focşeneanu, Stan, and Vulcănescu: 1995–1999) and, as a result, a whole generation of secondary school students could benefit from the modern methodology in the textbooks at the same time. The initial syllabus designed in Plymouth underwent several changes that reflected the development of the writers' own thinking in relation to the balance between innovation and tradition in the content of the textbooks. Some of the features were completely novel for an English textbook in Romania. Very importantly, the books retained aspects that reflected the traditional values attached to the culture and civilisation of the English-speaking world and placed them within a modern methodology perspective. Two years after the end of the project, in the face of strong competition, the *Pathway to English* series was the teachers' and students' first choice for instructional materials.

A further major project output was the creation of a group of specialist syllabus designers and textbook writers. As a result of their development in the project context, they were able to extend, transfer, and diversify their professional skills and act more generally as change promoters.

According to an evaluation assessment in 2000, the Romanian textbook project revived the British Council's interest in this area and influenced some of the emerging textbook projects of the time in other countries.

Lessons

Interim and end-of-project evaluation reports and the analysis of the feedback from the ELT community demonstrated that the Romanian textbook project went far beyond its initial aims and provided a learning context for all involved.

There are many learning points that emerged from our work. These relate to educational projects in general and can be of benefit to large categories of ELT professionals. However, I will mention here only those that I find more directly relevant to the textbook project experience.

- Textbooks are powerful triggers of educational reform, but there is a need for systematic and integrated reform in other areas of education such as the curriculum, teacher training, and examinations, if educational change is to be effective and long-lasting. There is great mutual benefit in establishing strong working partnerships between local and English native speaker professionals. In the Romanian textbook project, this 'best-of-both-worlds' formula was achieved by the sensitively handled collaboration between Romanian authors, the Romanian project manager, UK consultants, and UK publishers.

- Tight project planning is necessary; it lowers the risks that project implementation entails. However, there should always be some contingency planning and room for adjustment, particularly in the case of national innovative projects that are bound to challenge existing systems. The Romanian textbook project would not have survived without the trust and support of the project's senior management, who never failed to believe in the project and its team.

- The greatest and most long-lasting impact of educational change can be achieved by promoting innovation together with respect for local tradition. One of the challenges of innovation as sustained improvement is the successful management of the link between the existing stability, the 'fit' situation, and the evolutionary clashes, the 'split' situation. (Kennedy 1999a).

- Time and detailed attention given to the selection of team members pay off in that they ensure commitment, ownership, and efficiency. Capacity building, which should be an aim at the project concept stage, should be consistently developed throughout all the stages of the project, as a long-term gain of any educational endeavour. Initial training in the specific area of the project should be followed by continuous on-the-job training, in order to prepare team members for a complex and sometimes fluctuating project route, and to ensure that their development is based on first-hand experience. At present, years after the inception of the project, the Romanian textbook writers continue to engage with and manage innovation in wide areas of education, and to be at the forefront of the ELT scene in Romania and transnationally.

Acknowledgements

Finally, I would like to acknowledge the contribution of my colleagues to this project:

Lower secondary level: Alaviana Achim, Liana Capotă, Ecaterina Comişel, Felicia Dinu, Alice Mastacan, Ruxandra Popovici, Elena Teodorescu.

Upper secondary level: Rada Bălan, Miruna Carianopol, Ştefan Colibaba, Cornelia Coşer, Veronica Focşeneanu, Vanda Stan and Rodica Vulcanescu.

British Council project directors: Adrian Odell, Roy Cross, Lesley Hayman, Jeremy Jacobson and UK consultants: Rod Bolitho, Sue Mohamed.

Case 13:
Implementing the pilot stage of English in Action in Bangladesh: Negotiating the route to sustainable improvement in ELT classroom practice

Mike Solly and Clare Woodward

The project

English in Action (EIA) is a programme requested by the Government of Bangladesh in response to the poor English language skills of the population. The project's purpose is 'to increase significantly the number of people able to communicate in English to levels that enable them to participate fully in economic and social activities and opportunities' (English in Action Project 2008: 5).

EIA is a nine-year project funded by the UK Department for International Development (DfID) with the following partners: BMB Mott MacDonald, the Open University (OU), the BBC World Service Trust (BBC WST), Friends in Village Development Bangladesh (FIVDB), and the Underprivileged Children's Education Project (UCEP). EIA is involved at primary and secondary level in the government school system, as well as in non-formal settings through UCEP and FIVDB schools. It also targets a mass adult audience through the BBC WST's EIA products.

Stage – implementation

In the 18-month pilot phase from March 2010, EIA worked with around 700 primary and secondary school teachers across Bangladesh. The teachers work in the project in pairs from each school, and 10 schools are grouped together in a local district *(upazilla)*; the 20 teachers meet for monthly cluster meetings. A similar model will be applied in the next phase, 2012–15, when 12,500 teachers will join the project. These teachers will continue to work with peers in schools and come together six times a year. The facilitators, in turn, are to be supported by ELT/teacher training experts or core trainers.

In this paper, we focus on the implementation of the pilot stage of the project and the challenges that have been encountered in introducing resources and materials. We should also stress that our focus is on the schools' part of the intervention, a particular area of responsibility for the OU, and not on the adult learning element that was the particular responsibility of the BBC WST.

Story

Bangladesh has had a very traditional approach to English language teaching, focusing on teaching about the language rather than how to use it effectively. As Oliveira says:

> In general, teacher training is confined to situations in which teachers are exposed to theories about teaching, abstract discussion about general issues, or are being directly taught. Seldom do they have the opportunity to watch and interact with their peers – a fundamental tool for the creation of a learning community. (Oliveira 2007: 101)

Concerns have been expressed about the inability of students and adults to communicate effectively in English (for example, Chowdhury and Ha 2008; Hamid and Baldauf 2008; Hamid, Sussex, and Khan 2009).

A number of ELT improvement projects came about as a result of this concern, including the Government of Bangladesh's English Language Teaching Improvement Project (ELTIP 1998–2002), which helped introduce a more communicative framework in schools. EIA came into being as a result of the recognition that these earlier projects, while providing a foundation for improved teaching and learning, were not enough, and a more comprehensive and sustainable intervention was required.

The time span of the project meant that, during the pilot, a number of different classroom materials, technologies, and participatory ways of creating and reviewing materials and the support for using them could be explored, monitored, and evaluated, in order to have a greater understanding of what would be most appropriate and sustainable at the later embedding phase of the project.

However, a number of clear parameters were set by the Bangladeshi Government. Crucially, EIA had to work within the existing course book and assessment system. The revised course book (English for Today) was itself a product of earlier methodological reforms in English teaching in the ELTIP project and adopts a broadly communicative approach to learning. However, almost all teachers teach the book in the rote-learning way that is the cultural norm. A lesson, for example, designed to practice listening and speaking skills, while strengthening the use of the present perfect, but set around the story of Anne Frank's diary, would be seen by teachers as a lesson about Anne Frank's diary, in which a reading passage needed to be learnt by rote. More significantly still, the assessment system reflects this notion of writing an exam paper on 'the book'.

Materials

There were some differences of focus in the production of primary and secondary materials. For primary, the concentration was on introducing materials directly into the classroom and closely supporting the curriculum of the existing course book. Many primary school teachers in Bangladesh receive no training prior to entering the classroom and have little English language understanding, which results in the children receiving minimal modelling of good communicative language practice.

To give the children and teachers access to clear and accurate English, all participating teachers received an iPod loaded with classroom materials and provided with speakers. The materials on the iPod support the content of the textbooks and code-switches between Bangla and English to ensure that the children understand the context within which the English dialogues are set. There is also an activity guide for every lesson in the EFT (English for teachers) primary course books. The recycling of taught items from the course book is also embedded into these new primary audio materials. The iPod contains files of classroom language for the teachers to practise and video of good classroom practice to discuss in their cluster meetings. This is accompanied by a range of visual resources that the teacher uses alongside the audio.

The secondary classroom context is somewhat different, as the teachers are specialist teachers of English and all have degrees, with many holding an MA or M.Ed. The emphasis here is on practice-based teacher professional development. Through the iPods, bilingual multimodal materials are delivered which engage teachers in practical activities. The programme also encourages teachers to reflect on activities, adapt them to their own contexts, and gain confidence in ELT. Teachers are not expected to have native-like fluency in English and are encouraged to use Bangla when necessary. As with primary, there are files with classroom language and video of classroom practice. These devices can be used in the classroom, as many textbook dialogues, readings, poems, and songs have been recorded.

To get the most benefit from the secondary materials, we encouraged reflective learning in the programme. This was incorporated into exercises in the materials, but, in addition, an assessed non-compulsory OU course in reflection, MYTEC (Make Your Teaching Experience Count), was created to support the materials.

Support

The dilemma was to find a sustainable balance between materials support and mediated support. Ultimately, a blended approach was taken: materials on the MP3 players, hard-copy teacher guides, classroom materials, peer support in the schools, monthly cluster meetings, and classroom visits. Peer teacher facilitators (TFs), who also have contact with each other and other EIA stakeholders via mobile phones, facilitate these meetings and classroom visits. In the latter stages of the pilot, SMS (short message service) was used to encourage teachers to try out activities in their classrooms and reflect upon successes and challenges.

The TFs are supported through a range of mechanisms. As with the teachers, they are in pairs, with two supporting each set of 20 teachers; they also receive support from one of nine teacher development co-ordinators (TDC), who assist and advise the TFs on strategies for the meeting and have a handbook containing guidelines on maximising their role and techniques to apply when facilitating the cluster meetings.

Stakeholders: A teacher's journey

Having described the materials that were produced for the pilot stage of the project and how they were built around the existing curriculum and materials to create a more communicative way of teaching English, rather than teaching about English as a content subject, and having explained how the support system promoted this learning, let us now look at the project through a teacher's eyes.

Yasmeen Chowdhury is a 35-year old primary teacher from the semi-rural area of Jessore in Southern Bangladesh. In early 2010, her primary school was selected as one of 340 pilot schools for EIA. Yasmeen had previously taken part in a number of English methodology workshops, where she had been told about 'communicative English'. She understood that this meant getting her students to talk more, but she remained very unsure about how to do it.

In February 2010, with the other English teacher from her school, she attended a three-day workshop that brought together 60 primary teachers. There was much excitement on Day Two of the workshop, when the teachers were all given an iPod and a speaker for the classroom, with videos of Bangladeshi classroom activities and audio that could be used in every lesson. Yasmeen had seen on the video how the children loved this material and she left the workshop eager to try it in her classroom. She also felt more confident about her English, as she had used it far more than ever before.

At the end of the workshop, Yasmeen was asked whether she would like to play a special role in the programme as teacher facilitator, helping to run the monthly day-long cluster meetings that would take place over the next year, bringing together 20 teachers from her region. She would be supported by the teacher development co-ordinators and through two training workshops.

It took Yasmeen some time to understand her role as a teacher facilitator and exactly what 'peer support' meant; she felt that she could have had a little more help in this, but she contacted TDCs and other TFs on her mobile phone when she had concerns and slowly came to comprehend her role of supporting teachers. The two workshops held in Dhaka, which brought together all the TFs, were also very helpful.

In addition to the cluster meetings, there were also two workshops during the programme; these gave teachers the opportunity to share experiences, demonstrate techniques, and discuss the problems they encountered. For example, several teachers had difficulties charging their speakers properly for use in the classroom, as their schools had no electricity, and some people did not understand the relationship of some of the materials to the course book. In the final workshop,

Yasmeen learnt that this was not really the end of the programme, as there would be continuing cluster meetings held from time to time over the next year.

Yasmeen now feels more confident about using different techniques in the classroom, and her students' attendance has improved. She knows she has a lot further to go in her development as a teacher but hopes that what she has learnt will be sustained though continued contact with other teachers. Both she and her students also use English much more than before and they love the audio in the classroom. This is not only her experience, as all the research carried out during the pilot phase has come to the same conclusion.

Lessons

As with any pilot project, it has been crucial to document and examine all the areas where we have been successful and ensure, as we scale up in the next stage of the project, that we learn from the areas where there have been difficulties.

One major lesson learnt was that we tried to do too much, with the consequence that some of the teachers felt overwhelmed by the sheer volume of 'stuff'. In Bangladesh, classroom materials are scarce, and if you have them, you use them. Some of the EIA materials were produced as additional classroom aids, which caused some confusion, with teachers expressing concerns about how to relate all of the materials to specific parts of the course book. The lesson here is the need to be explicit about learning outcomes, even to the level of explaining why, in a picture provided for a particular lesson, there is a mango and not an apple on the tree when 'mango' was taught three weeks ago! In secondary, where the concentration was on teacher development through the demonstration and discussion of classroom techniques, there was a demand for more direct classroom materials. What we have learnt is that the strategy we adopted for primary (tying classroom materials very closely to the course book) needed to move a little more towards secondary (less material and more concentration on reflection and teacher development) and the strategy adopted for secondary has moved considerably closer to primary.

The second lesson was that, while mobile technology was essential in leveraging the delivery of both classroom materials and teacher professional development, the iPod was not sustainable. These have now been replaced by Nokia C1-01 mobile phones, which cost around £30 and are fitted with a 4GB micro SD card pre-loaded with the EIA materials. Some teachers who already own phones with SD card slots may simply be given the pre-loaded SD card.

Finally, a generic lesson learnt was to be specific about the scale of what can be achieved at various points of the project – and make sure that this is clearly shared with all the implementers of the project. Although we knew we had to demonstrate improvement in both the students' English language use and in the delivery of appropriate communicative teaching by teachers, we were halfway through the pilot when we found a clear way of expressing that in terms of what we would hope to see as a success measure at different stages. Once this was produced, there was a much clearer shared understanding of what we had achieved.

Although it is important to be cautious, as the project approaches the next phase, the results achieved strongly suggest that peer-supported, practice-based learning, leveraging mobile technology both to bring ELT resources into the classroom and provide professional development to teachers, could be an effective model for providing ELT training at scale to large numbers of teachers.

Case 14:
The Oman BA Project:
ELT change implementation, process or event?

Martin Wedell

The project

Until the mid-1990s, teaching and learning in Omani schools was content-focused, teacher-centred, and emphasised rote learning. Assessment was conducted entirely through examinations which largely tested memorisation.

In 1996, the Omani Ministry of Education (MoE) launched a major policy initiative, *Reform and the Development of General Education*. Its goal was to create a 10-year system of Basic Education that would provide Omani citizens with the knowledge and skills needed to participate in the changing global and local economy and job market. The principal strands of the reform programme included:

a. moving towards teaching materials and pedagogy which adopted a student-centred approach and supported the development of transferable skills

b. ensuring that assessment was, at least in part, continuous

c. allocating increased teaching time to key subjects such as science, mathematics, Arabic, and English

d. supporting the efforts to implement (a) and (b) by the existing 9,000 Omani teachers qualified to diploma level, by upgrading their qualifications to first-degree level

e. increasing the proportion of all teachers who were Omani citizens.

The first group of teachers chosen under (d) above were Omani English teachers. In 1999, an agreement was drawn up between the MoE and the University of Leeds to upgrade the qualifications of the approximately 1,000 Omani diploma-holding English language teachers to a Bachelor of Arts (BA) in Teaching English to Speakers of Other Languages (TESOL). The agreement ran through to 2008 and provided for six overlapping cohorts to study for their BA part-time over three years. Each cohort had members from across the country and was divided into a number of regional groups. Participants retained their roles as practising English teachers in their schools throughout the programme. Inputs were provided to the whole of each cohort during summer and winter schools, and teachers were entitled to day-release from their schools each week to meet each other and a full-time MA-qualified Regional Tutor. The day-release sessions provided weekly opportunities for teachers to discuss their attempts to implement or adapt ideas from the summer/winter schools in their classrooms with colleagues from the same regional context and to obtain resources for and advice on writing their BA assignments.

Stage – implementation

This case study focuses on one key strand of any ELT change initiative – the provision of contextually appropriate teacher support and development – and highlights some beneficial results for the outcomes of the initiative as a whole that can arise when implementation is (at least implicitly) recognised to be 'a process, not an event' (Fullan 2001:34).

Story

From the very beginning, two features of the way in which the BA project was planned and one feature of the context in which it took place supported its implementation. These features are, in my experience, rarely present in ELT change initiatives worldwide. I discuss these one by one.

The project timescale

From the very beginning it was stated that the project and its funding would continue for a nine-year period. At national level, leadership and management of the BA project was shared between Oman and Leeds. The benefits of the long project timescale were, in this case, maximised by the stability of the project leadership personnel on both sides. In effect, both sides were able to develop a thorough understanding of the aims of the project and of how these might be achieved over the project lifetime. At local level, the Regional Tutors, (employed for three years, one cohort at a time) were the project representatives with whom the students had most frequent contact. The great majority of these also remained with the project for at least one full cohort, providing a stable source of local leadership for participants of each cohort.

This stability of leadership and management over time enabled the people involved on both sides to get to know each other well, develop good, trusting personal relationships, and so establish ever more effective communication systems. It also meant that there was sufficient time for the MoE (which commissioned and funded the project) to recognise that the project leadership was competent and thus feel able to delegate ever more decision making to the project level. This, in turn, supported and enhanced relationships between leaders, enabling more informed development of coherent systems such as summer/winter school monitoring and reporting systems.

The information provided by such systems, over the extended project timescale, enabled Leeds-based leaders, tutors, and materials writers to develop a more thorough than usual understanding of the project (Omani) school and cultural context. This understanding informed the constant revision of programme materials and assessment practices, which, although desirable for any initiative, only becomes feasible and obviously worthwhile when the implementation process will clearly last for some time.

The length of the project timescale helped to highlight an important truth in any such ELT change project context. Awareness of what an educational change means in practice and of what this implies for how it may best be supported is an evolving process both for change planners and leaders, and for those (teachers, head teachers, and local education officials) who are expected to implement change in classrooms. The generally short lifetimes of most international joint ELT projects make the development of such awareness among all participants much less likely.

Teachers remained full members of their schools while studying on the BA project

Throughout their studies, all teachers taught four days a week at their schools. Structuring the project in this manner had positive effects on the success of the project. Teachers had ample opportunity to consider the appropriateness or otherwise for their own contexts of the ideas and practices that the programme introduced. The comments from their teaching experiences generated through discussion during their weekly day-release sessions also contributed more or less directly to the teaching materials revision process which was such a constant feature of the project.

Equally importantly, their continued presence in their schools and the consequent need for their head teachers to be contacted to agree their day-release played an important part in raising awareness of the project and of the wider educational reform of which it formed part. Since head teachers had to be approached to obtain permission for project members to have day-release for the three years of their study, they could not remain totally unaware of the BA project or the wider reform. The Omani educational hierarchy, like most others, is top-down. Heads had to be approached by regional-level educational administrators and/or supervisors-teacher trainers. Their need to convince heads to release their teachers meant they too needed to be aware of the purpose of the project and of its role in the wider reform. Since the project lasted for such a long time, graduates from earlier cohorts provided information and advice for their colleagues in later cohorts and for head teachers about what participation on the BA project entailed and what degree of adjustment to established working patterns was needed. Anecdotal evidence suggests that these informal contributions were often highly influential, given the tendency in Omani society to share experience orally in social gatherings. Overall, therefore, the need to negotiate teachers' day-release and the increasing number of project graduates in schools contributed to raising national awareness both of the project and its aims, and (more indirectly) of the direction which changes within other subjects in the curriculum would follow.

Harmony between project processes and goals and those of the wider educational reform

The changes to the teaching and learning of English which the project would introduce to teachers were consistent with changes being proposed across all Basic Education subjects. This affected positively how teachers experienced the change process. Teachers studying on the project worked in a school environment in which colleagues, heads, supervisors (and perhaps even parents and learners) were unlikely to be hostile to the changes they were trying to implement. Their daily work setting was, thus, one that was at worst neutral and at best positive about their attempts to change some of what happened in their classrooms. This is rarely the case in the many contexts where curriculum changes are limited to English classes only.

The 'whole-system' nature of the reform also positively affected several aspects of the project design. The teaching materials (textbook) that the teachers used were broadly consistent with the aims of the reform. Extracts from these could, thus, be used by programme designers/module materials writers to support/illustrate BA teaching inputs and as the basis for teachers' practice tasks back in their school classrooms. Similarly, the principles and practices of assessment introduced as desirable on the BA programme matched the assessment principles espoused by the educational reforms. As a result, over time, the project became more clearly seen as linked and relevant to what was (supposed to be) happening nationally in Basic schools across Oman. This led to a mutually supportive relationship between the project and the wider reform.

Lessons

State education systems introduce educational changes as considered appropriate and necessary for their national contexts. However, over recent decades, changes to the teaching of English across such systems worldwide have been unusual in the extent to which they have shared a goal: the development of school learners' communication skills.

In most contexts, the achievement of such a goal entails substantial adjustment to existing teaching and learning beliefs and behaviours for teachers and all those who may directly or indirectly influence their implementation attempts. The extent of adjustment required amounts to a process of re-culturing (Fullan 2007, Wedell 2009), during which implementers alter long-established professional (and possibly personal) behaviours, and eventually also beliefs about professional roles and responsibilities. Such a process takes time.

Much of the literature that comments on the outcomes of ELT innovations in different parts of the world (for example, Al Hazmi 2003, Nunan 2003, Chacon 2005, Waters and Vilches 2008, Ong'ondo 2009), alongside anecdotal evidence from postgraduate students, suggests that few state-system ELT change initiatives have in fact enabled the development of their learners' communication skills. One reason for the lack of success referred to in both formal and informal reports is the lack of communication and understanding between what Fink (2000) calls the 'two solitudes': *the policy makers*, whose planning often appears to give little consideration to supporting the re-culturing of those who are expected to make change visible in classrooms *(teachers and others)*.

It would be untrue to say that these 'two solitudes' were never apparent during the BA project. However, as the discussion of the supportive features above hopefully shows, over time, 'leaders' were able both to develop a fuller understanding of how best to support implementation in context and to act on that understanding in terms of adjusting teaching approaches, module content, and assessment formats to suit implementers' needs better.

Such supportive features are rarely present in the many international ELT projects which:

- are situated in contexts where the changes expected in English classrooms represent the first stage of some possible future transition from an existing 'transmission based' (Young and Lee 1984) version to some version (usually poorly defined) of a more learner-centred/interactive approach to learning and teaching across the wider education system

- continue to view the introduction of a 'communicative curriculum' as a simple event that can be rapidly completed and, therefore, plan with a short-term (often three-year) commitment to funding and leadership

- provide (usually only some) teachers with minimal (often short-term and off-site) training and do little to raise awareness of the changes and their implications among those whose attitudes and responses affect teachers' implementation experiences

- consequently expect successful implementation to take place in school contexts which understand little or nothing about the rationale for, or practical implications of, the change, and where change goals may be in direct conflict with what heads, learners, and their parents believe is needed to pass the unchanged examinations against which society measures teaching-learning success.

The above 'case' suggests that, if those responsible for initiating national ELT reforms hope to see evidence of their new ELT curriculum with its focus on communication skills being implemented in most classrooms, they would be wise to plan for a medium- to long-term process. Additionally, their attempts to change how English is taught are more likely to be successfully implemented if they are part of a 'whole-system' change, in which similar pedagogical changes are introduced to teaching and learning across all school curriculum subjects. Finally, initiatives need to be structured in ways that make direct and indirect support for implementers (heads and local administrators, as well as teachers) available over time. Planning that bears such issues in mind will make it more likely that the 'parts' of and the 'partners' within the whole system will be mutually supportive and so provide a positive context for the re-culturing process that will be needed if (versions of) the desired changes are ever to become visible in the majority of classrooms (Wedell 2011).

The cases:
Monitoring and
evaluation

Case 15:
Measuring the impact of the PROSPER Project in Romania: A learning experience

Mirela Bardi

The project

PROSPER (Project for Special Purpose English in Romania) was set up in 1991 with the broad aim of improving the level of English proficiency of future personnel in key sectors of the Romanian economy and public life such as engineering, economics, public administration, and medicine. Upgrading and diversifying the teaching/learning of English for Specific Purposes (ESP) in major tertiary education institutions represented a major step in achieving the project aim. Through its diverse professional activities, the project has had effects and implications which have extended well beyond the language classroom.

The project brought together teachers from various institutions and enabled them to work together to accomplish tasks that were relevant to everybody working in ESP, regardless of the institution of origin. Participation in project events has helped teachers to develop skills in areas such as syllabus and course design, textbook writing, classroom research, teacher training, and educational management. Working together to achieve common goals created a professional culture among ESP teachers, who shared the same values and confronted the same set of problems in their local environments. The project proposed its own structures, activities, channels of communication, roles, and responsibilities. It did so at a time when Romanian institutions were beginning to strive to generate new modes of working which were more flexible and open to novelty. Above all, the project created opportunities for learning and development, and aimed to make the need for continuous improvement irreversible. The project members had the freedom and responsibility to make the project work for themselves.

Stage – monitoring and evaluation

This case study focuses on the monitoring and evaluation of the project. This was the most complex and challenging project activity, with the study of impact being carried out over a period of three-and-a-half years (1996–99). The study aimed to capture evidence of expected and unexpected project impact on the teaching/learning process and on the major stakeholders involved: teachers, students, foreign languages departments, the British Council as the managing institution, and members of the ESP teaching profession in Romania.

This case study sets out to discuss the main aspects of the impact study process and to highlight the lessons learnt by the project team from the actual experience of conducting the study. I will argue that the lessons derived from this experience were both personal and institutional, in the sense that aspects of process management may inform the practice of managing innovation projects.

Story

We aimed to do a study of impact, rather than a standard end-of-project evaluation, because we felt that this latter kind of evaluation was, in a sense, too narrow and maybe too much linked to the original objectives of the project. For such a vast project as PROSPER (spanning over nine years and involving 16 universities), a study aiming to document impact on the numerous categories of stakeholders seemed to be more appropriate and more likely to yield valuable information. Although doing an evaluation was included among the project outputs, the decision to do an insider-led evaluation and the shape of the study depended on the way the project had evolved since its initial design. The collaborative project culture of consulting and involving project members in decision making about project events, and the need to continue and diversify the professional development of the project team were the main reasons for the choice of participatory evaluation, which was regarded as a new learning opportunity.

Rationale and design

The design of the study took account of two main features that differentiate impact studies from other forms of evaluation: the need to gather comparable data and to discuss unexpected ripple effects. In our case, the comparable data came from two sources. One was the baseline study done at the beginning of the project, which describes the situation as it was before the project influence began; the other was the data we collected during the impact study from institutions which were not involved in PROSPER. Impact was, therefore, measured both in terms of how the PROSPER group of institutions had changed when compared with the pre-PROSPER profile and in terms of how the impact of PROSPER had made that group different from groups of teachers who were not affected by the project.

The impact study became a project in its own right. It was an attempt to conduct participatory evaluation, with the project members designing the study framework and carrying out all the stages in the research process: drafting, trialling and revising the instruments, collecting the data, and analysing and writing up the results. However, the complexity of the study represented a considerable challenge for the team, which was entirely unprepared to do evaluation research on a large scale. As the impact study consultant observed at the time of the study publication: 'There is virtually no literature in language education on the design of an actual impact study' (Alderson 1999). The situation may have changed in the meantime, but the lessons we learnt while doing our impact study will hopefully be useful to others who may want to replicate the process or aspects of it.

The impact study also involved outsiders in various roles. The key presence was the impact study consultant, who provided professional and emotional support to a team lacking research training. Critical friends were also called on along the way, and their opinions and advice helped the team distance themselves from their own work and consider it through the perspective of a potential readership.

Methodology

The project team identified the areas of project impact through a brainstorming exercise. In terms of the teaching/learning experience, PROSPER was expected to have had an impact on teachers, students, classroom processes, materials and resources generated by the project members, and testing procedures. Impact was expected to have crossed the border through contacts with ESP project teams in other countries.

Data collection instruments were designed and administered by the impact study team, with one department being responsible for a particular instrument. We started with the collection of quantitative data through a set of five questionnaires (teacher, student, ex-student, employer, and management questionnaires) and a classroom observation schedule, and continued with qualitative data (case studies of graduates and group discussions with members of the core PROSPER departments). Research was carried out in PROSPER and non-PROSPER institutions, and the response rate was very high, as a result of direct administration during institutional visits by members of the impact study team. The following table provides a snapshot of the research instruments and the number of respondents for each of those:

Research instrument	No. of respondents	Response rate
Teacher questionnaire	104 PROSPER and 51 non-PROSPER teachers	92.4%
Classroom observation schedule	59 PROSPER and 25 non-PROSPER classes	100%
Student questionnaire	1,039 PROSPER and 449 non-PROSPER students	100%
Ex-student questionnaire	101 PROSPER and 51 non-PROSPER ex-students	92.7%
Employer questionnaire	46 respondents	76.6%
Case studies of graduates	4 PROSPER and 4 non-PROSPER graduates	
Departmental group discussions	8 institutions (98 PROSPER teachers participated)	92.8%
Comparative analysis of teaching materials	2 PROSPER, 2 pre-PROSPER, and 1 non-PROSPER locally developed textbooks	
Comparative analysis of tests	58 PROSPER, 15 pre-PROSPER, and 17 non-PROSPER tests	
Statements of ripple effects	6 statements from language centres directors, department managers, and managers of ESP projects in the region	

Table 1: Research instruments and respondents

Analysis of the data involved discussing the meaning of the results in terms of the presence or absence of expected impact, and thus trying to detect trends in the innovation process. The team returned to the assumptions underpinning the instruments and reconstructed the rationale of designing the instruments in that particular way. Writing up the study required refocusing and refining the interpretation as well as re-evaluating our project experience. In this recursive process, the innovation was reflected upon and redefined in terms of its meaning for the project team, while efforts were also made to communicate it to the wider professional community.

Lessons

As I have mentioned already, the process of carrying out the PROSPER impact study was essentially a learning experience for the project members – both in terms of their professional practice and of project management. Through its learning outcomes, it consolidated the expertise of the project team, as well as the process of implementing change.

Naturally, the process was not smooth. It involved co-ordination of several institutional teams (each in charge of developing one research instrument) and merging presentation and analysis of all results into a coherent study. Work in small institutional teams alternated with whole-team meetings where everybody had a chance to understand how their work fitted into the wider picture and how the study was coming together. All concerns about the research process - design and administration of instruments, and analysis and interpretation of results – were voiced and addressed during the whole-team meetings. The presence of the impact study consultant at these large meetings facilitated the search for solutions. In retrospect, one can confidently say that seeking solutions together was a form of experiential learning. Team members developed their research skills by engaging with every aspect of the research process in a continuous problem-solving process. The value of experiential learning will be discussed further in this section.

Responsibility and project ownership
The team became involved in the study out of a sense of responsibility towards the project and its successful completion, as well as out of a sense of responsibility towards their own professional development. In our experience, responsibility and ownership are closely connected, and they highlight the complex ties that can exist between projects and project teams, ties that cannot be 'managed' through a technical process. Managing projects is very much about building commitment and strong relationships among people and, from a manager's point of view, it is worthwhile investing in generating and maintaining commitment. Ownership takes time to build, and it was the whole participatory project culture, reinforced over years, that had created that strong sense of ownership.

Interest in the task
The team commitment was fuelled by the interest in the task itself. The task was perceived as interesting and worthwhile but also as contributing to project cohesion. It was an appropriate end-of-project task and an opportunity for project members to find out whether their beliefs about the success of PROSPER were

actually confirmed by data. A useful lesson for project management is that projects need to give the opportunity to the project teams to investigate and reflect on what they have achieved by taking part in the project. Project evaluation can be carried out as a developmental rather than an accountability exercise. In our case, working together to carry out a task that was perceived as valuable by all team members and for whose implementation everyone had clear responsibilities strengthened the feeling of team belonging and identity.

Learning outcomes and learning sources

The team motivation to carry out the study was reinforced by a sense of progress and accomplishment both in relation to the study itself and to team members' own development. The team members developed new skills and new ways of thinking about teaching and research, and increased their awareness of teaching circumstances in many other institutions. While we cannot predict the range of skills that every team member developed, my insider knowledge enables me to make a fair assessment of the impact study experience learning outcomes. The following table indicates the range of skills that participants may have developed, together with the possible sources of learning.

By engaging in the research process, sharing ideas, and discussing work with the whole team, and by talking to other teachers and observing their classes, participants were able to extend and enhance the following skills:

- Professional skills
  - teaching skills
  - research skills
  - critical thinking
  - project management skills

- Social skills
  - communication skills
  - interpersonal skills
  - teamwork skills
  - strategic competence
  - coping with challenging/unexpected situations

- Awareness of
  - the PROSPER team
  - other teachers and teaching circumstances
  - one's own abilities.

Participants learnt for themselves, but also for the group, in the sense of developing abilities for collaborative work. I believe I can justifiably claim that one major aspect of learning was reinforcing the sense of group identity and of confidence in what people can achieve by working as a group.

The role of the team

Learning from experience is another major theme of the impact study process. The team learnt by conducting the research process, but also by making decisions about the process. Uncertainty was present along the road, but the moments when solutions were being sought turned out to be valuable learning experiences.

The team itself was a major source of learning: learning from peer opinions, from team discussions and decision-making, as well as from the good work or mistakes of colleagues. The presence of the team was often a source of energy, because all the members were motivated by a common purpose. We need to be aware, though, that sometimes, feelings of group belonging may actually limit the freedom of individuals, precisely because of the desire to belong and to be accepted. In project management terms, our experience indicated that teams can be both a source of strength or confidence and a source of pressure for some of their members.

Process management

Accomplishment of such a complex task required relentless co-ordination. Apart from the challenge of conducting valuable research, there was also the challenge of managing the process in a way that ensured the quality and coherence of the work. One key aspect of the management process was the provision of support whenever the team or individual members needed it. Support often came through a joint quest for answers (what some of the team members called 'indirect training'), rather than through offering solutions, but what mattered was addressing the issues as they came up. It needs to be said that the project managers were members of the research team and fulfilled both a professional and an administrative role. Involvement of project managers in the research process increased the team's confidence in their ability to supervise the process competently, while making the managers themselves more knowledgeable about the demands of the research process and the needs of the team. In terms of project management lessons, one could say that, in the case of very demanding tasks, it is important for project managers to have an overall view of progress and to pull the strings together when needed, but they can only do so if they fully participate in task completion. Accomplishment of their managing role (planning and organisation of meetings, setting deadlines, and communicating with team members) was, in our case, facilitated by full professional involvement in the research process.

Managing change and managing learning

Change and learning are two key themes that describe the process and outcomes of conducting the study by the project team. They often appear in tandem in the literature of change management, where change seems to be identified with learning experiences:

> Change is fundamentally and profoundly about learning – the two are linked in a way that makes them symbiotic. (O'Sullivan and West-Burnham 1998: 45).

In our experience, an essential aspect of change management is to create opportunities for those involved to develop, to gain new insights into themselves and their circumstances, and to empower them to improve those circumstances, if they feel the need to do so. Change becomes sustainable when participants internalise the experience and translate it into the way they work, into patterns of behaviour and belief, and into perceptions of their role. This process of assimilating or rejecting elements of innovation is essentially a process of learning, and carrying out an impact study was a worthwhile and rewarding learning experience for the PROSPER team.

The following are some of the key management lessons derived from our experience:

1. Project ownership and responsibility are constantly created through the whole project culture of participation, sharing, and transparency. They are the result and also evidence of a participatory culture which needs to be built throughout the project lifetime.

2. Project managers have a crucial role in facilitating communication among team members and in ensuring that there is complete transparency, for all team members, about the implementation process. Communication and transparency generate better understanding and facilitate the process of task implementation.

3. It is very difficult to plan for learning, as learning outcomes of complex project activities are wider than initially envisaged. The role of management is to suggest tasks that are perceived as meaningful by the project teams and to facilitate participation and involvement.

4. Projects that respond to a perceived priority need are more likely to mobilise team effort and commitment.

5. Project teams do not emerge by mandate or team-building exercises, but are consolidated in the process of working together to accomplish a task perceived as meaningful/rewarding.

6. Delegation of responsibility to project teams has an essential role in their learning, as more responsibility generates more commitment and eventually more learning.

Innovations and change can be planned in a more or less rational, linear way, with identification of problems and needs, the planning of action, implementation of the plans, and evaluation of results (Fullan and Stiegelbauer 1991; Burnes 2000). Although these stages are useful in guiding our thinking, it is simplistic to assume that implementing an innovation is a matter of following the predesigned steps in a process. Essential variables such as the values and attitudes of project members can determine unexpected courses of actions and outcomes.

Change can, therefore, be regarded less as a rational, technicist process and more as contextually sensitive and involving human variables. The management of change will be specific to each situation, will require recognition of the fact that change involves human variables such as trust, confidence, and feelings of insecurity, and will move towards a more people-oriented, participatory approach to project management. On the basis of the PROSPER experience, I can, therefore, suggest a paradigm of project management that regards the process of change as a process of learning, not just a method of changing organisational structures and practices.

Case 16:
The challenge of monitoring and evaluation in Sri Lanka

Lesley Dick

The project

English was rejected in post-colonial Sri Lanka in favour of a Sinhala Only policy. Currently, though, as Lo Bianco argues in his Sri Lankan language policy history, '... the English comeback is remarkable. The language that once provoked fragmentation is now a key to reconciliation' (Lo Bianco 2011: 52).

Further, as Kennett confirms, '...recent amendments to the constitution have brought English back as a link language and English continues to be used as the language of management in public service and of international development' (Kennett 2010: 319). As Popovici discusses elsewhere in this volume, English literacy creates access to education, information, and technology, creates social equality and cohesion, and promotes local and international communication. In Sri Lanka, inequality of English teaching in urban and rural areas is evident: rural English teachers lack English language proficiency, up-to-date methodology, and often suitable materials and facilities.

The Council for Business with Britain (CBB) English Language Teaching (ELT) Project is an in-service programme for English language teachers designed by the British Council and carried out in association with the Sri Lankan Ministry of Education. A non-profit, non-political organisation focused on expanding bilateral trade links between Sri Lanka and the United Kingdom, CBB has HSBC as principal sponsor, and the project demonstrates its corporate social responsibility. Its goal is to upgrade the English skills of pupils; this is to be achieved through equipping teachers with the skills to deliver high-quality English teaching in their real-life low-resource classrooms. Additionally, the project seeks to redress the imbalance in quality between rural and urban English education with its design as a distance-learning training project that can benefit teachers in rural and urban areas equally. Importantly, from the Ministry of Education's perspective, the project works within existing school structures and curricula, focusing on long-term, sustainable development, rather than short-term, expensive, resource-based inputs.

Stage – monitoring and evaluation

This case study focuses on the monitoring and evaluation process in the project. The design of the project, which started in 2005, has, after an initial change from short-term weekend workshops to distance teacher training course, changed little from the pilot. The most challenging aspect has been the successful monitoring and evaluation of the impact on classroom teaching skills and on pupil learning. Lessons learnt here point to the importance of Kirkpatrick's four levels of evaluation (Kirkpatrick 1998).

Story

The project narrative is one of a continuing valiant attempt at monitoring and evaluating. The challenges of the four phases summarised in Table 1 will be presented in turn.

	Phase 1	Phase 2	Phase 3	Phase 4
Impact	Aug-Oct 2005	2006-2007	2007-2010	2010-2012
RESCs[1] involved	6	8	26	28
Mentors trained	0	16	40	1
Teachers trained	150	48	378	323
Pupils reached	12,000	3,840	31,200	42,043

Table 1: Project phases

Phase 1

CBB first approached the British Council in April 2005, with a desire to improve school leavers' English language skills. The project was short-term and low-cost. The 2005 Hornby School *English in the Workplace* was cascaded in six rural areas through weekend workshops targeting secondary English language teachers. The project aimed to train two teachers to cascade the workshops further. It was partly successful: high turnout in some areas; in others, low. Monitoring and evaluation were, in Kirkpatrick terms, level 1 ('reaction'): response questionnaires and attendance, plus informal evaluation by British Council and local trainers. While questionnaires were overwhelmingly positive, low turnout was disappointing. Informal response revealed the root cause: the timing (weekend) clashed with private teaching and led to loss of earnings.

Phase 2

For Phase 2 the British Council proposed a pilot which adapted their existing Teaching Knowledge Test (TKT) Course run by the Teaching Centre as Sunday teacher training workshops for local teachers, into a distance teacher training course. The RESCs, with their national geographic coverage, became the obvious choice as training centres. With CBB consultation, eight districts were selected on the basis of geographic spread. Two RESC trainers from each were chosen to complete

---

[1] Regional English Support Centres. These are funded by the Ministry of Education and their role is to support primary and secondary teachers in their district in training and resources.

the six-month face-to-face course in Colombo and Kandy, receive mentor training, and then mentor six teachers on the distance course. On the basis of monitoring and evaluation, CBB would decide on whether or not to expand the project.

The primary focus was on measuring the impact on the participants, in Kirkpatrick terms, level 2 ('knowledge'). Monitoring was based on attendance and quality of support for the distance course. Geographic participant spread made it challenging to evaluate. The future mentors attended a TKT face-to-face workshop every Sunday. The British Council trainers could monitor attendance and workshop performance, and report any problems quickly.

Monitoring the distance course was more problematic. It was imperative that British Council trainers could evaluate mentoring skills and study session supervision. British Council trainers visited RESCs once per module to ensure effective mentoring by the RESC trainers and provide them with opinion to ensure their development. Invaluable opinion was collected on materials, tasks, and study sessions. As a direct result of the RESC visits, two extra face-to-face workshops were delivered, portfolio tasks were reworked, two distance course units were revised, and a longer 10-hour mentoring course was developed.

Questionnaires were also used for monitoring both courses. While informative, they tended to be skewed by the inherent Sri Lankan reluctance to give negative opinion. This, plus the distance course participants' stated isolation, prompted the project manager to explore ways of both collecting more accurate opinion and creating a more collective spirit. A focus group at the annual ELT conference became the forum for participants to share views and to collect opinion. TKT as an international guideline and a motivator for participant success was revealed here. To counteract mentor isolation, weekly telephone contact was maintained, ensuring issues were swiftly responded to. This frequent contact built strong relationships and led to more effective monitoring.

Teacher and mentor evaluation used TKT exam performance as the measurement of success. The aim was 80 per cent with band 3 or above and this was easily achieved on the pilot. While this measured 'knowledge', it did not measure 'behaviour' (Kirkpatrick level 3). To demonstrate this, a portfolio was added: for each unit, teachers completed a portfolio task designed to apply the learning to the classroom and evaluate it. Portfolios were monitored by mentors, submitted to the British Council after the course, evaluated, and awarded a pass, weak pass, or strong pass depending on task completion and quality. While the portfolios were evidence of classroom impact, there was no direct evaluation of classroom or pupil performance. Nevertheless, exam results were excellent; portfolios demonstrated evidence of classroom impact; opinion questionnaires were positive; and CBB agreed to extend funding for three years.

Phase 3
Phase 3 saw the project expand from eight to 26 RESCs and from 16 to 40 mentors, who supervised the training of 378 teachers. With this expansion came monitoring and evaluation challenges.

Project coverage increased geographically. Monitoring every RESC module by Colombo-based British Council trainers was financially unrealistic. To reduce costs and to provide evidence of classroom impact, two changes were made. Peer moderation visits replaced British Council trainer visits in 2008. Mentors submitted visit reports for project manager moderation. This proved successful (and much cheaper) and encouraged RESC co-operation. Classroom observation (Kirkpatrick level 3) was also added. Mentors, after becoming a standard part of mentor training, observed three teachers each, before and after the course. Initially seen as developmental and general evidence of progress, these lesson observation reports were later compared to reveal behaviour change, for example, increases in learner-centredness. These were included in the portfolio for end-of-course evaluation.

The funders wanted RESCs in the north and east of Sri Lanka included; the security situation (the civil war having ended in May 2009), therefore, impacted on monitoring and evaluation. In the east, future mentors were traveling to Kandy from Batticoloa and to Colombo from Trincomalee every weekend; ensuring their safety was imperative. In the north, travel to and from Jaffna was severely restricted for local residents. In 2008, the Jaffna RESC co-ordinators commenced the distance course; experienced trainers, they completed the course with the teachers they were mentoring. The delivery of the materials before the course and the administration of the exam after the course by British Council trainers were the only times the RESC was monitored.

Alongside expansion, costs were increasing. The funders wanted better impact measurement and more return on investment. However, they argued against TKT as an evaluation tool because of the exam fees (the most expensive part of the project, despite discounts from Cambridge and the British Council). The case for keeping TKT as an international guideline of participant success was argued strongly on the grounds that the previous questionnaire and focus groups' results revealed the high motivation provided by the Cambridge exam.

While the primary evaluation tool focused on the impact on teachers themselves, the funders wanted evidence of direct impact on the pupils' English language skills. Three evaluation methods were proposed. Testing pupils of project teachers before and after the course using practice KET/PET (Key English Test/Preliminary English Test) tests was rejected as too expensive, because of the oral testing fee of British Council teachers. The O and A level results of schools involved in the project were rejected, as the low numbers of project teachers in any school meant their direct impact on results was impossible to determine. The third method involved collecting school data on the project teachers' classes and comparing this with parallel grades: any noticeable improvement in average marks could be attributed, at least in part, to training. This was accepted.

No primary data had been collected on project teachers' schools or grades. It was now added to application forms and a more detailed database kept. In 2009, the British Council approached the Ministry of Education to assist in obtaining student results for the 2008–09 year end school term English exam, for a sample of project teachers. A data collection form was produced for grade 9 and 10 project teachers and those in parallel classes. Two sets of results were compared and analysed: one for December 2008 exams before training; one for December 2009 exams after training. Unfortunately, the project design did not readily lend itself to direct classroom impact evaluation of pupil performance. Aside from teaching methodology, other factors could have influenced pupils' performance: lack of an examined speaking component (since the project emphasised speaking skills); general disruption to teaching schedules during the year and teacher absence; lack of exam credibility; poor exam design; and internal issues leading to statistical 'manipulation'. Nevertheless, the conclusion was that the CBB ELT programme led to a positive effect on examination performance by pupils in the two grades. The data supplied, though, led to such a small sample size that conclusions could only be tentative.

Phase 4

In this phase, we saw the inclusion of the RESC in Vavuniya, an area devastated by the civil war. A total of 155 teachers sat TKT in January 2011. Between July 2011 and March 2012, 28 RESCs will run the distance course for 168 teachers.

The monitoring and evaluation of Phase 4 reflects finally the four levels of Kirkpatrick. Level 1 ('reaction') is evaluated through questionnaires. Teachers' beliefs that the distance course is relevant, appropriate, and of good quality, that self-access materials are easy to access and use, that they will apply course methods and have an action plan showing how and when, and that they will recommend the course to their peers are measured. Level 2 ('knowledge') is evaluated through self-assessment and test. In addition to the aim of 80 per cent achieving TKT band 3, their confidence in using communicative methodology and in mentor support is measured. Level 3 ('behaviour') is measured through questionnaire and observation. Questionnaires provide evidence of teachers adding two new activities to classroom practice and an increase in the percentage of classroom English used by teachers and pupils. End-of-course observations hope to demonstrate more use of communicative methodology and tasks than earlier observations. An extra observation three months after the course to evaluate evidence of settled behaviour is also included. Finally, level 4 ('results') is evaluated. At the recruitment stage, a sample of teachers in schools with parallel classes to theirs have their pupils sit the Oxford Placement Test with an additional speaking component before and after the course. By using control groups, as Phillips argues (2003: 117), the impact of the training can be isolated. These results will be compared to give a more accurate measurement of pupil impact. Although there are problems involved in using experimental and control groups for the evaluation of project outcomes in social change projects, as reported by Pawson and Tilley (1997), there is a political need to provide hard numbers.

Lessons

This project story reveals the importance of having a detailed monitoring and evaluation plan, complete with needs and objectives matched to data collection methods, and a schedule in place from project inception. Zikri, in her discussion of the Egyptian curriculum development project in this volume, concurs. A very careful definition of project scope (and, therefore, of evaluation scope) at the outset is essential. This is also confirmed by Mathew in this volume. Similarly, the need for baseline evaluation in the opening stage of the project is crucial. On the one hand, if your goal is to improve the English skills of pupils, then evaluate that. Evaluating anything else will not reveal true impact. To do this, data collection must be planned and organised from the outset. Here primary data was not initially collected on schools and grades, and thus pupil evaluation was slowed down. On the other hand, although improving student performance might be a long term goal, the immediate project outcome is only going to be improved teacher performance. While this latter is observable and open to evaluation within a reasonable time frame, evaluating student outcomes is (a) very long-term and (b) involves so many variables that are outside the project's control that it is very difficult to evaluate it meaningfully.

Data collected and human resources used should be exploited fully. Here, mentors observed teachers and wrote lesson reports before and after the course, but this data was initially only used as a progress record. Only much later were closer comparisons of the observation reports done on individual teachers to reveal behaviour change. The difference between behaviour change and settled behaviour change was not considered until Phase 4. Had it been built in earlier, stronger impact data would have resulted.

Data collected must be reliable, valid, and accurate. Considerable time and effort were devoted to collecting data on pupil performance from the Ministry of Education without a convincing enough result. Despite the use of a control group, too many other factors could have impacted on pupil evaluation. Although attempts are being made to use control groups more effectively, their use could be seen as a fundamental flaw.

Regular and good methods of communication are essential: while response questionnaires can provide valuable information, face-to-face communication in the form of focus groups can deliver more useful and unpredictable information. This was evident in the informal response in Phase 1, which allowed the project manager to assess accurately the root cause of low turnout, and in the information gleaned from the focus groups in Phase 2. Only the information on the importance the teachers attached to the University of Cambridge exam prevented a potentially disastrous situation from developing when CBB wanted to jettison the TKT exam.

An equally valuable lesson is the unexpected benefits of regular monitoring. While the RESC visits were developed as a mentor performance check, they became a valuable mentor support vehicle, a strong relationship builder of trust between RESCs, Zonal Districts of Education, and the British Council, an information and resource basket to dip into, and a contributor to the strengthening of the respect local teachers had for RESC staff.

This project discussion hopefully points the way for more effective future project monitoring and evaluation.

Case 17:
Understanding washback:
A case study of a new exam
in India

Rama Mathew

The project

The Central Board of Secondary Education (CBSE) undertook a major curriculum renewal project in 1988, namely the CBSE-ELT Project, for English Course A (meant for English-medium students) at the secondary level. The main objective of the project was to improve teaching and learning of English in Classes IX and X with a focus on the development of language skills in communicative situations. The special feature of the project was the intensive involvement of teachers from CBSE schools in all aspects of curriculum development, i.e. designing the new syllabus, the preparation of teaching materials, the new testing scheme and sample papers, and the training manual for orienting teachers to the new curriculum. The new *Interact in English* package[1] was introduced in Class IX in 1993. Before the launch of the new course, about 2,500 teachers (out of about 8,000 teachers who taught at this level in the country) were trained through a 10-day INSET programme by teachers trained for the purpose. The new Class X Board exam was held in March 1995.

Stage – monitoring and evaluation

The Central Institute of English and Foreign Languages (CIEFL), Hyderabad, in keeping with its mandate to improve the standards of teaching English and foreign languages and to conduct advanced training and research in language and literature in India, undertook a national-level study from 1993–97 to monitor, evaluate, and support the CBSE's curriculum renewal project. The national outreach afforded by the CBSE network and its engagement with curriculum renewal were of interest to the Institute. This phase of the project, known as the Curriculum Implementation Study[2] (CIS), was located in the Evaluation Department at CIEFL, which provided professional expertise with assistance from other colleagues in the Institute. The case study presented here focuses on the monitoring phase of the project.

---

[1] This consisted of three books: the Main Course Book (MCB), the Work Book (WB), and the Literature Reader (LR), along with the Teachers' Book (TB) and listening materials on cassettes with the tape scripts in the TB.

[2] The project was funded by the UK Department for International Development (DfID), through the British Council India, while CIS was funded by the CBSE and DfID.

Story

The Curriculum Implementation Study

The main objective of CIS was to study how the different aspects of the curriculum, the new textbooks, the testing scheme, and teacher education unfolded in different types of classrooms, including the washback effect of the Board exam, and to provide continuing support for a more effective implementation of the curriculum. It also enabled teachers to become researchers in their own classrooms with a view to helping them develop professionally.

Key features of CIS

CIS was essentially insider/teacher-oriented and involved teachers in the studying of the different aspects of curriculum-as-reality (how the curriculum unfolded in everyday classroom activities), as opposed to curriculum-as-intention (the syllabus/textbooks as documents) or curriculum-as-product (the language proficiency of students revealed through end-of-course exams). Teachers gathered ongoing reports from classrooms, teachers, students, principals, and parents about the different aspects of the curriculum through a variety of procedures, i.e. classroom observations, interviews, questionnaires, field notes, informal and formal discussions, and examination of student scripts and documents. The study involved all the stakeholders in order to help them to understand the curriculum holistically from different perspectives and in the process to raise their awareness about and illuminate curricular processes. It was also believed that this kind of involvement would give them a sense of ownership and ensure sustainability beyond the life of the project.

The study was developmental with built-in flexibility, which allowed changes and extensions, as and when a need was perceived. Each stage was built on the previous one, on the basis of the evidence collected and lessons learnt. The short needs-based programmes that were organised responded immediately to the needs, felt and expressed, in a particular region, for a particular group, for a particular purpose. Further, the research design made it possible for teachers (and other stakeholders) to take part in the study at any stage, in various capacities, including carrying out action research in their own classrooms. It disseminated the interim results of the study at regular intervals to various stakeholders in ways that were intelligible, meaningful, and usable. The study also made an outsider perspective possible through the involvement of faculty members and research scholars from CIEFL, ELT institutes, and university departments, who looked critically at the different components of the curriculum.

The Final Report gives details of the entire CIS (CBSE-ELT Curriculum Implementation Study 1997). The case study presented here focuses on one aspect, i.e. ways in which the new assessment scheme was received by schools and teachers, and the nature and extent of the washback on different aspects of the curriculum and on stakeholders.

The new assessment scheme

The Board exam at the end of Class X was a paper-pencil test for 100 marks. The breakdown was as follows:

Section	Types of texts/tasks	Book(s) that help	Marks
Reading	3 unseen texts with questions (factual, literary, discursive)	MCB	30
Writing	4 tasks (2 short and 2 long)	MCB	30
Grammar	4 tasks	WB	15
Literature	5 tasks	LR	25

Table 1: Breakdown of Board exam

In Class IX, Continuous Assessment (CA) was assigned 60 per cent, which included informal and formal assessment of conversation (listening and speaking) skills, assignments, unit tests, and half-yearly exams, while the final exam was assigned 40 per cent. This was recorded in students' report cards and communicated to them; for Class X, however, although the same kind of oral assessment was recommended, the final Board exam was the sole indicator of students' success in the exam.

The story unfolds

The baseline study of Class X (1993–1994) showed that teachers and students were quite unhappy with the 'old' curriculum. The teaching/learning in the classroom and out-of-class activities revealed a strong negative washback of the 'old' heavily content-oriented/memory-based exam. Teachers and students were engaged in the monotonous task of revising, learning by heart teacher-interpreted content, and rehearsing mock exams. Obedience and discipline were expected of a Board class, just as it was the responsibility of the Board-class teacher to complete the syllabus as soon as possible so that revision could begin. Since the exam pressure left them with no alternative but to co-operate with each other to fulfil their self-assigned duties, *there was no time for achieving (language) objectives*[3]. However, everyone strongly felt that a learner-centred, skills-based curriculum, with tests that tested language skills would provide the much needed challenge, 'self-learning' techniques, and variety, even for the weak learners. Both teachers and students were clearly unhappy that they had missed the chance of being part of the 'new' curriculum. This, then, was the CBSE climate when the new curriculum was introduced.

The study of Class IX showed a consistent and definite shift towards a communicatively oriented classroom from year 1 (1993–94) to year 3 (1995–96) in different types of schools in different regions of the country. While teachers developed a slightly better understanding of the rationale of the communicative approach *vis-à-vis* the role of textbooks in year 3 compared with year 1, the idea of MCB and WB as resource books that aided skills development and were, therefore, useful for doing

---

[3] Text in italics is a direct quotation from the data.

Sections A and B in the exam paper was not apparent in teachers' reported data or actual work in the classroom. MCB was seen to have too many activities that were lengthy and repetitive and, therefore, arbitrarily dropped.

Alongside this, efforts on the part of teachers, rather than students, at meeting the exam demands a whole year later were clearly visible. Writing was more product-oriented and received less time and attention than other areas. Literature and grammar classes were content/form-focused, largely teacher-led (with teacher explanations and marginal student participation), which students, on the whole, found dull and boring. The time spent on literature, which increased to about 40 per cent in year 3, was disproportionate to what the exam mandated (25 per cent), with a lot of explicit exam preparation. Completing the syllabus, i.e. the prescribed textbooks, was seen by teachers and principals as a main measure of teacher competence.

While everyone appreciated the new assessment scheme for its inherent worth, classroom-based assessment by and large did not concretise the concept of formative evaluation. Teachers' poor understanding of the area and lack of necessary skills combined with inadequate administrative support seemed to affect the implementation of the scheme to quite an extent. That said, all the stakeholders seemed quite positive in their attitude to change when they made suggestions for better implementation: more teacher orientation, better infrastructure, change to be introduced from primary classes, oral exams in Class X Board exam, among others.

The first year of Class X (before the new exam) revealed quite a communicatively oriented class, although all the stakeholders expressed a good deal of anxiety about the exam and spent a substantial amount of their time and effort in revising the lessons and rehearsing mock exams. The study of Class X after the exam (1995–96) revealed exam preparation as the most crucial activity which was separate from teaching; since oral assessment was not part of the final assessment, it was not done or done half-heartedly, especially in privileged schools where the students' language proficiency was high.

Problems in the exam and in its different uses surfaced as the study progressed:

1. The exam scheme had about 45 per cent devoted to rehearsed tasks.

2. The different versions of question papers meant for Delhi/other regions and for outside India were not equivalent.

3. All those who were trained in marking did not mark exam scripts and vice versa.

4. Teacher-made tests used for classroom-based assessment were poorly constructed, although they mirrored the exam pattern in every respect.

5. The Board's policy of providing only total scores, as opposed to section totals, did not give the necessary response to the stakeholders about what kind of teaching/learning in class resulted in what kind of scores.

The needs-based workshops, such as analysis of teacher-made tests, item writing/banking, assessment of oral skills, and marking writing, succeeded in problematising the issue and developed prototype materials and tasks. Apart, however, from identifying key people who could take the ideology of CIS forward, reaching out to thousands of teachers spread across the country was beyond its brief. Therefore, the washback of a less skills-based exam but a largely skills-based course was not entirely positive, as had been expected, although all the stakeholders were quite happy with the new curriculum, which, in turn, reflected the extent to which they accepted the change.

This was only a partial picture that emerged in a majority of urban/well-resourced[4] schools; it was clear that the new curriculum/exam had not addressed the problems of weak students, especially in remote areas and under-resourced schools. In regions such as Arunachal Pradesh, where only the CBSE's Course A is available (which most people concede is not relevant to their needs), the situation was one of a distorted version of the new curriculum and lower scores in the first Board exam. If less proficient learners had to pass and a measure of teacher accountability was the pass percentage in his or her class, recourse to a results-oriented methodology was the only proven alternative. Therefore the MCB was not used until late, i.e. February, or not touched at all, since it was outside the syllabus. Teachers felt quite confident, from past experience, in handling the texts from the LR for exam purposes. The request for more exam-type formats, i.e. integrated grammar tasks, was therefore not without reason. This was corroborated by the analysis of answer scripts of the first Board exam: it showed that students with low scores from regions such as Guwahati and Allahabad had scored almost all of the 25 marks in the literature section and the remainder in B3 and B4 writing tasks which demanded prior knowledge of texts from MCB, but had left out Reading and Grammar sections.

A positive washback of the Class X curriculum was, to some extent, evident in Class XI. Teachers and students wanted their classes to continue to be communicative. They did not like to go back to the old style of teaching, where the meaning of the text, fixed by the teacher, was explained until all the students understood it. Teachers found themselves unable to use old books in new ways, because of the inherent limitations of the texts for adapting for communicative tasks/exercises. The washback of the slightly revised Class XII exam, however, was not apparent. Therefore, what everyone desperately wanted, before all the good things done in Classes IX and X were undone, was a change to books that promoted the development of language skills and an exam scheme that incorporated an oral component. The urgency of this demand also reaffirmed the degree of acceptance the stakeholders had shown of the new curriculum in Classes IX and X.

In sum, then, it appeared that the new curriculum, given the constraints of the new exam, was not entirely satisfactory, especially for weak learners, as opposed to what was envisaged through a communicative curriculum. The conflict that emerged because of dichotomies in the seen-unseen components of the question

---

[4] Well-resourced schools and under-resourced schools are not necessarily dichotomous, but represent a continuum in terms of infrastructure (for example, tape recorders in working condition, cyclostyling facilities), adequate number of teachers with high motivation and language competence, students who are not first generation learners, and school management that believes in quality education and provides support to teachers.

paper, language-literature issues, lengthy question-cum-answer papers only for English, among others, had neutralised, to quite an extent, the work done during the project and CIS. A recommendation made to the CBSE by the study was that concerted efforts should be made to support the enormous amount of progress that motivated and committed teachers were making, before the negative impact of the changed curriculum became firmly established.

Lessons

Given the magnitude and complexity of the curriculum change, which marked a major departure from secondary Boards' textbook revision exercises, the project demonstrated a model of curriculum reform at the secondary level. The teacher-as-researcher approach to monitoring and supporting the curriculum change in different types of schools for different types of students, with all stakeholders participating in it willingly, was a unique experiment that other curriculum projects could adopt with suitable modifications.

There seemed to be at least two related issues that CBSE should have addressed: first, the assessment scheme did not capture what transpired in class, thus making the test a de facto curriculum (Shohamy 1997), different in nature and scope from the official curriculum. This negated the impact considerably, hampering, in the process, the confidence the stakeholders had gradually built up. Even if a sudden switch to a completely skills-based exam was not practical, a change in stages should have been conceived of and carried out, but this was not on CBSE's agenda. Further, since the needs of the weak learner had not been adequately met, the question of how the Board, with its reputation of being elitist, should/can be equally successful with all types of schools and regions had to be examined. Alternatively, was this a realistic goal and, if not, should CBSE's outreach be redefined? The CIS illuminated the macro and micro aspects of curriculum implementation, especially from a bottom-up perspective, and, therefore, the stakeholders, it seemed, were equipped to take on such a challenge.

The second factor which hampered effective implementation was the stage at which the innovation was introduced. Given the high-stakes nature of a single, summative, paper-pencil exam at the end of secondary school, Class IX, everyone felt, was too late for any radical change to be initiated. They saw the change as piecemeal and felt constrained to resort to time-tested, results-oriented methodologies. An area where the impact of the Board exam was felt most was the way the scheme percolated to lower classes, especially in private schools, since it was beyond the purview of CBSE. The adoption of the three textbooks (MCB, WB, and LR) for the same exam scheme from Class I onwards, and the use by scores of private publishers of the project team members as materials writers and trainers, to ensure the curriculum worked in practice, give some indication of how the innovation spread. Private schools with more educated and aware parents were, thus, more influential in turning the innovation to their advantage. The weak learner and teachers in under-resourced schools in this enterprise were just passive recipients of the innovation.

A clear message from this experience for the future is the following: it is essential that a Board clearly define, at the beginning of the project, the scope of such a project and ensure that the agreed brief is satisfactorily completed; in addition, it will have to respond to the expressed and felt needs of its stakeholders during the project and incorporate changes along the way, by going beyond a *logical framework* (see Tribble 2000 for details), especially when the project is located within a stakeholder approach to curriculum renewal. Here, it was definitely possible to introduce an evaluation scheme that included a component of oral skills in its high-stakes test, in keeping with the communicative curriculum which emphasised oral skills in the classroom, by which teachers and other stakeholders were more than persuaded. Similarly extending the innovation to lower classes in a systematic, project mode was a necessity without which everyone felt let down. This, then, was a case of lost opportunity, which one needs to be guarded against in future endeavours.

One aspect of the philosophy of CIS which, in my view, was significant was the high level of engagement of the main project 'users'. The project provided the space for teachers and other stakeholders (including me, as Project Director) to interpret the curriculum changes according to their own local realities, to feed those interpretations directly into needs-based workshops, and to provide their personal insights during events such as review workshops, and national and international seminars. The international seminar held in 1995 stood out for its exuberance, professional commitment, and 'passion', as a participant put it, and was an example of how the insider-teachers wrested the podium away from the outside-experts and shared their myriad (research) experiences in an academic forum. For a project of this magnitude to become an evolving curriculum (as opposed to a static one), teachers' (and other stakeholders') voices need to be heard and acted on. While the notion of collaboration within and outside schools was kept alive during CIS, what kind of communication network would need to be set up after the life of the project? It seemed that time-bound projects had to finish their work and move on. This was more true of CBSE and the British Council than CIEFL, an organisation with continuing research interests. That CBSE had expended a lot of its time and attention on English and now had to think of other subjects was not in keeping with the principles of a grass-roots-level project. There were the issues of the roles and responsibilities required of the three organisations in order to ensure sustainability that should have been negotiated early on the project.

The lessons learnt from the exercise, however, can feed into a more sensitive and viable curriculum than has been possible thus far. Indeed, the formative nature of the study has activated the notion of dynamism in the curriculum and has accommodated the changing context, rather than treating it as a top-down prescription to be executed in its entirety. The individual strengths of teachers will need to be co-ordinated and supported at school, and the school in turn will need to be supported by outside agencies, if the notion of 'evaluation as a development tool' is to be concretised in meaningful contexts. It seems that the gap between curriculum-as-intention and curriculum-as-reality can be closed only through a research and development approach to one's own teaching and that long-term improvement of education hinges on the effective utilisation of curriculum research.

Postscript

The CBSE changed its exam scheme in 2005 with the following breakdown: Reading (20), Writing (30), Grammar (20), and Literature (30). It was more memory-based than in 1995, a clear regression in 10 years. A tracer study done in 2001, three years after this study officially ended, revealed that, although there was no longer any dialogue between different stakeholders, some teachers continued to create learner-centred classrooms and adopt a research approach to their teaching. They were system-free, silent innovators working in isolation (Mathew 2006).

Case 18:
Redirecting a curriculum development project in Egypt

Mona Zikri

The project

Egypt's longest-ever ELT project ran from 1975 to 1991. It was sponsored by the British Council, UCLA (University of California, Los Angeles), the Binational Fulbright Commission, and the Faculty of Education (FoE) of Ain Shams University. It focused on an ad hoc committee proposal for 'developing ELT in Egypt' through the 'revision of curricula and textbooks in conformity with the language needs of Egypt and individual Egyptians' ([1]Ad Hoc Proposal 1975: 4). A key new body, the Centre for Developing English Language Teaching (CDELT), was established and affiliated to the English Department of the FoE.

Three curriculum development projects can be identified. They were classified as CDP I: materials development, CDP II: research, and CDP III: a staff development scheme.

However, the design of the project lacked a needs assessment, well-defined objectives, and adequate planning. Also, the project's change theory had three flaws:

- the adoption of a prescriptive approach by expatriate experts

- the rationale for reform's focus on 'product', not 'process'

- the failure to recognise the 'social context' of the reform.

The CDPs succeeded in developing curricula, but failed on two fundamentals of reform: building ownership and improving capacities. The new curricula were not adopted. Recognition of the importance of the social context of reform led to a redirection of the project in its final years. Limited success was achieved with the improved performance of professionals, but there was no impact on systemic change. CDELT did not achieve ELT reform in Egypt, although it served temporarily as a professional development hub.

---

[1] Documents no longer exist but are quoted from Zikri 1991. They will be cited as (Doc: date) without bibliographical citation.

Stage – monitoring and evaluation

This case study focuses on the monitoring and evaluation (M & E) system for CDP. An adequate M & E system is crucial to a project's success and sustainability, especially one with challenges of design and implementation. In fact, a truly iterative project need not be ideal at the design stage, but should have enough flexibility to evolve according to needs, guided by assessment findings. This case study examines the validity of formative and summative evaluations throughout the 16 years of the project, and their success and failure in solving problems and redirecting project goals.

Story

The low impact of continuing evaluation on project outcomes

Although the project had models of formative and summative evaluations, as well as output and implementation assessment, systematic M & E was not yet a common practice when the project began. The validity of the assessment practices, their impact on progress, and the project's sustainability and results will be examined in this paper.

Evaluation is just one of a set of problem-solving interventions, but it is a crucial tool for adjusting plans and making progress towards positive results. During its first decade, CDELT evaluations had little impact on progress, lacking tactics and strategies, and, in the absence of clear objectives, there were no standards to measure progress against. In some cases, problems were identified, but no action was taken to address them. Eventually, an ethnographic approach to evaluation was adopted, providing insight into and solutions to issues, and supporting the project to enable it to achieve limited success. The features of the evaluations were:

- **Inadequate tools/lack of instruments:** In 1978, the testing expert specified revision issues, which in fact denoted the absence of formative evaluations throughout CDP I, since there existed 'no clear defined measurable objectives, no criterion of mastery established, no concurrent programmes were available, no proficiency measures...' (Henning: Doc: 1978). In 1979, the first evaluation report stated that shortcomings in staff assessment in relation to subject matter expertise were being 'informally made'. No mechanisms were set for formative evaluation through the 'continual approval' of stakeholders (Bowers et al.: Doc: 1979). In general, evaluation results were based on inconclusive evidence. For example, there was a conclusion that students' attitudes towards English had changed after the trial because 'they often used English in the corridors' (Hudson and Melia 1981: 144), without any comparison with the state before the trial.

- **Disregard for Egyptian involvement:** Project continuity depended on the English department's acceptance of the courses. However, two reviews dated 28 May 1981 show a dispute between the Centre and the department chair, the 'Principal Investigator' of the project, who rejected the materials, stating that senior staff could not support materials they had not been allowed to examine, let alone develop. The British team leader disregarded the allegations, admitted the atmosphere was 'worrying', but decided to proceed with publishing irrespective of the department's decisions. Senior staff members from Ain Shams, Assiut, and Tanta universities confirmed the department's complaints that expatriates did not acknowledge context, regulations, or the local work culture (Hudson and Melia op.cit.). This terminated collaboration between CDELT and the department.

- **Evaluations not supporting the adjustments:** Evaluations reflected issues that resulted from a lack of proper project design, but a lack of planning persisted throughout the three stages, with plans and objectives sometimes appearing after materials were actually produced. Needs and context analyses were absent. Implementation was built on assumptions that were tested by trial and error. Thus we find:

1. **CDP I:** The British team leader reported that the project and scope of teaching materials were poorly defined. Initial bad planning had led to constant confusion about aims and objectives (Melia: Doc: 1982). D. Loos, a team member, stated: 'In piloting our materials this year, we had to face the fact that our materials were going to be used under conditions which we considered to be less than ideal... Our initial response was (1) the materials were not designed for such use...' (Loos et al 1983: 34). However, this negative evaluation was not acted on, and the project's chance for enhanced impact was lost.

2. **CDP II:** No materials revision or summative reviews had been conducted for first and second year materials. These would have supported the design of a 'research paper' project to develop the second phase of the CDP. After the completion of 24 research papers, an evaluator reported that the research was 'too theoretical and impractical to support developing materials' (Nelson: Doc: 1984).

3. **CDP III:** Poor design, constant lack of planning, and unsupportive evaluation negatively affected project results right up to the end. However, a summative assessment found materials to be of high quality and Egyptian professionals to be well versed in the materials and methodology. It recommended that research attachments should be replicated, as local expertise was the only way to disseminate the use of the materials (Robinson: Doc: 1990). In fact, this echoed the views the Department Chair expressed in 1981. The British team leader, in his concluding report, confirmed these findings, but raised the problem that such work could not be sustained, since planning for building local expertise should have been developed earlier (Smith: Doc: 1990).

- **Limitations of external evaluations:** J. Morley and B. Coffey's report praised the materials but, in assessing their applicability, their views were divorced from the realities of the education context (Doc: 1982). For example, the materials were found to be incompatible with 'non-ideal' situations, while in fact the norm for Egyptian classes was 'non-ideal'. This undermined the validity of the materials. The sole Egyptian evaluation by G. Saad Eldin, Y. El Ezabi, and A. Farghali was generally positive towards the materials, with some criticisms and reservations. However, issues were defined and solutions proposed, but not implemented (Doc: 1982).

Evaluations did not capture implementation issues

Evaluations focused on the curriculum products but did not capture the flaws in the implementation process. In fact, CDELT had potential success factors that were not utilised, including the potential for sustainability and institutionalisation as an Egyptian entity, an ideal duration of 16 years to effect change, distinguished ELT professionals supporting the projects, and the establishment of partnerships. Implementation issues included:

- The work management style was prescriptive. The foreign 'experts', researchers from outside the system and culture, saw themselves as innovators with sole control of design and implementation, in isolation from stakeholders and cultural constraints.

- Plans for sustainability were not inbuilt. Handover was on the agenda, but the key roles were unquestionably played by expatriates, with no plans to develop Egyptians to take over in these roles. Finally, it became evident that the transfer of posts to Egyptians was the way to Egyptianise CDELT (Holliday: Doc: 90).

- A high turnover of expatriates supported a rigid adherence to short term plans. British Council experts held two- or three-year contracts. Newcomers picked up from where their predecessors had left off, guided by and following up on short-term plans with insufficient time or institutional memory to interact with the context. Consequently, issues persisted throughout. It was not until the final phase, when the expatriate expert had an extended contract of five-years, that issues were identified and addressed.

A shift in assessment approach redirected the project

As British involvement was ending, the project still faced the dilemma of how to disseminate and institutionalise the materials. Sustainability, capacity development, and human attributes were emerging issues. As the social constraints became evident, the initial assumption that curriculum development (CD) was the route to reform became invalid. A. Holliday, language co-ordinator (1985-90), set new objectives, changing the focus from curriculum reform to developing Egyptian 'change agents'. Changed work practices ensured that Egyptian 'colleagues' and expatriate 'consultants' collaborated, and the value of capacity development, partnership, and ownership became evident. Understandings emerged about the power of social context, cultural biases, and socio-physical conditions.

Holliday introduced new monitoring practices, collecting information by 'ethnographic classroom observations, discussions, consensus building, and stakeholders' opinions, and means and needs analysis of the social context' (Holliday: Doc: 1985, 1987, 1988, 1989, 1990), with results that supported the redirection from CD to staff development.

Practices included:
- First-hand on-site investigations. This included observing as well as teaching classes. New vital observable phenomena emerged concerning students' behaviour and local staff status.

- Feedback. Egyptian staff provided opinion as experts in their fields.

- Assessment of materials. Visiting specialists and local senior academic staff were involved in discussions and agreement on materials and approaches.

Lessons

Throughout 1983–93, research by different CDELT team members reflected lessons learnt, many of which formed new principles for international ELT support.

CDP I: Bowers (1983) recognises that successful design and implementation must take into consideration the following lessons learnt:

- The uniqueness of project context. The measures for innovation which were acceptable in one context were not appropriate for another. Thus, every CDP represents a unique attempt to initiate change. It is necessary to consider the unique physical, cultural, linguistic, and psychological variables in project design and implementation.

- The relationship between design, planning, and monitoring. In order to compensate for the short planning phase of projects and cope with problems arising during implementation, Bowers advocates that monitoring and evaluation should drive a flexible process of adjustment.

- The negative impact of conflict. Bowers describes the CDELT crisis as 'disputes over project management' that negatively impacted on results. He recognises that CDPs that fall into the trap of excluding stakeholders will fail on this essential human factor, more than on any other.

- Cultural interaction between expatriates and host cultures. It is necessary, in a multilingual world, where 'our (the West's) contemporary ethic values and practices [have a dominant status], to mediate between these and alternative ethics and ways of acting, both generally and in educational terms… [and] to make common our knowledge and share our uncertainties' (Bowers 1985: 255-57).

- Clear objectives and stakeholder collaboration. Projects must have a managed set of priorities, objectives, timescales, and balances between external expertise and local inputs.

CDP III: CDELT offered multiple lessons, as reflected in Holliday's research (Doc: 1987, 1988, etc. and Holliday 1991, 1997, and 2005). The impact of social constraints in project development was crucial. He argued for 'appropriate methodologies for different social contexts of education'; advocated shifting the 'destructive notion of cultural imperialism' to a more collaborative analogy of a 'marketplace' where 'all partners are equal' (Holliday 1997: 7). Lessons learnt included the impossibility of conducting CDPs without regard to the host's social context, and ownership. Appropriate project design necessitates information collection and continuing ethnographic means analysis. Sustainability requires good planning, built into projects, for a local counterpart to take over.

Conclusion

Egyptian academics who were involved with the Centre during the last project phase have managed to evolve some small-scale professional networking and adopt improved ELT practices, but there was no reform infrastructure to support long-lasting systemic changes in ELT.

Broad lessons learnt can be summed up as follows:

1. Project design must be flexible and based on needs.

2. Reform is a process with 'results', not a product with 'outputs'.

3. Crucial to success are issues of ownership, capacity development, and incorporation of the social context through 'appropriate methodologies'.

4. Valid monitoring and evaluation systems should inform project designers, implementers, and policy makers on how best to achieve results.

The cases:
Embedding and
dissemination

Case 19:
The English Language Teachers' Association (ELTA) project for newly-qualified teachers in Azerbaijan

Sue Leather

The project

The British Council ELTA project aimed to address the needs of newly qualified secondary school teachers of English in a number of countries in southern Europe and the Balkans. It was originally targeted at Turkey, Greece, Bulgaria, Armenia, Romania, Georgia, Azerbaijan, and Macedonia. However, though some of the research into the needs of teachers was done in Armenia and Greece, as well as other countries in the region, only four countries eventually took part in the full project. Those countries were Romania, where the project was 'owned', Georgia, Macedonia, and Azerbaijan. The project was initiated in 2005 and handed over to local partners in April 2008.

The perceived need at the outset of the project was that newly qualified teachers (NQTs) in these contexts were ill-equipped by their university education and pre-service training for working as teachers in schools. Most of their training was academic in nature, and little attention was given to their needs in terms of dealing with the practicalities of working with pupils or supporting the teachers as they settled into their positions in schools. The goal of the project, therefore, was not only to provide effective training for the NQTs, but also to provide the means, through a flexible, self-access resource pack, to support them in-service.

The project included research into the needs of NQTs in the countries involved in the project, the development of the resource pack for them, trainer training, and delivery of the training to the teachers by local trainers.

The project today

In Azerbaijan, about 500 newly qualified teachers have benefited directly from training since the project started. A further 100 have benefited indirectly by cascade training. In 2011, the project is still going strong in Baku, where the number of NQTs who are eager to take part in the training has never declined. The demand is also strong in the regions, though lack of material support has meant that it is not delivered face to face there, much to the disappointment of AzETA (Azerbaijani English Teachers' Association). This brings to the fore a common dilemma in change projects, namely insufficient funding fully to carry the project forward in the medium to longer term, once initial donor funding is no longer available. In this way, it could be said that the project has not fully embedded, though AzETA do at the very least have an effective continuing course 'product' that they can present to possible future funders.

Stage – embedding and dissemination

In this case study, I will look at the embedding and dissemination stage of the project, particularly at the stage where British Council funding ended and the project was handed over to local partners. I will examine factors which led to successful embedding and dissemination in one specific context – Azerbaijan – focusing specifically on the factors that led to success.

Experiences and issues which I consider to be of interest or importance will include: matching of project aims and local context; the nature of the target group; suitability of materials; effective partnering; processes and procedures, and leadership and management. I will include an update of the project in Azerbaijan today.

Story

Matching of project aims and context

An important factor in the successful embedding and dissemination of the project in Azerbaijan was the effective matching of project aims and context. The feeling among key participants from both the British Council Azerbaijan and the main partner, the local Azerbaijani English Teachers' Association, is that the project addressed, and continues to address, a real need in the local context. The British Council's in-country ELT consultant, who worked alongside the programmes manager on the project, described pre-service training for teachers in Azerbaijan as being based on the old Soviet model. This makes it top heavy with theory and very light on the practical issues of teaching and up-to-date interactive methodology. The British Council's project manager, initially ELT country co-ordinator for the project, suggested that the main challenges for NQTs in Azerbaijan are lack of resources, modern teaching methodology, managing the classroom, and lack of confidence. The project aimed to address all these factors through highly practical training and through the resource pack. According to AzETA and the British Council, there are about 200 NQTs per annum graduating from universities in Azerbaijan, and they all continue to be in need of the training and the resource pack. This has clearly made the embedding of the project easier.

Target group

Another reason that may have led to successful embedding has been the members of the target group themselves. In *Planning for Educational Change*, Martin Wedell points out that one of the main reasons why educational changes fail is that 'the change causes teachers to worry, because it expects them to use new practices that require a different classroom management style' (Wedell 2009: 45). By their very nature, the teachers in the target group had very little classroom experience anyway and were arguably more open to change than teachers who had been teaching in a particular way for many years. While these NQTs still had to fit in with their school cultures to an extent, their youth and relative lack of experience may well have made them more open to change.

Choice of partner
An additional factor which was critical for the effective embedding and dissemination of the project was choice of partner. The key partner for the project was chosen by competitive interview. Before the project started, the British Council Azerbaijan already had well-established links with the local Teachers' Association, AzETA. It therefore seemed natural to choose AzETA as key partner for the project, especially since it had, as the British Council ELT consultant said, 'the capacity and the ability to deliver'. Local Departments of Education and the Ministry of Education were also partners. The British Council made a point of raising the profile of AzETA with the Ministry of Education.

Within AzETA, an NQT Special Interest Group (SIG) was set up during the initial stages of the project. A professional trainer within AzETA was appointed as co-ordinator of the SIG, under the leadership of the TA (Teachers' Association) head. The NQT co-ordinator had a special understanding of the needs of NQTs and was keen to develop training for them. In addition, the co-ordinator and another trainer from AzETA attended trainer training for delivering the project training materials in the summer of 2006, given by the international consultant to the project. The AzETA trainers thus became, in effect, the master trainers of the project. This enabled AzETA to develop ownership early in the life of the project.

Choice of trainers
As I have detailed above, the initial choice of trainers was important. Once these AzETA trainers had received training with the resource pack, the British Council then proceeded to select the regions and trainers to pilot the NQT course in Azerbaijan. In late 2006, a trainer training session was held in the capital, Baku. Six trainers from that group were then selected to work on the project in the three pilot cities of Baku, Sumgayit, and Ganja. The two master trainers worked in Baku, another two trainers worked in Sumgayit, and two more in Ganja. The training was then delivered to NQT participants in instalments between January 2007 and mid-2008, each separate training session being focused on different modules from the resource pack. All the training was closely monitored by the British Council project manager in Baku and two other appointed observers in Sumgayit and Ganja. All observers gave responses to the trainers.

This staged assimilation of trainers and roll-out of the training during the implementation phase seems to have been successful in providing AzETA with a good model of how the training could be managed. The monitoring and responses during the phase of the project which was supported by the British Council also ensured that the Teachers' Association and the trainers felt guided and supported, which made handover much easier.

Resource pack

The resource pack *Steps to Success* was used in the training of trainers and then in the delivery of the training to NQTs. It was written by the international consultant as a result of research done into the needs of NQTs in the region and in consultation with local trainers. In it, there were 12 topics under four main headings: classroom skills and competencies; developing skills; materials and resources; and developing as a teacher. In addition, there were trainers' tips for each topic and other resources such as observation sheets. The intention was for the pack to be user-friendly for both trainers and teachers, with plenty of ready-made activities. Steps to Success was effectively a first-aid kit, offering easy-to-follow solutions to problems that NQTs face in their first year of teaching. As the resource pack was delivered in the regions, evaluation was gathered from participants and incorporated. The practicality of this resource pack went a long way towards making its embedding and dissemination successful.

Leadership and management

As can be seen from the comments above, leadership and management factors contributed greatly to the successful embedding and dissemination of the project in Azerbaijan. From the British Council side, there was careful selection of trainers by the project manager, in consultation with the Teachers' Association, and trainers chosen were diligently and professionally monitored. This monitoring process gave AzETA a clear model of how training was to be organised and provided. Before handover, the British Council and AzETA carefully planned what was to happen and what the objectives were; the British Council leadership also attended all project board meetings. Without this constant support and involved partnership, it is doubtful whether the handover and the period after handover would have been so successful. The effective leadership of AzETA and its NQT Special Interest Group was also key.

A teacher's story

What of the newly qualified teachers themselves? How did they experience the project? Looking at the project through a teacher's eyes will give us insight into how it was received by the target group.

Amalya is a 23 year old newly qualified teacher in a secondary school in Baku. She attended the training which was held every Saturday for 12 weeks in the AzETA office at Baku Slavic University, starting November 2008.

The topic of the first session was 'Managing your classroom and your students'. In the session, she was able to discuss with her trainer and colleagues some of the difficult issues that arise for young teachers in state secondary schools. One of the most challenging problems is how to control teenagers in class, as there is not much age difference between teacher and students. There were a lot of good discussions on that topic, and Amalya found it a great relief to learn that she wasn't the only teacher with discipline problems. She also found it fascinating to meet colleagues from different institutions in Baku.

The second session of the training was on 'Planning lessons and courses'. At university, Amalya had found lesson planning boring, but here she discovered how crucial producing a good lesson plan was to her work. She also experienced 'micro-teaching'.

The next topic was 'Grammar and vocabulary presentation, and practice issues'. In that session, she picked up some fresh and exciting ways of presenting grammar. She also learnt about how to use lead-ins effectively, to get students ready to learn.

Further topics included teaching the four skills, teaching about culture, using visual aids, and the important topic of assessment. The final part of the course was about professional development. Here, Amalya and the other participants discussed how to develop as teachers and how they could support one another once the course was finished.

During the course, Amalya gave three workshops for other teachers in her school, telling them about the new ideas she was learning. She found that very stimulating, as it was her first experience of running a workshop for teachers.

Overall, Amalya felt that she had learnt a lot from the course. Perhaps the most important thing, she felt, was that it was possible to make training sessions – and lessons – both hard work and fun. She was also very happy about how practical everything was. She was able to try out ideas and activities immediately with her students.

Lessons

There are a number of lessons that emerge from this brief study of the embedding and dissemination stage of the ELTA project for newly qualified teachers. They are:

1. *The project needs to meets a real need in the local context.* Clearly, making sure that the project aims are suited to the context is crucial. In the case of the project in Azerbaijan, the extensive research and consultation that took place before project initiation made sure that this was the case.

2. *The right partner needs to be chosen to take the project forward.* AzETA proved to be the ideal partner to take the project forward. It already had professional trainers, provincial branches, and a desire to address the needs of NQTs in the country. Crucially, also, the project seemed to fill a need already identified within AzETA.

3. *The key partner(s) must develop ownership early in the initiation stage of the project.* AzETA set up a Special Interest Group for NQTs early in the life of the project. Trainers were also involved at an early stage and became the master trainers of the project. The communication between the British Council and AzETA seems to have been very good, enabling ownership from the outset.

4. *The project resources must be well suited to the real needs of the target group.* The Steps to Success resource pack proved to be very popular with the target group because of its user-friendliness and highly practical nature. It was well suited to the needs of the participants, largely because it was based on extensive research and consultation.

5. *There must be a good management model of how to deliver the project.* The way that the project implementation was handled by British Council managers showed a good, principled approach to training delivery. There was an effective monitoring and reports system. All this gave a good model to local partners for the delivery, monitoring, and evaluation of training, which, in turn, made dissemination more effective.

Case 20:
Embedding change in state education systems in Brazil: The Paraná ELT project

Christopher Palmer

The project

The Paraná ELT project ran from 1999 to 2002, with the British Council being invited to manage this ambitious three-year project at the request of the State Secretary of Education, State of Paraná, Brazil, with funding coming from the World Bank. The focus was on improving the language and teaching skills of teachers of English in the southern Brazilian state of Paraná.

The project had a number of dimensions, including a language improvement programme, a distance learning teacher training programme using resources created by the Open University, a tailor-made internet-based English course, immersion courses at a specialist Teachers University (Universidade do Profesor), a BBC radio course adapted for local radio, methodology courses in the United Kingdom, a tailor-made programme for the best teachers designed to embed the programme into the educational context of the state education system, and, finally, the formation of local self-help groups.

The progress of each teacher was measured by means of tests from the University of Cambridge Local Examinations Syndicate (UCLES) which were administered before and after participation.

The client, the State Government of Paraná, expressed great satisfaction with the outcomes of the project, which succeeded in raising the levels of English language and the teaching capacity of some 2,875 teachers from all parts of the state. The project attracted particular attention for its range of innovations, not least its use of distance learning methodology. Success can be measured in requests from other subject areas for a similar programme, requests for replication from other Brazilian states, and the number of papers the project generated, especially from teachers themselves.

Stage – embedding and dissemination

This case study will focus on how the project team attempted to embed the achievements of what became a three-year project into the education system in Paraná and promote its success and possible replication across the country.

Story

The challenge

Every project has to overcome internal and external challenges, and the Paraná project was no exception. These can be divided into two categories: those external to the project and those resulting from the project itself, which I refer to here as internal challenges.

External challenges:

- **Funding**
  Funding was based on provision of results on a year-by-year basis with the following year's funding only released several months after the start of the year. This created a challenge for planning and continuity.

- **Political uncertainty**
  There were several periods of political uncertainty in which the very position of the State Secretary of Education was under threat and these had a direct impact on the team and the state teachers.[1]

- **Local opposition**
  Foreign interference in a local issue was an accusation used on several occasions to undermine the integrity of the project. Even amongst some of the partners, there were those who questioned the whole ethos of allowing an organisation such as the British Council to lead a project of this kind, despite their track record.

  Notwithstanding the impact of these external factors which threatened the project itself, it was the internal factors which had to be addressed, if lasting impact was to be achieved.

Internal challenges:

- **Low self-esteem amongst teachers**
  The first challenge was the low expectation of teachers. At the start of the project, language teachers were the only group of teachers not to have benefited from training and access to the resources offered by the Teachers University, the Universidade do Professor in Faxinal do Céu. An initial needs analysis indicated that the language level of teachers was very low and, furthermore, teachers' self-esteem appeared to be at rock bottom. There

---

[1] In fact the State Secretary of Education lost her job during the second year of the project for a period of several months, only to be reinstated after the Governor could not find an adequate replacement. She was finally dismissed in a political shake-up prior to the elections and was not replaced.

would clearly not be any short-term fixes, and any long-term impact would be dependent on building self-esteem to a level that would allow self-expression and ownership of their own learning (see next point).

- **Dependency culture**
Making teachers independent learners was the next most challenging task. However, in view of the project's uncertain life expectancy, it was essential to instil the learning skills which we hoped would give teachers the encouragement to pursue their learning with or without a 'project'.

- **System failures**
Another challenge was the fact that the State Secretary of Education saw the failure of the teachers as being the direct result of failures in the university teacher education system. This was highly disputed by the universities themselves, and it was clear from the outset that no teacher training solution could be either successful or sustainable unless the universities were involved, as the project proved.

- **Size and reach**
A final challenge facing the project was the problem of size. There were over 4,500 teachers of English spread across a state which is four-fifths of the size of the United Kingdom. To deliver training to them all and give all teachers an equal chance to participate would involve a wide network of delivery partners (universities) and a model largely based on distance learning. Distance learning was relatively new to Brazil, and we had been warned that Brazilian culture, where self-discipline and autonomous learning were not considered common attributes of teachers, was not conducive to such an approach. The project was to prove this a myth.

The response
To meet these challenges the project team focused on a number of strategies:

- **Feel-good factor**
The feel-good factor was fundamental to addressing the issue of low self-esteem. From day one of the project, when 500 teachers came to the Teachers University to give their views on the training model being envisaged, it was apparent that raising self-esteem would be a significant factor in embedding the benefits. The fact that this project was focusing on state teachers of English for the first time had an immediate impact, but to sustain this impact, both the management team and the delivery partners had important roles to play. Whether through individual study programmes or the shared opportunities in Faxinal do Céu and the United Kingdom, creating a strong group dynamic was fundamental to raising self-esteem and promoting a sense of can-do.

- **Autonomous learning**
Turning teachers into independent learners is challenging if the pervading culture is one of dependency. The starting point for tackling this had to be the universities and building the skills of the university trainers in managing autonomous learning. This was achieved through a series of workshops.

■ **Capacity building of trainers and trainees**

Universities had traditionally implemented pre-service and in-service training, but the perception was that this had not been successful. It was not within the Project Manager's remit to delve into the basis of this perception but, as the only training bodies in existence capable of managing teacher training at a state level, it was clear that universities would have to be strengthened if the improvements in teacher education were going to be embedded. Through the creation of a university supply network, building their capacity through a number of trainer training programmes, and involving representatives in the project consultative committee, not only did this allow for much better communication and exchange of skills and knowledge amongst them, but it also enhanced their own sense of worth within the system, in that they were able to influence the development of the regional project directly. In all, the project enhanced their abilities and strengthened their reputation within the state and across Brazil.

■ **Developing learning skills**

As I have previously mentioned, the question of size and reach was addressed by adopting a distance education approach, with periods of self-study interspersed with fortnightly meetings with tutors, where the focus was less on teaching new content and more on such matters as managing learning and assessing needs, celebrating successes, and dealing with learning problems. The internet and radio English courses also helped to enhance teachers' sense of managing their own learning. Both courses were optional additions which grew in popularity over the life of the project. This brought the twin benefits of making teachers more independent in their learning and less dependent on others for input, and also the building of a sense of self-worth and achievement which would continue well beyond the project itself.

The final countdown

As we approached the third year, it became evident to the management team that the project would not continue beyond three years, with the prospect of a change of government growing increasingly likely. To ensure a positive legacy beyond the short-term gains of better teaching and improvement in student performance, we needed to create the conditions for continued self-development. For this, we needed to identify leaders amongst the teachers who could act as catalysts, co-ordinating local initiatives such as self-help groups, modelling good teaching behaviours, taking the message to the outside world through participation in state and national events, and, most importantly, finding a voice as the English language teachers of Paraná. This would need different structures and types of training to be put in place.

■ **Special Interest Groups**

With the State Secretary of Education's support, these were established across the state. This allowed teachers to meet and conduct group learning and other activities together. It also helped them plan and engage in professional events at state and regional level[2].

---

[2] Response from teachers (2011) indicated that some of these groups still exist at the time of writing.

The textbook project

Teachers consistently said that the textbooks they had were no longer adequate. With the help of publishers, a group of teachers and university lecturers participated in a textbook evaluation project. Although this did not culminate in the purchase of textbooks, the skills acquired by those involved meant they were in a better position to evaluate materials and later choose which resources they wanted to use in their classes[3].

Pathmakers

The *Pathmakers* programme was designed for a group, largely self selected, who wanted to help make the Paraná ELT project sustainable. The programme specifically addressed issues of self-esteem, leadership, and action. It was run three times over the final year of the project and was so popular that, by the end, the university teachers were asking to join in – this perhaps representing the final breakdown of barriers between the perceived 'carriers' of knowledge, in this case, universities, and the 'consumers of knowledge', in this case, the teacher-learners. It was no surprise that several of these teachers subsequently gave papers at conferences, including one who gave a joint presentation with the author at the annual IATEFL Conference in the United Kingdom. Furthermore, some of these teachers went on to do Masters degrees, join university departments, write articles for journals, and, in an ultimate act of self-empowerment, write to the incoming State Secretary of Education arguing for the continuation of the project and extolling the benefits that had been gained in its lifetime[4].

Dissemination and replication

Throughout the life of the project there was widespread interest from neighbouring Brazilian states and further afield. Towards the end, project managers were giving regular presentations at conferences and to state governments. These culminated in a presentation to all state ministers of education. This resulted in direct interest from the states of Pernambuco, Bahia, Santa Catarina, and Tocantins, where a major project was subsequently conducted.

Lessons

People and relationships

Relationship management is extremely important when dealing with a very complex set of stakeholders and participants, involving institutions, government, individuals, and communities. For all the available technologies, nothing can replace direct human contact when there are major issues to resolve, and investing time in managing relationships is not, as it is often perceived, time wasted, but time gained in achieving your goals.

---

[3] Textbooks were subsequently introduced under the new state government.

[4] Although the project was not continued under the new government, the new State Secretary of Education stated that it was one of the best he had ever seen managed by an external organisation..

Trust

Trust is extremely important when distances and numbers are great. Building trust is not easily achieved and trust can normally only be developed over time. Fortunately, in this case, the author had been working with the state universities for three years prior to the project, which allowed more immediate acceptance. Gaining the trust of the State Secretary of Education was also important, especially since her initial position was that the programme should not be conducted through the universities, because they were the problem. The team had to earn trust in order to build the space to develop the programme without constant scrutiny[5]. Moreover, the State Secretary of Education also had to convince the teachers[6].

Empowerment and shared ownership

Concentrating power in the project management team does not promote independence and autonomy, and does little for building trust. It stifles individuals and creates pressure at the centre. By empowering both delivery partners and teachers to take responsibility, confidence and engagement grow and the project is strengthened.

Self-belief and conviction

Without strong self-belief and conviction on the part of project managers and stakeholders, projects are likely to fail. Self-belief and conviction will carry project teams through adversity and take partners, sponsors, and participants (teachers) along with them.

Emotional intelligence

Systems and planning are extremely important, as I have outlined above, but dependence on them will not guarantee success. The use of emotional intelligence, or rather emotional leadership, and the ability to respond sensitively to situations and particularly to people are ultimately what makes a difference.

I will leave the final word to the former State Secretary of Education, Alcyone Saliba, who made improvement in the quality of English language teaching the flagship project of her mandate and who, the author understands, to this day continues to receive e-mails in English from teachers extolling the virtues of the programme:

> *If I ever had the opportunity again, not only would I set up the ESL*
> *programme with a few improvements; I would also use that design/approach*
> *for other teaching areas, starting with (Portuguese) language.*
> (Personal communication 2011)

---

[5] The fact that meetings between the Project Manager and the State Secretary of Education became more infrequent was evidence of the growing confidence and trust in the programme. 'I know how well things are going: I hear it from the teachers every time I speak to them, because they now speak to me in English' (the State Secretary of Education).

[6] When the project was proposed to 500 teachers at the first consultation meeting, one of the first questions was: 'Can we really believe you?'

Acknowledgements

My thanks go to everyone involved in the ELT project in Paraná who provided opinion on its legacy, particularly my former colleagues, Vanessa Andreotti, Ines Carnielleto, Thaisa Andrade, and Maria Tognato, and state teachers such as Joina Almeida, who remain living proof of everything the project sought to achieve. I would also like to thank Alcyone Saliba, former State Secretary of Education for Paraná, for having the vision in the first place and lastly my British Council colleagues, Adrian Odell and Michael Houten, who played their own parts in the success of the project.

Case 21:
An early years bilingual schools project: The Spanish experience

Teresa Reilly

The project

In 1996, the Spanish Ministry of Education, in partnership with the British Council, introduced a pilot *Early Bilingual Education Project* (EBEP) in 44 state schools throughout Spain. 15 years later, there are 120 primary and secondary schools participating in the project, with a total of 30,000 pupils aged between 3 and 16. The model developed through the project also serves as an example of good practice for regional governments in Spain which are developing similar programmes. With close to 1,000,000 pupils in state schools throughout the country studying a form of bilingual education, a number of language professionals consider that the approach is bringing about a transformation in language education in the country and challenging existing perceptions of how children may best learn a foreign language.

Bilingual education

There is considerable debate globally on what constitutes a 'bilingual' person: in the Spanish EBEP, the outcomes specify that, by the age of 16, pupils are proficient, literate English second language users, confidently able to communicate with age-appropriate native and non-native audiences. In addition, in subject areas taught in English such as science and geography, it is expected that pupils will achieve the same results as their monolingual peers. And finally, though they have had less exposure to teaching in Spanish, their competence in L1 (first language) will be equal to those of their monolingually educated counterparts.

It is worth noting that the project was designed with a whole-school approach, with 40 per cent of time dedicated to teaching through English. There is no selection of pupils in primary schools: the children, all from state schools and many from a background of social or economic challenge, continue through nursery school to primary and on to secondary.

Stage – embedding and dissemination

EBEP Spain has recently completed a three-year independent evaluation study directed by Professor Richard Johnstone and jointly funded by the two major stakeholders, the Spanish Ministry of Education and the British Council.

The task of the evaluation team was to collect high-quality evidence through classroom observations, reports, and questionnaires in order to learn whether the project was achieving its objectives. The evaluation itself had three aims agreed with the stakeholders. The principle aim was to provide research-based evidence of pupils' language proficiency as demonstrated through the study of subject areas and their achievements in Spanish. The findings in the report provide examples of how the project aims with regard to language proficiency are being achieved and often superceded. The second aim was to gather evidence within the project, at school and classroom level and at project administration level, which would provide examples of good practice leading to success. This case study highlights the major societal and provision factors identified as part of the second aim which have contributed to successful project embedding.

Story

Societal Factors – political will and parental demand

There were a number of good reasons for the Spanish Ministry of Education to adopt a new approach to the teaching of English. There is a widely held conviction in Spain that competency in English is of growing importance in permitting young citizens to take their place, academically and professionally, in an increasingly global world. In addition, there has been dissatisfaction with levels of English at the end of secondary education, in spite of the fact that teaching a foreign language to children from the age of eight has been mandatory since 1992. This political will for change, continuing over the 15 years of the project and accommodating changes of government, and the demand from parents of children in state education for a bilingual approach, have been instrumental in the long-term embedding and dissemination of the project. This might best be appreciated by noting that the impact of the initial EBEP has led to a demand from parents for extended provision of early bilingual education in state schools: most regional Ministries of Education in Spain, which have had devolved responsibility for the management of education since 2000, have now established similar models of EBEPs.

Provision Factors – strong partnership between the Ministry of Education and the British Council

The project was set up with an agreed high-level strategy document stating the roles and duties of each partner, and the expected outcomes, and stressing the need for sufficient time for the project to embed itself bottom-up from primary and then into secondary schools, before expecting the impact to become manifest.

A Joint Ministry/British Council steering committee, convening annually, has overall responsibility for strategy decisions. This board, in turn, appoints two project managers, one from each organisation. They are members of the steering committee and advise on strategy decisions using the knowledge they have acquired from working in both strategic and management roles. Their roles include:

■ management of the jointly allocated budget

■ analysis of needs and outcomes, and taking appropriate decisions on project planning, development, and training

- co-operation and collaboration with regional governments in Spain, international examination boards, research and evaluation teams, universities, teacher trainers, and school management teams

- facilitation of continuous professional development (CPD) for teachers

- leading on curriculum design and implementation

- recruitment of supernumerary teachers

- website development and production of an annual magazine *Hand in Hand*.

Provision Factors – continuity and commitment
For schools, this is not an opt-in/opt-out programme. Schools put themselves forward voluntarily, but if accepted, they had to commit to remain for the duration of the programme: the full impact of an EBEP approach would not necessarily be apparent until the second or third cohorts had completed their tertiary education. Before a school was accepted, meetings with the two project managers were held with all parties involved: head teachers, Spanish and English teachers, inspectors, and parents were all expected to commit to supporting the initiative during the nine years from nursery school through to the end of primary. Extensive information was provided on project implications and guidelines were supplied for parents. In addition, at the time the project was established, there was agreement with the participating secondary schools that the pupils from the primary schools would continue to receive a bilingual education. Finally, two evaluation studies were built into the planning, and there was an agreement that pupils aged 16 would be prepared for specific IGCSE (International General Certificate of Secondary Education) examinations.

Provision Factors – integrated curriculum
A significant amount of time (40 per cent) is allocated to learning through English from the age of three, in a number of academic subjects such as geography, science, and history, in addition to English language and literacy. There were initial concerns from school management and parents as to what exactly the children would be studying in each language and how standards of Spanish were to be maintained: these concerns were highlighted in an early evaluation study (Ministry of Education, Culture, and Sport and British Council 2000). The report emphasised that teachers were doing excellent work, that the standards of the first cohort (seven and eight-year-olds) were good in both languages, but that too much was being expected from teachers by requiring them constantly to adapt the existing Spanish curriculum to meet the demands of a bilingual classroom.

The recommendation of the evaluation team resulted in the production of special curricula approved by the Ministry of Education (Boletín Oficial del Estado 2000) and designed in three stages: nursery school, primary, and secondary. One of the strengths of the various curricula is that, though shaped by the Ministry of Education and the British Council, they draw very largely on the experience and expertise of classroom practitioners, Spanish and English teachers, from the project schools. Evidence gathered from classroom research and observation and the

Evaluation Report (Dobson, Pérez Murillo, and Johnstone 2010) highlights the fact that the curriculum is an essential tool in providing confidence that standards are being maintained in the 120 schools.

Space does not permit a detailed analysis of the curriculum, but it is worth noting that a basic principle has been the emphasis on the early introduction of reading and writing, and a focus in all three stages on the development of authentic literacy skills to promote an underlying competence in language acquisition and learning of subject knowledge, and an increasing capacity for reflective skills.

Provision Factors – teacher provision and continuous professional development (CPD)

When the project was established in 1996, Spanish teachers in primary schools generally had a relatively low level of competence in English. The decision was therefore taken to recruit several native-speaker/Spanish bilingual primary school teachers (not EFL teachers) per school to deliver the English part of the curriculum.

However, a school project which depends solely on the 'foreign expert' would be unsustainable, financially and culturally: for the 15 years of the project there has been a focus on quality CPD for Spanish teachers teaching through English. The courses are not a reflection on teachers' skills, focusing rather on an awareness that the bilingual classroom requires a different mental framework and methodological approach that complements their skills and helps overcome difficulties. Support needs to be continuing: there is often a mismatch between the expectations of a teacher before teaching in a bilingual environment and the reality of the classroom. Overcoming the initial conviction that they were not good enough and that only the native-speaker teacher could teach literacy and subjects in English has been a challenge, but Spanish teachers of English have gradually taken on more responsibilities for teaching, mentoring, and now teacher training within the project, and often beyond.

The blend of supernumerary teachers and Spanish teachers has brought benefits to the schools, not the least of which is the added dimension of other cultures and teaching experiences. This considerably enriches the lives of the children and the culture of the schools and local communities.

Lessons

There is no single model of bilingual education, but what successful models have in common is that they illustrate an understanding of the underlying principles of bilingual education and are applied and evaluated appropriately in their own particular contexts. This section of the study focuses on key learning points in the Spanish project which policy developers might find useful when designing similar projects.

Key stakeholder partnerships, long-term political buy-in, commitment to strategic change, and good ground-level management and support are essential, non-negotiable components.

Understanding the underlying principles of early bilingual education is essential: both languages are of equal importance and the focus is on education through the medium of English, not the teaching of a foreign language as a subject. Stakeholders, especially politicians and parents, must recognise that patience is required, that education in two languages is a long process, and that traditional EFL tests may not be the most effective way of reflecting the benefits and impact of the bilingual classroom and bilingual child.

The curriculum is a fundamental standardisation tool. No two projects will develop in the same way and, for some situations, a special curriculum may not be an option. However, in the EBEP, all parties agree that, once the curriculum was in place with a clear focus on the importance of literacy, standards rose, inspectors and parents were reassured, and teachers felt they had the tools to achieve results. The curriculum motivates and challenges, encourages continuity, collaboration, and networking, and addresses issues such as diversity and assessment.

Sufficient and continuing funding needs to be secured for continuing teacher support. Teachers participating in such innovative projects deserve support in understanding how the underlying principles of bilingual education impact on their classroom practice: they need time to develop appropriate resources, reflect on their practice, carry out classroom research projects, and network and attend training courses, meetings, and conferences.

An external evaluation process should be built in at agreed stages of the project, the results of which should encourage further sustainable implementation/ dissemination.

Conclusion

There are issues within the bilingual project in Spain which remain to be resolved, not least of which is gaining official recognition at European level for the achievements in education of young bilinguals. There is also the challenge of addressing the needs of the 10 per cent of pupils whom the evaluation study (Dobson et al. op.cit.) identifies as not clearly benefitting from a bilingual approach. There is, however, convincing evidence that, for the other 90 per cent, the objectives of providing an enriched model of education in two languages are being delivered within the model.

It is hoped, through this short case study, that the points raised and challenges overcome in the EBEP project may be of interest to educational institutions seeking sustainable ways to raise standards in language teaching in the early stages of education.

Conclusion:
Lessons learnt

A summary of key lessons from the case studies

Paul Woods

In this chapter we bring together a treasure trove of good advice on examples to follow and pitfalls to avoid from four out of the five continents, covering all stages of English language project planning and implementation, from the initial stages of scoping a project through to evaluation, follow-up, and sustainability. This should not be seen as a substitute for a thorough reading of the articles and cases, but we hope that it will prove useful as a summary of the accumulated experience reported in this volume.

Project design

Understand the context

Identify contextual drivers for change before undertaking any design process, recognising and acknowledging personal drivers, and involving end-users in the design process (Whittaker). This theme is taken up by Reilly, who identifies the twin pillars of political will and parental demand as reasons contributing to the success of the Early Bilingual Education Project in Spain, and to its embedding and dissemination. In the Indian Tamil Nadu Project, master trainers adapted plans and materials to make them suitable for teachers in their local context.

Wedell argues that a whole-system approach to educational change is more likely to succeed. In Oman, the changes introduced by the BA Project were consistent with changes being proposed across all basic education subjects. The environment was thus at worst neutral and at best positive towards the changes the teachers were implementing. Wedell points out that this is rarely the case in the many contexts where curriculum changes are limited to English classes only.

The ELTA Project in the Balkans and south-east Europe was based on extensive research and consultation. It established that pre-service training was top-heavy on theory and addressed this contextual issue by providing practical training and a resource pack for newly qualified teachers (Leather). By contrast, Zikri attributes the failure of curriculum development projects in Egypt in the 80s and early 90s to a lack of appreciation of the uniqueness of project context: it is necessary to consider the unique physical, cultural, linguistic, and psychological variables in project design and implementation. The Egyptian curriculum development project had three fatal flaws: the adoption of a prescriptive approach by expatriate experts; the rationale for reform being focused on 'product', not 'process'; and failure to recognise the social context of reform. This meant that the project succeeded in developing curricula but failed to build ownership and develop local capacity.

In another context, O'Donahue advises, 'Go with the flow.' This is advisable and less stressful than trying to impose alien procedures which may not be acceptable or appropriate to the local context.

Allow adequate time for planning, design and implementation

This can involve ensuring that you do not underestimate the length of time which will be needed to design or redesign a course if an iterative approach is used (Whittaker). Zikri quotes Bowers (1983) on the relationship between design, planning and monitoring: to compensate for the short planning phase of projects and cope with problems which arise during implementation, monitoring and evaluation should drive a flexible process of adjustment. In Spain, stakeholders, especially politicians and parents, had to recognise that patience was required and that education in two languages is a long process (Reilly). O'Donahue points out that change takes time and effort, and so one should not expect to see results overnight. If the results of the programme involves changes in beliefs or attitudes, it will depend very much on where the teachers are at the beginning of the programme and how far they may need to travel. Patel also asserts that large-scale projects need adequate time for planning, preparation and implementation, and suggests that, where a project involves major systemic change, it is advisable to use learning points from a small-scale pilot before going to full implementation.

Many projects worldwide which have focused on developing school learners communication skills have failed because of lack of understanding and communication between what Fink (2000) calls the two 'solitudes' – policy makers on the one hand and teachers on the other. On the basis of his experience in Oman, Wedell suggests it would be wise to plan for a medium- to long-term process, which is part of a whole-system change in which similar pedagogical changes are introduced across all curriculum subjects. Initiatives need to be structured in ways that make direct and indirect support for implementers (head teachers and administrators, as well as teachers) available over time, providing a positive context for the reculturing process which is needed if the desired changes are ever to become visible in the majority of classrooms. The Omani BA project was planned to cover a nine-year period from the outset. The benefits of the long project timescale were maximised by stable project leadership on both sides, while regional tutors generally stayed with the project for at least a full three-year cohort. This stability facilitated trusting personal relationships and ever more effective communications systems. Awareness of what an educational change means in practice is an evolving process for both planners and implementers. However, the generally short lifespans of most international joint ELT projects make the development of such awareness among all participants much less likely (Wedell).

Work constructively with partners

Walter gives an example from Russia, where the Russian textbook project was conceived of as a Russian-British partnership from the outset. This enabled the project to weather the political storm which affected the British Council in Russia. However, partnership arrangements which unduly favour the other partner are best avoided. The partner initially chosen for the Russian publishing project had their own agenda and had to be replaced (Walter).

In Spain, a strong partnership between the Ministry of Education and the British Council set up a project with a high-level agreed strategy stating the roles and duties of each partner, the expected outcomes, and the need to allow sufficient time for the project to embed itself bottom-up from primary and then into secondary schools before expecting its impact to become manifest (Reilly). Leather emphasises the importance of choosing the right partner at the outset and allowing them to develop ownership early in the life of the project. In the case of AzETA, the project filled a need already identified by the partner.

Avoid ill-considered top-down decision-making

There is a need for greater awareness of the dynamics at work in policy formulation. For example, in Simpson's case study on Rwanda, there was a top-down process in which a key decision on language policy, whether to give priority to the mother tongue on pedagogic grounds or English as a result of political or personal/ professional considerations, was taken by the government. Tensions between political and socio-economic drivers of reform and pedagogic principles informed by international research and best practice need to be resolved early on. In Rwanda a decision taken in 2009 to go straight for English as the language of instruction in Primary 1 was later reversed, in 2011, creating significant challenges (Simpson). In Malaysia, the government announced in mid-2002 that mathematics and science would be taught through the medium of English from January 2003. This 'extremely bold decision' received varied reactions from education professionals as well as the general public, but six years later in July 2009 the policy was officially reversed (Patel).

Ensure continuing access to decision makers

This can be done through informal and informal networking (Crossey). Setting up a joint steering committee is another useful strategy. In the Spanish project described by Reilly, a joint Ministry of Education/British Council steering committee, convened annually, had overall responsibility for strategic decision making. This Board, in turn, appointed two project managers, one from each organisation, who were members of the steering committee and advised on strategic decisions, supported by their knowledge gained from working in both strategic and management roles. In the Indian Tamil Nadu project (O'Donahue), extensive dialogue took place between the three project partners, and clear communication channels were established in the project initiation stage.

Managing change

Create opportunities

An essential aspect of change management is creating opportunities for the development and empowerment of those involved. Change becomes sustainable when participants internalise the experience and translate it into the way they work, into patterns of behaviour and belief. This process of assimilating or rejecting elements of innovation is essentially a process of learning. Project ownership and responsibility are constantly created through the whole project culture of participation, sharing, and transparency (Bardi).

Encourage collaboration and pay attention to the environment

O'Donahue reminds us that it is the people and not the policies that effect change. We should not underestimate the physical comfort of trainers and trainees, or the importance of selecting venues that offer the best possible facilities. In Korea, INSET was seen as something done by superiors to inferiors, rather than a collaborative shared enterprise (Hayes). However, in India, collaboration meant recognising each other's expertise, listening to each other, valuing each other's inputs, and moving forwards together towards a shared goal. O'Donahue advises taking considerable care and attention when building up a working relationship and opening effective communication channels with those you are relying on for smooth implementation. She advocates identifying the most effective mode of communication, and adapting and using modes most effective and acceptable to the given environment, 'whether this means using cloud computing or carrier pigeons'.

Stakeholder buy-in

Allow sufficient time for dialogue

Create time and space for dialogue between decision makers and language policy experts, before key policy decisions are taken. If this does not happen, an information gap may be created in which decisions made by government officials may not be well informed on issues pertinent to language in education (Simpson).

Avoid mismatches in perceptions

Mismatches in perception can be at the heart of many problems. Thus, in the Peacekeeping English Project, the Polish authorities wanted native-speaker teachers who would genuinely represent UK life and culture, while the UK Ministry of Defence wanted NATO-standardised testing and overall reform of curricula (Crossey). In Korea, administrators saw a need for language improvement via INSET, rather than improving teachers' pedagogic skills. These divergent perspectives on the most productive forms of INSET, teacher capabilities, and classroom needs led to a low take-up of generously funded INSET places (Hayes). In Tunisia, there was potential for misunderstanding and conflict arising from the way terminology was interpreted in different ways depending on the perspectives of the agencies and people using it. Technical terms need to be recognised as a means to an end, but can be refined and altered to suit the planning context (McIlwraith).

Be transparent

Beware of neglecting to share conclusions of scoping/design studies with the host government or agency. In Peacekeeping English in Poland, this led to politicisation and lack of local buy-in (Crossey). In Tunisia, where the British Council wanted to use APM-based methodology, but the Ministry preferred PRINCE2, the project ended up with two project plans, one for the donors and the other for the MoE and beneficiaries (McIlwraith). Scholey advises not to get too hung up on project documents and to avoid what Holliday calls 'naïve notions of mutuality' and 'the appearance of agreement with regard to project documentation'.

Build consensus amongst stakeholders

Scholey advocates shared ownership of decision making. This avoids the risk of 'seeing others in our own terms, not theirs' (Holliday). In India, agreeing partners' specific roles at the outset of the programme laid the foundation for a plan which recognised each organisation's expertise and set the scene for reciprocal learning. An environment of mutual trust and respect was created through consultations and meetings involving key stakeholders working at different levels in their organisations (O'Donahue). Patel points out that the inclusion of key stakeholders in initial discussions and continued planning will create a sense of investment and ownership, and these individuals and/or groups are more likely to help towards achieving goals and results.

Build trust and engagement
Ensure buy-in of people such as head teachers and others who are in a position to obstruct changes in curriculum, methods, and teacher training, and get involved with the same people over the lifespan of the project, getting to know them well and building trust (Scholey). Building trust is not easily achieved and takes time. The team in Paraná had to earn the trust to build space to develop the programme without constant scrutiny (Palmer).

In India, master trainers and teachers both needed to be convinced that the proposed changes to be made would have beneficial effects. They needed to know 'What's in it for me?' and also what the intended change in classroom practice might look like. Residential courses allowed participants to be fully engaged, to have time to reflect, and to form new friendships and bond together as a teaching community. Meeting participant expectations is also a crucial factor for success (O'Donahue).

Remember, however, that concentrating power in the project management team alone does not promote independence and autonomy, and does little for building trust. By empowering both delivery partners and teachers to take responsibility, confidence and engagement grew and strengthened the whole Paraná project (Palmer). Palmer emphasises that relationship management is very important when dealing with very complex sets of relationships. Nothing can replace direct human contact, and time invested in managing relationships is not, as it is often perceived, time wasted, but time gained in achieving your goals. Schools in the Spanish bilingual education project put themselves forward voluntarily, but had to commit themselves for the duration. Head teachers, inspectors, and parents were all expected to commit to supporting the initiative during the nine years from nursery school through to the end of primary (Reilly).

Leave the hard nuts to your local counterpart to crack
In the China PETT Project, the British Council and Guangdong Department of Education provided funding and made policy, while the University of Leeds and GTCFLA were executives and supervisors. It was wise for the British Council, when dealing with local government, to act as a funding provider, but let the Guangdong Department of Education take the role of policy maker (Lin Hong).

Avoid the negative impact of conflict
In Egypt, disputes over project management negatively impacted on results. Projects which fall into the trap of excluding key stakeholders will fail on this essential human factor more than any other. Projects must have a managed set of priorities, objectives, timescales, and balances between external expertise and local inputs (Zikri).

Managing external and internal risks

Recognise external risk factors

Political uncertainty can be an external risk factor over which a project can exert no control. Uncertainty over political leadership in Paraná had a direct impact on the project team and teachers. Local opposition to the ethos of allowing an external agency such as the British Council to lead a major change project threatened to undermine the integrity of the project (Palmer). In Rwanda, where English is a means to regional integration and economic development, and is replacing French as the language of instruction in schools, ELT reform competes for time, attention, and resources with other major educational developments, with the risk of more change in the making than the system can cope with, and the added risk that the quality of individual reforms may be jeopardised by their number and a lack of capacity and funds to implement numerous large-scale changes concurrently (Simpson).

Mitigate internal risk factors

Internally, the Paraná ELT project faced challenges, including low self-esteem amongst teachers, a culture of dependency, which meant making teachers into independent learners was a challenging task, and systemic failures such as the perception that the university pre-service system was not successful, plus the size and scope of a state-wide project which dictated a model based largely on distance learning (Palmer).

Project funding

Secure funds up front and be creative

Ensure projects are fully funded for the full duration from the outset. In PEP Poland, an annual funding cycle meant there was no commitment to fund for longer than the next 12 months, which made the activity and presence highly political (Crossey). In the Paraná ELT project, funding was based on delivery of results on a year-by-year basis, with the following year's funding released only several months after the start of the year. This created a challenge for planning and continuity (Palmer). In Spain, sufficient and continued funding needed to be secured for continuing teacher support. Teachers needed time to develop appropriate resources, reflect on their practice, carry out classroom research projects, network, and attend training courses, meetings, and conferences (Reilly). In China, teachers from remote areas could not afford to pay travel and accommodation costs to attend training in the provincial capital, but this problem was resolved creatively by having trainers from the capital move around from city to city (Lin Hong).

Project structures and systems

Adopt appropriate structures and models

A light non-institutional structure with fixed-term contracts for staff provided for flexibility in planning the PEP project in Poland (Crossey). Scholey advises against using a cascade model of training, which he asserts can be unreliable, and proposes a model of change which involves using materials development combined with project-trained teachers as materials writers and thus agents of change. Lin Hong, however, describes a successful cascade model in China, where instead of putting all effort into 'localising' foreign trainers, the PETT project shifted its approach to training local trainers, using a cascade approach.

Palmer reminds us that systems and planning are extremely important, but emotional intelligence, or rather emotional leadership, and being able to respond to situations and people are ultimately what makes a difference. Clear and transparent two-way communication channels helped build an atmosphere of trust and ownership in India, where all stakeholders and interested parties were equally valued. A 1,500-strong closed user group mobile network allowed free access to anyone at any level at any time in an environment where access to the internet and emails is extremely limited. This allowed instant communication, and text messaging became the modus operandi (O'Donahue).

Organising cascades

Adapt the training package for cascade training each time to suit local circumstances. In the China PETT project, trainers were grouped in threes, with trainers from teacher training colleges (teacher trainers), who had a superior command of English and knowledge of ELT theory, and who led the cascade training, working together with *JIAOYANYUAN* from education bureaux in charge of local teacher training and 'backbone' English teachers from primary schools who acted as examples for other teachers to follow (Lin Hong).

In India, the limitations of the cascade model of training were fully recognised, but because of the large numbers involved and the vast geographical reach, direct teacher training was not an option. Mitigating the risk of using a cascade was a shared concern, and on the basis of the previous experience of the partner organisations, strategies for minimising transition loss were embedded into the implementation plan. Master trainers in India were strategically paired up to deliver the cascade programme. This meant less was lost in transmission, strengths of individuals were recognised, and those less confident were supported by their peers (O'Donahue).

Integration

In the Romanian textbook project, the link between textbooks and teacher training was strengthened, and a complex training project was set up with new textbooks closely integrated with projects to train teachers, trainers, inspectors, and university lecturers (Popovici). The whole-system approach adopted in Oman meant that there was a mutually supportive relationship between what was taught on the BA programme, the textbooks used in schools, and the assessment principles being applied by wider educational reform (Wedell).

People management

Assign clear roles and responsibilities

Clearly set out and communicate the agreed roles and responsibilities of all those involved, and when action is demanded, do it quickly and effectively, and expect all others involved in the programme to do the same (O'Donahue). Pay attention to the choice of trainers, staged assimilation, and leadership and management. AzETA developed ownership of the southeast Europe ELTA project at an early stage and set up a SIG for NQTs (Leather).

Facilitate learning

On the basis of the PROSPER experience in Romania, Bardi suggests a paradigm of project management that regards the process of change as a process of learning, not just a method of changing organisational structures and practices. Project managers have a crucial role in facilitating communication among team members and ensuring there is complete transparency, for all team members, about the implementation process. Communication and transparency generate better understanding and facilitate the process of task implementation. Bardi asserts that project teams do not emerge by mandate or team-building exercises, but are consolidated in the process of working together to accomplish tasks perceived as meaningful/rewarding. Delegation of responsibility to project teams has an essential role in their learning, as more responsibility generates more commitment and, eventually, more learning.

Stay in touch with reality

Students on the Omani BA project continued to teach four days a week in their schools. This allowed them to consider the appropriateness or otherwise for their own contexts of the ideas and practices being introduced. It also raised awareness more widely of the project and the educational reform of which it was part (Wedell). It is important for project managers to have an overall view of progress, but they can only do so if they fully participate in task completion. In the Romanian PROSPER project, accomplishment of their management role (planning and organisation of meetings, setting deadlines, and communicating with team members) was facilitated by full professional involvement in the research process (Bardi).

Build capacity and confidence

Build capacity of trainers as well as trainees. In Paraná, a university supply network was created and capacity built through training programmes (Palmer). Capacity building should be consistently developed, with initial training in the specific area of the project followed by on-the-job continuous training. Time and detailed attention given to the selection of team members pays off in that it ensures commitment, ownership, and efficiency (Popovici). One of the strengths of the curricula developed in Spain by the Early Bilingual Education Project was that, though shaped by the British Council and Ministry of Education, these drew very largely on the experience and expertise of classroom practitioners, Spanish and English teachers, from project schools (Reilly). Make use of the feel-good factor to address teachers' low self-esteem, promoting a sense of can-do (Palmer).

Don't forget the learners

Patel reminds us that teachers are the main agents of change, but often we forget those at the heart of the change process, those at the very core of the change we want to bring about: the students. Ensure that students are active participants in the process and not just passive recipients, and that the change is implemented at a level and pace that will build their confidence and motivate them to want to learn.

Project implementation

Allow time for embedding new ideas

Allow time for reflective collaboration on experience and newly acquired skills and knowledge, and provide in-school follow up to short INSET courses. In Korea, there was no follow up, and observation was not linked to the INSET course content in a way which would assist teachers in putting into practice what they had learnt on the course (Hayes). Do not, however, try to do too much: in the Bangladesh English in Action Project, some materials were produced as additional classroom aids. This caused confusion about how to relate all the materials to specific parts of the course book. There is a need for compromise between tying materials very closely to the course book and having less material and allowing time for teacher reflection and development (Solly and Woodward).

Standardise the approach

Standardise delivery across centres to provide comparable learning opportunities. In Bosnia and Herzegovina, centres had initially developed their own blended learning courses independently of each other, which led to huge differences in outcomes (Whittaker). In Spain, the curriculum was a fundamental standardisation tool which gave a clear focus on the importance of literacy. The curriculum motivated and challenged, encouraged continuity, collaboration, and networking, and addressed such issues as diversity and assessment (Reilly). In Poland, there was initially a lack of standardisation, which was resolved when a curriculum framework was laid out by the National Council of Teacher Education. This allowed for standardisation but gave sufficient space for flexibility (Komorowska).

Introduce major changes gradually

Change takes effort, energy, time, and sometimes courage. One big change can be substantial, two daunting, but three can be completely overwhelming. There is a strong argument for implementing one initiative first, laying its foundations, and then building on it with other initiatives over time, rather than implementing too many initiatives at one time (Patel).

Materials and technology

Involve carefully selected local authors

Walter advises taking care over the selection, development, and management of authors, and ensuring author teams are well distributed across a country or region by having a regional strategy and disseminating materials widely. Having a regional network built in from the start ensured appropriateness and acceptability of the finished materials in the Russian textbook project, while the fact that the Romanian textbook project was written locally was central to its success. A major output was a group of specialist syllabus designers and textbook writers who were able to extend, transfer, and diversify their professional skills and act as change promoters (Popovici).

Keep materials practical and useful

In the southeast Europe ELTA Project, the resource pack produced by the project was suited to the real needs of the target group (Leather).

Use appropriate technology

Technology can be problematic. In Bangladesh, mobile technology was essential in leveraging the delivery of both classroom materials and teacher development, but the iPod was not sustainable. It was replaced by a cheap Nokia mobile fitted with a 4GB micro SD card preloaded with project materials. The results achieved in the Bangladesh pilot project strongly suggest that peer-supported, practice-based learning, leveraging mobile technology both to bring ELT resources into the classroom and to deliver professional development to teachers can be an effective model for delivering English language training at scale to large numbers of learners (Solly and Woodward).

Project embedding and dissemination

Identify and create champions

In Paraná, teachers were identified who could act as catalysts, co-ordinating local initiatives such as self-help groups, modelling good teacher behaviours, and getting wider exposure for the project though participation in state and national events. The Pathmakers programme addressed issues of self-esteem, leadership, and action, and broke down the barriers between universities, which had been seen as carriers of knowledge, and teachers, who had been seen as consumers of knowledge. Towards the end of the project, as the message spread via conferences across Brazil, other states became interested, including Tocantins, where a major project was subsequently implemented (Palmer). In Spain, it was necessary to overcome the initial conviction teachers had that they were not good enough and that only the native-speaker teacher could teach literacy and subjects in English. This was a challenge, but Spanish teachers gradually took on more responsibilities for teaching, mentoring, and then teacher training, both within the project, and often beyond (Reilly). In China, the project made use of 'teaching and research fellows' (JIAOYANYUAN) to ensure sustainability by organising training for teachers in their districts even after the official end of the project and any external funding (Lin Hong).

Celebrate success

Celebrate and communicate success and provide ongoing support for trainers and teachers to enable them to continue growing after the initial programme has concluded (O'Donahue).

Ensure sustainability

Sustainability can be enhanced from the outset by embedding a project in a nexus of mutually supportive projects. A nexus of complementary projects can magnify the success of individual projects (Walter).

Project evaluation

Start with a plan

Dick emphasises the importance of having a detailed monitoring and evaluation plan – complete with needs and objectives matched to data collection methods – and a schedule in place from project inception. Similarly, the need for baseline evaluation in the opening stages of a project is crucial. In Sri Lanka, primary data was not initially collected on schools and grades, and thus pupil evaluation was slowed down. The ELTA project in southeast Europe provides a good management model for project delivery and evaluation, and incorporated effective monitoring and feedback systems from the outset (Leather). Two evaluation studies were built in from the start of the Spanish Early Bilingual Education Project, plus an agreement that pupils aged 16 would be prepared for specific IGCSE examinations (Reilly). Be specific about the scale of what can be achieved at the various stages of a project. In Bangladesh, the team were halfway through the pilot before they found a clear way of expressing what degree of improvement in students' English language use and in teachers' delivery of appropriate communicative teaching would be seen as a measure of success at different stages (Solly and Woodward).

Exploit all the available data

Data collected and human resources used should be exploited fully. In Sri Lanka, mentors observed teachers and gave feedback, but this data was initially used only as a progress record. Only much later were comparisons done on individual teachers to reveal behavioural change. Had this been built in earlier, much stronger impact data would have resulted (Dick).

Use focus groups

Focus groups can deliver useful and unpredictable information: in Sri Lanka, only teachers' views gathered from such groups prevented a potentially disastrous situation from developing when the partner wanted to jettison the Cambridge ESOL TKT exam on cost grounds (Dick).

Evaluate long-term impact

Evaluation of INSET courses should go beyond the teachers, trainer, and course itself and look at impact in terms of use of knowledge and skills acquired, and longer-term student outcomes (Hayes).

Avoid negative washback effects

Mathew highlights the importance of assessment and evaluation schemes capturing what goes on in classrooms. In India, the test became a de facto curriculum, different in nature and scope from the official learner-centred curriculum which the project was attempting to introduce. This negated the impact of the curriculum changes which the Central Board of Secondary Education was promoting.

Learn from previous mistakes

Flaws in the evaluation of the Egyptian curriculum development project identified by Zikri include: inadequate evaluation tools and lack of evaluation instruments, disregard for Egyptian involvement in the evaluation of materials produced by the project, and failure to incorporate the results of evaluation to support adjustments. Although CDELT had potential for sustainability and institutionalisation as an Egyptian entity (with an ideal duration of 16 years, involving distinguished ELT professionals, with established partnerships), the work management style of the foreign experts was prescriptive, sustainability plans were not built in at the outset, and a high turnover of expatriate staff led to rigid adherence to short-term plans. Only towards the end of the project was there a shift of emphasis from curriculum change to staff development of Egyptian change agents.

Monitor progress on a regular basis

Regular monitoring is important and can yield unexpected benefits. Monitoring visits in Sri Lanka, initially developed as a check on mentor performance, became a valuable mentor support vehicle, building trust, generating information, and developing the respect of local teachers for project staff (Dick). In the Indian Tamil Nadu Project, comprehensive monitoring and evaluation were undertaken throughout the programme by all three partners (UNICEF, Sharva Shiksha Abhiyan, and the British Council) at all levels. Monitoring visits by representatives of each partner organisation often coincided, and this led to shared key findings and agreement on subsequent action. Good relationships were built up by this close, on-the-ground, monitoring schedule. Observation and feedback from comprehensive monitoring and evaluation throughout the programme by all the partners at all levels of the cascade were essential, as this allowed information sharing both horizontally and vertically within and across the partner organisations (O'Donahue). Monitoring and feedback systems in Oman, where the project extended over a period of nine years, enabled Leeds-based leaders, tutors, and materials writers to develop a more thorough than usual understanding of the Omani school and cultural context.

Make evaluation itself a learning process

The process of carrying out an impact study was an important learning experience for PROSPER project members, both in terms of professional practice and project management. Seeking solutions together was a form of experiential learning in which team members developed their research skills by engaging with every aspect of the research in a continuous problem-solving process. Projects need to give project teams the opportunity to investigate and reflect on what they have achieved by taking part in the project – evaluation can be carried out as a developmental rather than an accountability exercise. In the PROSPER impact study, working together to carry out a task that was seen as valuable by all the team members strengthened the sense of team belonging and identity (Bardi).

Contributors

Contributors

Mirela Bardi

Measuring the impact of the PROSPER Project in Romania: A learning experience

Academy of Economic Studies, Bucharest

Dr Mirela Bardi is senior lecturer at the Academy of Economic Studies, Bucharest. She teaches Business English to undergraduates, as well as academic writing and qualitative research methodology to MA students. She worked for British Council Romania as manager of the PROSPER project, training ESP lecturers and co-ordinating the development of ESP textbooks. She also managed European Accession projects that contributed to the development of European Studies modules in Romanian universities. She completed an MEd in teaching ESP at University College Plymouth St Mark and St John, and a PhD in Linguistics at the University of Lancaster. She is very keen on developing her expertise in teaching academic writing to professional researchers, as one of her main current academic duties is training lecturers in the University of Economics, Bucharest in writing research for international publication.

Address for communication: **mirela.bardi@incontext.ro**

Rod Bolitho

Projects and programmes: contemporary experience in ELT change management

Norwich Institute for Language Education

Rod Bolitho is Academic Director, Norwich Institute for Language Education, and has been involved in consultancy to projects overseas for over 20 years. He has trained textbook and curriculum designers in and from Romania, Russia, Belarus, India, Ukraine, and Uzbekistan, where he is still actively engaged in the English Reform Project. He is also currently working on a British Council Continuing Professional Development (CPD) initiative in India, with vocational teachers in Romania, and on curriculum standards in the vocational sector in Austria. His interests include CPD, language awareness, and materials development. His most recent publication, co-authored with Tony Wright, is *Trainer Development*, published by www.lulu.com.

Address for communication: **rod@nile-elt.com**
rodbol44@yahoo.co.uk

MaryAnn Christison

Understanding innovation in English language education: Contexts and issues

University of Utah, USA

Dr MaryAnn Christison is a professor in the Department of Linguistics and the Urban Institute for Teacher Education at the University of Utah in the United States of America. She teaches courses in applied linguistics in the undergraduate and graduate programmes. She is the author of over 75 refereed articles on language teaching and second language research, and 17 books, including *Leadership in English Language Education: Theoretical foundations and practical skills for changing times* (with D. E. Murray), *A Handbook for Language Program Administrators* (Second Edition) (with F. L. Stoller), *What English language teachers need to know: volumes I and II* (with D. E. Murray), *Multiple intelligences and language learning,* and *Learning to teach languages.* Christison currently serves on the board of trustees for The International Research Foundation (TIRF), and she was President of TESOL 1997–98. She has been a classroom teacher for 36 years, teaching in elementary and secondary K-12 contexts and with adult learners in non-academic and university contexts. She has been a language teacher educator for 22 years, working with teachers in the United States and in over 30 other countries.

Address for communication: **mac@linguistics.utah.edu**

Mark Crossey

Peacekeeping English in Poland

British Council, Indonesia

Mark Crossey is currently Director of Programmes at British Council Indonesia, having worked for the British Council since 1994, when he was a teacher on the organisation's first Military English project in the Baltic States. He subsequently managed the Council's Peacekeeping English Project ('PEP') in Poland, before going on in 2005 to co-ordinate the global PEP programme at British Council London. The role offered the opportunity to explore and negotiate new PEPs in countries such as China, Vietnam, and Turkey. Mark is a strong believer in engagement with military and security forces by means of communicative and learner-centred language training programmes. He is also interested in language testing, as well as micropolitics in language training programmes and has published in both fields.

Address for communication: **mark.crossey@britishcouncil.org**

Lesley Dick

The challenge of monitoring and evaluation in Sri Lanka

British Council, Sri Lanka

Dr Lesley Dick has over 25 years' EFL teaching experience and 15 years' teacher training experience in Finland, Sri Lanka, Turkey, Italy, the United Arab Emirates, and Libya. She has also developed and managed Learning Centres for tertiary level educational institutions. She has worked in Sri Lanka with the British Council on and off since 1989. Currently, she is the English Language Teaching Projects Manager there, and is responsible for developing and delivering English language teacher training around the country in both the public and the private sector, and materials development for teacher training. She has a particular interest in initial teacher training, materials development, the challenges of working in low-resource environments, online teacher education, and mobile learning.

Address for communication: **lesley.dick@britishcouncil.org**

David Hayes

Planning for success: Culture, engagement and power in English language education innovation

Mismatched perspectives: In-service teacher education policy and practice in South Korea

Brock University, Canada

Dr David Hayes currently teaches in the Department of Applied Linguistics, Brock University, Canada. Before this, he worked on a number of long-term UK-funded educational development projects managed by the British Council in Sri Lanka, Thailand, and Malaysia. In addition, he has recently undertaken short-term consultancies on World Bank and Asian Development Bank projects in Vietnam, Thailand, and Sri Lanka, as well as working on British Council initiatives in Korea, Indonesia, and Vietnam. His primary interests are in educational development, the lives and careers of non-native speaking teachers of English working in their own state education systems, and the role of second language education in promoting peace in post-conflict societies.

Address for communication: **dhayes@brocku.ca**

Richard Kiely

Designing evaluation into change management processes

Centre for International Language Teacher Education, University College Plymouth St Mark and St John

Dr Richard Kiely is Professor of Applied Linguistics and Language Education at the Centre for International Language Teacher Education (CILTE), University College Plymouth St Mark and St John. He has worked as a teacher, teacher educator, consultant, and programme evaluator in Bangladesh, China, France, Malaysia, Mexico, Poland, South Africa, and Zambia. He has recently completed evaluation studies in CLIL (Pro-CLIL) and on the impact of initial teacher education programmes (TCL Cert TESOL). He is the author of 'Evaluation and learning in language programmes', in the *Handbooks of Applied Linguistics: Volume 6: Handbook of foreign language communication and learning,* and *Programme Evaluation in Language Education* (both with Pauline Rea-Dickins).

Address for communication: **rkiely@marjon.ac.uk**

Hanna Komorowska

The Teacher Training Colleges Project in Poland

Warsaw School of Social Sciences and Humanities, Warsaw University

Dr Hanna Komorowska is full Professor of Applied Linguistics and Language Teaching at Warsaw School of Social Sciences and Humanities and at Warsaw University. After the fall of communism, she headed the Expert Committee for foreign language teaching and teacher education reform in Poland. A former Vice-President of Warsaw University, the Polish delegate for the Modern Languages Project Group of the Council of Europe, and a member of the EU High Level Group on Multilingualism in Brussels, she is now a consultant to the European Centre of Modern Languages in Graz and co-author of the *European Portfolio for Student Teachers of Languages*. She publishes widely in the field of FLT methodology and teacher education.

Address for communication: **hannakomo@data.pl**

Sue Leather

The English Language Teachers' Association (ELTA) Project for newly-qualified teachers in Azerbaijan

Sue Leather Associates

Sue Leather is director of Sue Leather Associates, a group of ELT professionals providing consultancy and training for institutions and organisations worldwide. With a background in working with teachers, trainers, and educational managers to effect change in classroom practice, she has extensive experience of international ELT projects. She has worked with a number of organisations, including the British Council, the Soros Foundation, and the Open University. Her recent experience of ELT change processes includes: Lead Consultant to the British Council's ETTE (English for Teaching, Teaching for English) project, run in eight countries in Central and South Asia, from 2007–11, Lead Consultant to the British Council Romania's ELTA newly qualified teacher project, 2005–07, Lead Consultant to a large British Council curriculum change and training project in the former Yugoslavia from 2002–05, and Lead Consultant to a curriculum reform project in Kosovo in 2003.

Address for communication: **sue@sueleatherassociates.com**

Lin Hong

Making it work: A case study of a teacher training programme in China

Guangdong Teachers College of Foreign Language and Arts, China

Professor Lin Hong has worked in the field of ELT for over 27 years. She is Vice-President of Guangdong Teachers College of Foreign Language and Arts and currently teaches ELT methodology on the pre-service teacher education programme. Her major academic research interests are related to teaching English to young learners. Her recent teacher resource book is *Songs and Chants for Primary English Teaching*. She is also actively involved in teacher training projects, working with academic and governmental and non-governmental organisations. In the past few years, she headed several major provincial projects for in-service English teacher training, including PETT.

Address for communication: **linhong@gtcfla.net**

Hamish McIlwraith

Designing a 'Language-in-Education' planning strategy in Tunisia

McIlwraith Education

Hamish McIlwraith is owner of McIlwraith Education, a consultancy business based in Edinburgh that works worldwide with international agencies and partners including DfID, UNICEF, and the British Council to help governments, organisations, and institutions reach their education goals. Previously, he worked for over 20 years on ELT projects and as a university lecturer in Sudan, China, Brunei, and Bulgaria. He has a particular interest in curriculum, testing and assessment, teacher and trainer training, and the design and implementation of language policy. He is a former lecturer at Edinburgh University's School of Education, Moray House.

Address for communication: **education@mcilwraith.org**

Rama Mathew

Understanding washback: A case study of a new exam in India

Delhi University

Dr Rama Mathew is Professor of Education in the Department of Education, Delhi University, Delhi. Previously she taught at the Central Institute of English and Foreign Languages, Hyderabad, where, for more than twenty years, she was involved in English language education with specific focus on language teacher education and assessment. She was Project Director of a national curriculum evaluation study (1993–98), the CBSE-ELT Curriculum Implementation Study, which concretised the notion of the teacher as researcher in actual classroom contexts. She also co-ordinated a project on mentoring in collaboration with the Open University, UK, under the UKIERI scheme. She is currently co-ordinating the English Language Proficiency Course for the students of Delhi University in which loose-leaf materials meant for adult learners have been developed and students take proficiency tests at three levels that assess all their language skills. She has been a guest plenary speaker at several conferences in India and other countries, including the conference of the International Association of Teachers of English as a Foreign Language (IATEFL).

Address for communication: **ramamathew@yahoo.co.in**

Denise Murray

Understanding innovation in English language education: Contexts and issues

Macquarie University, Australia

Dr Denise E. Murray is Professor Emerita at Macquarie University, Australia, and San José State University, California. She was Executive Director of the AMEP Research Centre and of the National Centre for English Language Teaching and Research at Macquarie University for seven years. She was founding Chair of the Department of Linguistics and Language Development at San José State University for nine years. She was TESOL President in 1996–97. She has presented at conferences, conducted workshops, and consulted with governments, professional associations, and academic institutions around the world.

Her research includes the intersection of language, society, and technology; language education policy; and leadership in language education. She has published 17 books and over 100 articles. Her books include *Planning change, changing plans: Innovations in second language teaching; Leadership in English Language Education: Theoretical foundations and practical skills for changing times,* with M. Christison; *What English language teachers need to know: volumes I and II,* with M. Christison.

Address for communication: **denise.murray@mq.edu.au**

Clare O'Donahue

Change in Tamil Nadu, India

British Council, India

Clare O'Donahue has been working as a Senior Training Consultant for the British Council at its Chennai office in south India since January 2009. Before this she worked in the United Kingdom, first as a teacher and then as a manager of change during the adult literacy, language, and numeracy initiative *Skills for Life*. She has worked as a consultant to a sector skills council to develop initial teacher qualifications and in-service development programmes for post-16 teachers and trainers. Since joining the British Council (English Partnerships) in India, she has worked with the Tamil Nadu and Karnataka governments to implement large-scale teacher development programmes.

Address for communication: **clare.odonahue@britishcouncil.org**

Christopher Palmer

Embedding change in state education systems in Brazil: The Paraná ELT project

British Council, Saudi Arabia

Christopher Palmer is British Council Deputy Director Saudi Arabia. He has worked on or managed a range of ELT and education projects with the British Council, including the Polish Access to English (PACE) project in Poland, the British Council Culturas Inglesas-UCLES-British Council COTE project and the World Bank-funded Paraná State Education project. Before joining the British Council he worked as a teacher and teacher trainer in Italy, Spain, and Brazil, and spent four years working in the Department of Education at the University of York. More recently his education work has been focused on developing climate change education for schools.

Address for communication: **christopher.palmer@sa.britishcouncil.org**

Mina Patel

The ETeMS project in Malaysia – English for the Teaching of Mathematics and Science

Ten Education Consultants Sdn Bhd

Mina Patel has been Managing Director of Ten Education Consultants Sdn Bhd for the last three years. Before this, she worked for the British Council in Sri Lanka and Malaysia as a teacher, teacher/trainer trainer, and ELT projects manager. She has authored a resource kit for teachers based on graphic novels, for the Malaysian secondary school curriculum. Her interests lie in training methodology and affect in the world of ELT and education.

Address for communication: **minaten@hotmail.com**

Ruxandra Popovici

The Romanian Textbook Project: Learning together, driving reform

British Council, Romania

Ruxandra Popovici is English and Education Projects Manager for the British Council, Bucharest, Romania. Since joining the British Council in 1994, she has worked in the fields of English language teaching, teacher development, materials writing, content and language integrated learning, and intercultural education. She has co-authored a secondary EFL textbook series, a human rights textbook, and a democratic citizenship handbook for secondary schools, acting as project manager in all instances. She is also currently working in the field of English language teaching for vocational education.

Address for communication: **ruxandra.popovici@britishcouncil.ro**

Teresa Reilly

An early years bilingual schools project: The Spanish experience

British Council, Spain

Teresa Reilly has worked for British Council Spain for 35 years as a teacher, teacher trainer, teaching centre manager, and project manager. She has a degree from Edinburgh University, an MSc in Language Education from Aston University, a PGCE in primary education, and an RSA Dip TEFL. Since 1997, she has been Bilingual Projects Manager for the British Council, where her main role is to work in partnership with the Ministry of Education and Regional Governments in Spain to develop bilingual projects in state schools in Spain by bringing to these projects British Council expertise in teacher training and the development of bilingual curricula. She has worked with the British Council and Ministries of Education in Italy and Portugal on the initiation of pilot bilingual projects there. She has given seminars and workshops in bilingual education at conferences in Spain, the United Kingdom, and other European countries. She has recently been to Indonesia and Japan as a consultant on bilingual education at conferences and training seminars. She is now leaving the British Council to set up her own consultancy in bilingual education.

Address for communication: **teresamaryreilly@hotmail.com**

Mike Scholey

Materials design and development in English for the world of work in Turkey: Policy, strategies, and processes

Freelance ELT Consultant

Mike Scholey is a freelance ELT consultant and former senior lecturer in ELT at University College Plymouth St Mark and St John, where he taught on the MEd ELT/ESP and Trainer Development courses and developed a new MEd CLIL. He has worked in Russia as a consultant on the Presidential Management Training Initiative (RPMTI), the ESP Teacher Development project (RESPONSE), the Primary School Textbook project (Millie), and the North Caucasus Tolerance through Languages project. He worked on both the English Language Improvement (ELIP) and Key Skills for Women Teacher Trainers (KEYSWOTT) projects in Ethiopia, and was consultant for both the National Mozambique English Curriculum and the New Ukrainian University ESP Curriculum (with Rod Bolitho). More recently, he has worked on trainer development in Tajikistan, a vocational English Hotel and Tourism curriculum in the Comoros Islands, ELT textbook projects in China and Northern Cyprus, and latterly on textbook and INSET projects in Maharashtra, India.

Address for communication: **mike.scholey@yahoo.com**

John Simpson
Mind the gap: Language policy reform in Rwanda
British Council, Sub-Saharan Africa

Dr John Simpson is the British Council's Language and Education Adviser in sub-Saharan Africa. He currently assists the Rwandan Ministry of Education with its sector-wide transition to English-medium education, providing technical advice to the Rwanda English in Action Program (REAP). He also helps the Teacher Service Commission initiate reforms in teacher education, management and professionalisation. He has over 30 years' experience in language and education, including 15 years' in UK higher education and 10 years' in sub-Saharan Africa. Most recently, he has provided long-term consultancies on ELT reform to the Governments of Rwanda (2009– present) and Ethiopia (2007–08). His skills set includes policy development, situational assessment/needs analysis, strategic planning, quality assurance of service delivery, monitoring and evaluation, teacher education and professional development, learning materials, institutional capacity building, and promoting synergies between government agencies and development partners.

Address for communication: **john.simpson@britishcouncil.org**

Mike Solly
Implementing the pilot stage of English in Action in Bangladesh: Negotiating the route to sustainable improvement in ELT classroom practice
Open University, UK

Mike Solly is currently Senior Lecturer in Education at the Open University and is working on a large-scale ELT development project in primary and secondary schools throughout Bangladesh. He worked in ELT as a teacher and trainer in Eastern Europe, the Middle East, and the United Kingdom for over 15 years and for the last 10 has been involved in the management and delivery of a number of ELT projects. He has been co-ordinator of the IATEFL Global Issues Special Interest Group and has a growing interest in English language teaching, development, and mobile/virtual technologies. He is currently researching attitudes to English in rural Bangladeshi communities.

Address for communication: **m.g.solly@open.ac.uk**

Christopher Tribble

Editor

Overview

King's College, London

Dr Christopher Tribble has taught in primary, secondary and tertiary education in France, the United Kingdom, and China, and worked from 1993–95 as ELT Projects Manager for the British Council, Baltic States. He is currently a lecturer in the Department of Education and Professional Studies at King's College, London University, where he teaches courses in English for Academic Purposes, written discourse analysis, and the management and evaluation of innovation. He is also Visiting Professor at Université de Paris, Diderot, and a consultant and trainer in the design, management, and evaluation of education projects. He has a long-standing research and teaching interest in applied linguistics, with a particular focus on written communication and the use of computational corpus analysis and applications in ELT, and is the author of *Writing* (1996) in the OUP Teacher Education Series and *Textual Patterns* (2006) with Mike Scott. He is also a documentary photographer and has created extensive visual documentations for the British Council on the lives and professional experiences of English language teachers in many countries around the world.

Address for communication: **christopher.tribble@kcl.ac.uk**
www.ctribble.co.uk

Catherine Walter

Textbooks, teams, and sustainability in Russia

University of Oxford

Dr Catherine Walter is a Lecturer in Applied Linguistics at the University of Oxford and the leader of the distance Postgraduate Diploma in Teaching English in University Settings there. She is the Chair of the British Council's English Language Advisory Group and has advised the Council on English language teaching since 1998. Since her Presidency of IATEFL in the early 90s, she has been deeply interested in the exchange of knowledge between Eastern and Western European language educators. She has also written numerous English language teaching books with Michael Swan, the latest of which is the Oxford English Grammar Course series. Her research interests are in instructed language learning, teacher development, and reading comprehension.

Address for communication: **catherine.walter@education.ox.ac.uk**

Martin Wedell
The Oman BA project: ELT change implementation, process or event?
University of Leeds

Dr Martin Wedell is Head of International Education at the School of Education, University of Leeds, UK. From 1977–98 he lived and worked in Kenya, Saudi Arabia, China, and Hungary on state and private English language teaching programmes and/or UK aid projects. He continues to travel widely to countries attempting to implement changes to their existing ELT provision. He believes that, in most contexts, state system ELT policy change entails varying degrees of cultural change for the parts of and partners in that system. His particular interest is in understanding what this implies for the planning, designing, and provision of change implementation support for serving and novice state English teachers.

Address for communication: **m.wedell@education.leeds.ac.uk**

Claire Whittaker
Redesigning a blended learning course in Bosnia and Herzegovina: Introducing new technologies for ELT
Bell Educational Trust

Dr Claire Whittaker is the Head of Learning and Teaching at the Bell Educational Trust, where she is responsible for providing academic leadership and ensuring the quality of learning and teaching in Bell's UK programmes. She has a career of over 16 years in ELT as a teacher, trainer, and consultant. A significant part of this time was spent overseas, where she worked for International House and the British Council. It was while working on the British Council's Peacekeeping English projects in Ukraine, Uzbekistan, Tajikistan, Kazakhstan, Kyrgyzstan, and Bosnia and Herzegovina that she gained experience in managing ELT change processes.

Address for communication: **claire.whittaker@bell-worldwide.com**

Paul Woods
A summary of key lessons from the case studies
British Council, Southern Cone, Americas

Paul Woods has worked for the British Council since 1977 and is currently Regional English Adviser, covering the Southern Cone of the Americas, based in Buenos Aires. He previously held a similar role as the Council's English Manager for sub-Saharan Africa, where he helped develop the Teaching English Radio series. He has managed large-scale projects in ELT and education for a wide range of agencies, including the global Peacekeeping English Project, which covers 27 countries; curriculum development and teacher training projects in Mozambique, Tanzania, Sierra Leone, and Brunei; and ESP projects in the Philippines and Brazil. He has also been Director of the British Council in Mozambique and Botswana, managed the Education UK website, and in the mid-1990s was a Consultant in Language and Development in the British Council's Consultancy Group. His article 'The hedgehog and the fox: two approaches to the teaching of English to the military' was included in the anthology *Re-Locating TESOL in an Age of Empire*, published in paperback last year by Palgrave Macmillan.

Address for communication: **paul.woods@britishcouncil.org.ar**

Clare Woodward

Implementing the pilot stage of English in Action in Bangladesh: Negotiating the route to sustainable improvement in ELT classroom practice

Open University, UK

Clare Woodward is currently a Lecturer in Education at the Open University, working on a large-scale ELT development project in Bangladesh. She worked as an EFL teacher and trainer in South-East Asia, the Middle East, and the United Kingdom for 15 years. Having completed an MA in Distance Education, she then spent several years managing projects on the use of ICT and social networks with disadvantaged communities. She has an interest in international teacher development and m-learning, and is currently researching the role of SMS and reflective practice in teacher professional development.

Address for communication: **c.e.woodward@open.ac.uk**

Mona Zikri

Redirecting a curriculum development project in Egypt

Faculty of Arts, Helwan University

Dr Mona Zikri is Professor Emerita at the Faculty of Arts, Helwan University, with over 30 years' experience as an ELT professional. She holds a PhD degree in linguistics from Manchester University, UK. Her experience ranges from academia to education reform projects. During the 1980s, she participated in CDELT activities and finally held the position of CDELT language co-ordinator. She was subsequently Deputy Dean and Chair of the English department of Helwan University, where she introduced EFL curricular and professional development innovations. From 1998 her career shifted to development, as she was seconded to USAID and then to the World Bank, where she supervised multi-million dollar education projects, including an ELT reform project. From 2005–11 she was deputy director for the CIDA-funded primary education reform project and is currently seconded as the institutionalisation advisor to the CIDA-funded Early Childhood Education Enhancement Project.

Address for communication: **mzikri@eceep-cat.org**
zikrimona@yahoo.com

References

References

Achim, A., Capotă, L. (Book 5 only), Comişel, E., Dinu, F., Mastacan, A., Popovici, R., and E. Teodorescu. (1995–99) *Pathway to English*: Book 5. Bucharest: Editura Didactica si Pedagogica; Books 6, 7, and 8. Oxford: Oxford University Press.

Adamson, B. and C. Davison. (2008) 'English language teaching in Hong Kong primary schools: Innovation and resistance', in D. E. Murray (ed.). *Planning change, changing plans: Innovations in second language teaching*. Ann Arbor: University of Michigan Press.

Ajzen, I. (1988) *Attitudes, personality, and behaviour*. Milton Keynes: Open University Press.

Alderson, J .C. (1992) 'Guidelines for the evaluation of language education', in J. C. Alderson and A. Beretta (eds.).

Alderson, J. C. (1999) 'Introduction', in M. Bardi, G. Chefneux, D. Comanetchi, and T. Magureanu (eds.). *The PROSPER Project – Innovation in Teaching English for Specific Purposes in Romania: A Study of Impact*. Bucharest: British Council in association with Cavalliotti Publishing House.

Alderson, J. C. (ed.) (2009) *The Politics of Language Education: individuals and institutions*. Bristol: Multilingual Matters.

Alderson, J. C. and A. Beretta (eds.) (1992) *Evaluating Second Language Education*. Cambridge: Cambridge University Press.

Alderson, J. C. and M. Scott. (1992) 'Insiders, outsiders, and participatory evaluation', in J. C. Alderson and A. Beretta (eds.).

Al Hazmi, S. (2003*)* EFL teacher preparation programmes in Saudi Arabia: Trends and Challenges. *TESOL Quarterly* 37/2: 341-45.

Amin, N. (2001) Nativism, the native speaker construct, and minority immigrant women teachers of English as a second language. *The CATESOL Journal* 13/1: 89-107.

Andrews, S. (2001) The language awareness of the L2 teacher: Its impact upon pedagogical practice. *Language Awareness* 10/2-3: 75-90.

Andrews, S. (2003) Teacher language awareness and the professional knowledge base of the L2 teacher. *Language Awareness* 12/2: 81-95.

Arnold, E. and G. Sarhan. (1994) Ten tips for making ELT counterparting work. *ELT Journal* 48/1: 12-21.

Asian Development Bank. (2007) *Report and Recommendation of the President to the Board of Directors. Proposed Loan and Asian Development Fund Grant, Democratic Socialist Republic of Sri Lanka: Education for Knowledge Society Project.* Manila: Asian Development Bank.

Bajunid, I. (2000) 'Rethinking the work of teachers and school leaders in an age of change', in C. Day, A. Fernandez, T. E. Hauge, and J. Møller (eds.).

Baker, W. (2008) A critical examination of ELT in Thailand: the role of cultural awareness. *RELC Journal* 39: 131-146.

Bălan, R., Carianopol, M., Colibaba, Ş., Coşer, C., Focşeneanu, V., Stan, V., and R. Vulcănescu. (1995–99) *Pathway to English*: Book 9. Bucharest: Editura Didactica si Pedagogica; Books 10, 11, and 12. Oxford: Oxford University Press.

Baldauf, R.B. (2004) Language Planning and Policy: Recent Trends, Future Directions. *American Association of Applied Linguistics*: 1-8.

Bardi, M., Chefneux G., Comanetchi D., and T. Magureanu (eds.) (1999) *The PROSPER Project – innovation in Teaching English for Specific Purposes in Romania: a Study of Impact*. Bucharest: British Council in association with Cavalliotti Publishing House.

Bax, S. (1995) Principles for evaluating teacher development activities. *ELT Journal* 49/3: 252-61.

Beetham, H. and R. Sharpe. (2007a) 'An introduction to rethinking pedagogy for a digital age', in H. Beetham and R. Sharpe (eds.).

Beetham, H. and R. Sharpe (eds.) (2007b) *Rethinking Pedagogy for a Digital Age*. Abingdon, Oxon: Routledge.

Bennett, K.C., Hillyard, S., Malderez, A., and D. Wilson. (2009*) Report: China ELT Needs Analysis Consultancy*. Beijing: British Council.

Bentley, C. (2005) *Practical PRINCE2* (Third edition). London: Stationery Office.

Beretta, A. and A. Davies. (1985) Evaluation of the Bangalore Project. *ELT Journal* 39/2: 121-27.

Berg, G. (2000) 'Steering in and steering of the school', in C. Day, A. Fernandez, T. E. Hauge, and J. Møller (eds.).

Bilingual Education Project: Spain. (2010) *Evaluation Report*. Available at http://www.teachingenglish.org.uk/sites/teacheng/files/BEP.%20Inglés%20.pdf (accessed 28 December 2011).

Block, D. (2003) *Second Language Identities*. London: Continuum.

Boletin Oficial del Estado. (2000) Decree of April 5th 2000. *Boletin Oficial del Estado* 105: 16748.

Bolitho, R. (2002) Global Coursebooks, Local Contexts. *ETAS-English Teachers' Association Switzerland Journal* 19/2. 43-45.

Bolitho, R. (2005) 'British ELT and the mainstream', in B. Beavan (ed.). *IATEFL 2005 Cardiff Conference Selections*. Canterbury: IATEFL.

Borg, S. (2006) *Teacher cognition and language education: Research and practice.* London: Continuum.

Bowers, R. (1983) *Project planning and performance. ELT Documents 116.* London: British Council.

Bowers, R. (1985) 'General Issues', in R. Quirk, H. G. Widdowson, and Y Cantù. (eds.). *English in the world: teaching and learning the languages and literatures.* Cambridge: Cambridge University Press for the British Council.

Bray, T. and T. Luxon. (1999) 'The Role of Baseline Studies in ELT Projects', in C. Kennedy (ed.).

Brewster, J. (1999) 'Teaching English through Content: Supporting Good Practice', in C. Kennedy (ed.).

British Council. (2003) *English for Specific Purposes (ESP) in Ukraine: A Baseline Study.* Kiev: British Council.

British Council. (2008) *The English for hotels and tourism project, Turkey.* Available at http://www.teachingenglish.org.uk/elt-projects/english-hotels-tourism-project-turkey (accessed 3 June 2011).

Brumfit, C. J. (ed.) (1983) *Language Teaching Projects for the Third World. ELT Documents 116.* Oxford: Pergamon Press.

Burnes, B. (2000) *Managing Change – A Strategic Approach to Organizational Dynamics.* London: Pearson Education.

Burns, A. and J. Richards (eds.) (2009) *The Cambridge Guide to Second Language Teacher Education.* Cambridge: Cambridge University Press.

Burridge, T. (2010) *Why do Finland's schools get the best results?* Available at http://news.bbc.co.uk/2/hi/8601207.stm (accessed 2 August 2011).

Byram, M. (2000) *The interculture project: evaluation report.* Available at http://www.lancs.ac.uk/users/interculture/reports.htm (accessed 20 July 2011).

Canagarajah, A. S. (1999) *Resisting linguistic imperialism in English language teaching.* Oxford: Oxford University Press.

Canagarajah, A. S. (2002) 'Globalization, methods, and practice in periphery classrooms', in D. Block and D. Cameron (eds.). *Globalization and language teaching.* New York: Routledge.

CBSE. (1997) *ELT Curriculum Implementation Study. Final Report.* Hyderabad, India: Central Institute of English and Foreign Languages.

Chacon, C. T. (2005) Teachers' perceived efficacy among English as a foreign language teachers in middle schools in Venezuela. *Teaching and Teacher Education* 21: 257-72.

Chang, K., Jung, K., Hayes, D., Yeon, J., Kim, W. and B. Lee. (2010). In-service English teacher training program evaluation. *English Teaching* 65: 127-63.

Chang, K., Yeon, J., Kim, W., Jung, K., and D. Hayes. (2008) *Intensive in-service English teacher training program evaluation report.* Research Report CRI 2008-1-2. Seoul, Korea: Korea Institute for Curriculum and Evaluation.

Chapman, K. (2011) *Bye-bye PPSMI.* Available at http://thestar.com.my/education/story.asp?file=/2011/11/13/education/9878350&sec=education (accessed 13 November 2011).

Choong, K. F. (2004) *English for the Teaching of Mathematics and Science (ETeMS): From conception to implementation.* Kuala Lumpur: English Language Teaching Centre. Available at http://www.eltcm.org/eltc/Download/paperbank%20PDFs/English%20for%20the%20Teaching%20of%20Mathematics%20and%20Science%20paper.pdf (accessed 5 May 2011).

Chowdhury, R. and P. L. Ha. (2008) Reflecting on Western TESOL training and communicative language teaching: Bangladeshi teachers' voices. *Asia Pacific Journal of Education* 28/3: 305-16.

Christison, M. A. (2011) 'The L2 student advocate', in M. A. Christison and F. L. Stoller (eds.).

Christison, M. A. and D. E. Murray. (2009a) 'Introduction', in M. A. Christison and D. E. Murray (eds.).

Christison, M. A. and D. E. Murray (eds.) (2009b) *Leadership in English language education: theoretical foundations and practical skills for changing times.* New York: Routledge.

Christison, M. A. and F. L. Stoller (eds.) (2011) *A handbook for language program administrators* (Second edition). Miami: Alta Book Center.

Claxton, G. (1989) *Being a Teacher.* London: Cassell.

Coleman, H. (1992) 'Moving the goalposts: project evaluation in practice', in J. C. Alderson and A. Beretta (eds.).

Coleman, H. (ed.) (2011) *Dreams and Realities: Developing Countries and the English Language.* London: British Council.

Connell, J. P. and A. C. Kubisch (1998) 'Applying a Theory of Change Approach to the Evaluation of Comprehensive Community Initiatives: Progress, Prospects, and Problems', in K. Fulbright-Anderson, A. C. Kubisch, and J. P. Connell (eds.). *New Approaches to Evaluating Community Initiatives, vol. 2, Theory, Measurement, and Analysis.* Washington, DC: Aspen Institute.

Cook, R. S. (1986) 'Introducing ELT Curriculum Change', in R. Bowers (ed.). *Language Teacher Education: An Integrated Programme for EFL Training. ELT Documents 125.* London: British Council.

Country Report. Poland. (2006) *Language Education Policy Profile. 2005–2006.* Warsaw: Ministry of Education.

Crystal, D. (1997) *English as a Global Language.* Cambridge: Cambridge University Press.

Dadds, M. (2001) The politics of pedagogy. *Teachers and Teaching: theory and practice* 7: 43-58.

Day, C., Fernandez, A., Hauge T. E., and J. Møller (eds.) (2000) *The life and work of teachers: international perspectives in changing times.* London and New York: Falmer Press.

Day, C., Stobart, G., Sammons, P., Kington, A., Gu, Q., Smees, R., and T. Mujtaba. (2006) *Variations in teachers' work, lives, and effectiveness. Research Report RR743.* London: Department for Education and Skills.

Delbecq, A. L., Van de Ven, A. H., and D. H. Gustafson. (1975) *Group techniques for program planning: A guide to nominal group and Delphi processes.* Glenview, Illinois: Scott Foresman.

Department of Education. (2006) *Language – English. Lower Secondary Syllabus.* Papua New Guinea: Department of Education.

DfID (Department for International Development). (Undated) *Student Performance in National Examinations (SPINE).* Available from http://www.dfid.gov.uk/r4d/SearchResearchDatabase.asp?ProjectID=60615 (accessed 18 October 2011).

Dobson, M., Pérez Murillo, M. D., and R. Johnstone. (2010) *Bilingual Education Project: Spain: Evaluation Report.* Madrid: Ministry of Education and British Council.

Donaldson, G., Marnik, G., Mackenzie, S., and R. Ackerman. (2009) What makes or breaks a principal. *Educational Leadership* 67/2: 8-14.

Duke, C. (2002) *Managing the learning university.* Suffolk: Society for Research into Higher Education and Open University Press.

Dyer, J., Gregersen, H., and C. M. Christensen. (2011) *Innovator's DNA: Mastering the five skills of disruptive innovators.* Boston: Harvard Review Press.

Edge, J. (1988) Applying linguistics in English language teaching training for speakers of other languages. *ELT Journal* 42/1: 9-13.

Edge, J. (ed.) (2002) *Continuing professional development: Some of our perspectives.* Whitstable, Kent: IATEFL.

Elder, C. (2009) Reconciling accountability and development needs in heritage language education: a communication challenge for the evaluation consultant. *Language Teaching Research* 13/1: 15-34.

Ellis, L. (2002) Teaching from experience: A new perspective on the non-native teacher in adult ESL. *Australian Review of Applied Linguistics* 25/1: 71-107.

Ellis, R. (2009) 'Second language acquisition and teacher education', in A. Burns and J. Richards (eds.).

English in Action. (2008) *English in Action Project – Project Memorandum*. London: DfID.

Erling, E. J. and P. Seargeant (eds.) (2011) *English and International Development*. Bristol: Multilingual Matters.

Escamilla, K. (2009) English language learners: Developing literacy in second-language learners – report of the national literacy panel on language-minority children and youth. *Journal of Literacy Research* 41/4: 432-52.

European Commission. (2004) *Aid delivery methods: Vol. 1, Project Cycle Management Guidelines*. Brussels: European Commission.

Evans, L. (1998) *Teacher morale, job satisfaction, and motivation*. London: Paul Chapman Publishing.

Farrell, T. S. C. (2004) *Reflective practice in action*. Thousand Oaks, California: Corwin Press.

Farrugia, C. (1986) Career-choices and sources of occupational satisfaction and frustration among teachers in Malta. *Comparative Education* 22: 221-31.

Fillmore, L. W. and C. E. Snow. (2000) *What teachers need to know about language*. Paper for the US Department of Education Office of Educational Research and Improvement.

Fink, D. (2000) *The Two Solitudes: Policy Makers and Policy Implementers: Implications for Leaders*. Paper presented at the Annual Conference of the British Educational Management and Administration Society. Bristol (September 2000).

Fisiak, J. (1992) English language teacher training in Poland: Past legacy and present challenge, English – a world language. *Journal of the English Speaking Union* 2: 6–14.

Freeman, D. and K. E. Johnson. (1998) Reconceptualizing the knowledge-base of language teacher education. *TESOL Quarterly* 32/3: 397-417.

Fullan, M. (2003) *Leadership and sustainability: Systems thinkers in action*. Thousand Oaks, California: Corwin Press.

Fullan, M. (2007) *The new meaning of educational change* (Fourth edition). New York: Teachers' College Press.

Fullan, M. and A. Hargreaves (eds.) (1992) *Teacher Development and Educational Change*. London: Falmer Press.

Fullan, M. and S. Stiegelbauer. (1991) *The new meaning of educational change*. London: Cassell.

Gibson, J., Ivancevich, J. M., Donnelly, J. H., and R. Konopaske. (2009) *Organizations: Behavior, structure, processes* (Thirteenth edition). Boston: McGraw Hill-Irwin.

Gill, S. K. (2007) *Language and Cultural Identity: Balancing National and International Needs in Public Universities in Malaysia.* Paper presented at 19th International Conference on Higher Education, Cluj Napoca, Romania.

Gilpin, A. (1997) 'Cascade training: sustainability or dilution?', in I. McGrath (ed.). *Learning to train: Perspectives on the development of language teacher trainers.* Hemel Hempstead: Prentice Hall.

Government of Rwanda Ministry of Finance and Economic Planning. (2000) *Rwanda Vision 2020.* Kigali.

Government of Rwanda Ministry of Finance and Economic Planning. (2007) *Economic development and poverty reduction strategy: 2008–2012.* Kigali.

Government of Rwanda Ministry of Education. (2010) *Education Sector Strategic Plan: 2010–2015.* Kigali.

Graddol, D. (1997) *The Future of English?* London: British Council.

Graddol, D. (2006) *English Next.* London: British Council.

Green, R. and D. Wall. (2005) Language testing in the military: problems, politics, and progress. *Language Testing* 22: 379.

Greenwood, J. (1985) Bangalore revisited: a reluctant complaint. *ELT Journal* 39/4: 268-73.

Gu, Q. (2005) The perception gap in cross-cultural training: an investigation of British Council English language teaching projects in China. *International Journal of Educational Development* 25: 287-304.

Guangdong Department of Education. (2004) *Training Course of Primary English Teaching Techniques.* Guangzhou, Guangdong: Guangdong Higher Education Press.

Guba, E. and Y. Lincoln. (1989) *Fourth generation evaluation.* Newbury Park: Sage.

Gulyamova J. and N. Isamukhamedova. (forthcoming, 2012) English Reforms in Uzbekistan. *The Teacher Trainer* 26.

Hamid, M. O. and R. B. Baldauf. (2008) Will CLT bail out the bogged down ELT in Bangladesh? *English Today* 24/3: 16-24.

Hamid, M. O., Sussex, R., and A. Khan. (2009) Private Tutoring in English for Secondary School Students in Bangladesh. *TESOL Quarterly* 43/2: 281-308.

Handal, G. and P. Lauvas. (1987) *Promoting Reflective Teaching: Supervision in Action.* Milton Keynes: Open University Press.

Harmer, J. (2007) *The practice of English language teaching.* (Fourth edition). Harlow: Longman.

Harper, C. and E. de Jong. (2009) English language teacher expertise: The elephant in the room. *Language and Education* 23/2: 137-51.

Harris, J. and M. Conway. (2002) *Modern languages in Irish primary schools – an evaluation of the National Pilot Primary Project.* Dublin: Institiúid Teangeolaíochta Éireann.

Hayes, D. (1995) In-service teacher development: some basic principles. *ELT Journal* 49/3: 252-61.

Hayes, D. (1996) Prioritizing 'voice' over 'vision': reaffirming the centrality of the teacher in ESOL research. *System* 24: 173-86.

Hayes, D. (2000) Cascade training and teachers' professional development. *ELT Journal* 54: 135-45.

Hayes, D. (2004) 'Inside INSET: trainers' perceptions', in D. Hayes (ed.). *Trainer development: principles and practice from language teacher training.* Melbourne: Language Australia Publications.

Hayes, D. (2006) *An exploration of the lives and careers of teachers of English in state education systems in Sri Lanka and Thailand.* Unpublished PhD thesis, Centre for English Language Studies, University of Birmingham, UK.

Hayes, D. (2007) *The introduction of English into primary schools in Vietnam.* Unpublished consultancy report for the Ministry of Education and Training, Vietnam. Hanoi, Vietnam: British Council.

Hayes, D. (2010) Language learning, teaching, and educational reform in rural Thailand: an English teacher's perspective. *Asia-Pacific Journal of Education* 30: 305-19.

Holliday, A. (1991) From Materials Development to Staff Development: An Informed Change in Direction in an EFL Project. *System* 19/3: 301-308.

Holliday, A. (1992) Tissue rejection and informal orders in ELT projects: collecting the right information. *Applied Linguistics* 13/4: 403-24.

Holliday, A. (1994) *Appropriate Methodology and Social Context.* Cambridge: Cambridge University Press.

Holliday, A. (1999) 'Achieving Cultural Continuity in Curriculum Innovation', in C. Kennedy (ed.).

Holliday, A. (2005) *The Struggle to Teach English as an International Language.* Oxford: Oxford University Press.

Hu, G. (2005) Contextual influences on instructional practices: a Chinese case for an ecological approach to ELT. *TESOL Quarterly* 39: 635-60.

Hudson, T. and J. Melia. (1981) Methods and Materials: A Case Study. *Proceedings of the First National Symposium. CDELT.*

Hunter, T. (2009) 'Micropolitical Issues in ELT Project Implementation' in J.C. Alderson (ed.).

Ingvarson, L., Meiers, M., and A. Beavis. (2005) *Factors affecting the impact of professional development programs on teachers' knowledge, practice, student outcomes, and efficacy. Professional Development for Teachers and School Leaders.* Australian Council for Educational Research. Available at http://research.acer.edu.au/professional_dev/1 (accessed 2 August 2011).

Internet World Stats. (2011) *Internet usage statistics: The internet big picture.* Available at http://www.internetworldstats.com/stats.htm (accessed 15 July 2011).

Ismail, I. (2009) *English in the Teaching of Mathematics and Science Subjects (ETeMS) Policy – Implications for the Performance of Malaysian Secondary Schools in Mathematics and Science Subjects.* Available at http://www.edamba.eu/userfiles/file/Ismail%20Ihsan.pdf (accessed 28 November 2011).

Jacobson, J. (1995) 'Evaluation in the Romanian ELT Unischools project', in R. Kiely, D. F. Murphy, P. Rea-Dickins, and M. Reid (eds.). *Proceedings of second PRODESS (Project Development Support Scheme) Colloquium.* Manchester: British Council.

Johnstone, R. (2010) *Learning through English: Policies, Challenges, and Prospects.* London: British Council.

Kabel, A. (2009) Native-speakerism, stereotyping, and the collusion of applied linguistics. *System* 37: 12-22.

Kachru, B. B. (1986) *The alchemy of English: The spread, functions, and models of non-native Englishes.* Oxford: Pergamon Press.

Kanter, R. M. (1983) *The change masters: Innovation and entrepreneurship in the American corporation.* New York: Simon and Schuster, Inc.

Kaplan, B. and R.B. Baldauf. (1997) *Language Planning: From practice to theory.* Clevedon: Multilingual Matters Ltd.

Kennedy, C. (1988) Evaluation of the management of change in ELT projects. *Applied Linguistics* 9/4: 329-42.

Kennedy, C. (1999a) '"Fit" or "Split"? - Innovation and Best Practice' in C. Kennedy (ed.).

Kennedy, C. (1999b) 'The foreign trainer as change agent and implications for teacher education programmes in China', in C. Kennedy, C. Doyle, and P. Goh (eds.). *Exploring Change in English Language Teaching.* Oxford: Macmillan.

Kennedy, C. (ed.) (1999c) *Innovation and Best Practice.* Harlow: Longman.

Kennedy, C. (2011) 'Challenges for language policy, language, and development', in H. Coleman (ed.).

Kennedy, M. (1991) *An agenda for research on teacher learning* (National Center for Research on Teacher Learning special report). East Lansing: Michigan State University.

Kennett, P. (2010) 'English as a Tool for Conflict Transformation', in H. Coleman (ed.).

Kiely. R. (2008) 'The purpose, promise, and potential of teacher research', in M. Pawlak (ed.). *Investigating English Language Teaching and Learning*. IATEFL: University of Poznan.

Kiely, R. (2009) Small answers to the big question: learning from language programme evaluation. *Language Teaching Research* 13/1: 99-116.

Kiely, R. and P. Rea-Dickins (2005) *Programme Evaluation in Language Education*. Basingstoke: Palgrave Macmillan.

Kikuchi, K. and C. Browne. (2009) English educational policy for high schools in Japan: Ideals vs reality. *RELC Journal* 40: 172-91.

Kirkpatrick, D. L. (1998) *Evaluating Training Programs: The Four Levels*. San Francisco: Berrett-Koehler Publishers.

Komorowska, H. (1991) 'Second language teaching in Poland prior to the reform of 1990', in J. E. Alatis (ed.). *Georgetown Round Table on Languages and Linguistics*. Washington, DC: Georgetown University Press.

Komorowska, H. (2007) *Metodyka nauczania języków obcych w Polsce 1957–2007 (Foreign Language Teaching Methodology in Poland 1957–2007)*. Warsaw: Wydawnictwa CODN.

Kora, P. G. (2011) *Some home truths about the education reforms in PNG – Day 5*. Available at http://rausimobe.wordpress.com/ (accessed 2 August 2011).

Kushner, S. (1996) The limits of constructivism. *Evaluation* 2/2: 189-200.

Lamb, M. (1996) 'The consequences of INSET', in T. Hedge and N. Whitney (eds.). *Power, pedagogy, and practice*. Oxford: Oxford University Press.

Lamie, J. (2004) Presenting a model of change. *Language Teaching Research* 8/2: 115-42.

Lamie, J. (2005) *Evaluating Change in English Language Teaching*. Basingstoke: Palgrave Macmillan.

Leung, C. (2009) 'Second language teacher professionalism', in A. Burns and J. Richards (eds.).

Lindqvist, P. and U. K. Nordanger. (2007) (Mis?) using the E-Delphi Method: An Attempt to Articulate the Practical Knowledge of Teaching. *Journal of Research Methods and Methodological Issues* 1/1: 1-13.

Lo Bianco, J. (2011) 'A Friendly Knife? English in the Context of Sri Lankan Language Planning', in L. Farrell, U. N. Singh, and R. A. Giri (eds.). *English Language Education in South Asia: From Policy to Pedagogy*. New Delhi: Cambridge University Press.

Loos, D. et al. (1983) An Investigation of Problems and Solutions to Handling Large EFL Classes in Egypt. *Occasional Papers* 4. CDELT.

Lowenberg, P. H. (2002) Assessing English proficiency in the Expanding Circle. *World Englishes* 21/3: 431-35.

Lynch, B. (1996) *Language Programme Evaluation*. Cambridge: Cambridge University Press.

MacDonald, B. (1976). 'Evaluation and control of education', in D. A. Tawney (ed.). *Curriculum evaluation today: Trends and implications*. London: Macmillan Education.

Markee, N. (1993) The diffusion of innovation in language teaching. *Annual Review of Applied Linguistics* 13: 229-43.

Markee, N. (1997) *Managing Curricular Innovation*. Cambridge: Cambridge University Press.

Mathew, R. (2006) Tracing the After-life of Teacher Development Programmes: Reopening Closed Chapters. *English Language Teacher Education and Development* 9/Winter: 21-38.

Meixner, H. (2005) 'Gentle Warriors: Britain's Defence Diplomacy in Romania since 1990', in D. Deletant (ed.). *In and Out of Focus: Romania and Britain. Relations and Perspectives from 1930 to the Present*. Bucharest: Cavallioti.

Melia, J. P. (ed.) (1998) *Innovations and Outcomes in English Language Teacher Education – Proceedings of the PRINCE Conference, Popowo, Poland*. Warsaw: British Council.

Ministry of Education. (2001) *National English Curriculum Standard*. Beijing: People's Education Press.

Ministry of Education. (2004) *The Development of Education: National Report of Malaysia*. Kuala Lumpur: Ministry of Education.

Ministry of Education and Science of Ukraine. (2005) *English for Specific Purposes: National Curriculum for Universities*. Kiev: British Council.

Ministry of Education, Culture, and Sport and British Council. (2000) *Joint Spanish/ British Review of the Bilingual Project*. Madrid: Ministry of Education, Culture, and Sport and British Council.

Mitchell, R. and J. Hooper. (1991) 'Teachers' views of language knowledge', in C. James and P. Garrett (eds.). *Language awareness in the classroom*. London: Longman.

Muijs, D. and G. Lindsay. (2008) Where are we at? An empirical study of levels and methods of evaluating continuing professional development. *British Educational Research Journal* 34: 195-211.

Mukundan, J., Hajimohammadi, R., and V. Nimehchisalem. (2011) Professional Development Interest of Malaysian Math and Science Teachers in the English for Teaching Maths and Science (ETeMS) Buddy System. *Journal of International Educational Research* 7/1: 81-87.

Murphy, D. F. and P. Rea-Dickins. (1999) 'Identifying stakeholders', in V. McKay and C. Treffgarne (eds.). *Evaluating Impact*. Serial No. 35. London: Department for International Development.

Nor, F. M., Aziz, M. A., and K. Jusoff. (2011) Should English for Teaching Mathematics and Science (ETeMS) in Malaysia be Abolished? *World Applied Sciences Journal* 12: 36-40.

Norris, J. (ed.) (2009) Understanding and improving language education through Programme Evaluation. *Language Teaching Research: Special issue*: 13/1.

Norris, N. (1998) Curriculum evaluation revisited. *Cambridge Journal of Education* 28/2: 207-20.

Nunan, D. (2003) The impact of English as a global language on educational policies and practices in the Asia-Pacific region. *TESOL Quarterly* 37/4: 589-613.

O'Donnell, K. (2005) Japanese secondary English teachers: negotiation of educational roles in the face of curricular reform. *Language, Culture and Curriculum* 18: 300-16.

Oliveira, J. B. (2007) 'Brazil: Television-plus: Journalism in the service of teacher education', in H. Perraton, B. Robinson, and C. Creed (eds.). *International case studies of teacher education at a distance*. Oldenburg: BIS-Verlag.

Ong'ondo, C. (2009) *Pedagogical practice and support of English language student teachers during the practicum in Kenya*. Unpublished PhD thesis. School of Education, University of Leeds.

O'Sullivan, F. and J. West-Burnham. (1998) *Leadership and Professional Development in Schools*. London: Pearson Education.

O'Sullivan, M. C. (2001) The inset strategies model: an effective inset model for unqualified and underqualified primary teachers in Namibia. *International Journal of Educational Development* 21: 93-117.

Organization for Economic Cooperation and Development (OECD). (2001) *What schools for the future?* Paris: OECD.

Palmer, C. (1993) Innovation and the experienced teacher. *ELT Journal* 47/2: 166-71.

Pathmawathy, S. (2011) *PPSMI students given option to continue in English*. Available at http://www.brudirect.com/index.php/Malaysiakini/ppsmi-students-given-option-to-continue-in-english.html (accessed 5 November 2011).

Patton, M. Q. (2008) *Utilization-focussed evaluation* (Fourth edition). Thousand Oaks: Sage.

Pawson, R. (2003) Nothing as Practical as a Good Theory. *Evaluation* 9/4: 471-90.

Pawson, R. and N.Tilley. (1997) *Realistic Evaluation*. London: Sage.

Pennycuick, D. (1993) *School effectiveness in developing countries: A summary of the research evidence*. London: Overseas Development Administration.

Phillips, J. J. (2003) *Return on Investment in Training and Performance Improvement Programs* (Second edition). London: Butterworth Heinemann.

Phillipson, R. (1992) *Linguistic imperialism*. Oxford: Oxford University Press.

Phillipson, R. (2001) English for globalization or for the world's people? *International Review of Education* 47: 185-200.

Pillay, H. and M. Thomas. (2003) A Nation on the Move: Challenges in the Implementation of Major Change in Language Policy. *Asian Englishes* 6/2: 26-43.

Popovici, R. and R. Bolitho. (2003) 'Personal and Professional Development through Writing: The Romanian Textbook Project', in B. Tomlinson (ed.). *Developing Materials for Language Teachers*. London: Continuum.

Posel, D. and D. Casale. (2011) Language proficiency and language policy in South Africa: Findings from new data. *International Journal of Educational Development* 31: 449-57.

Prabhu, N.S. (1987) *Second Language Pedagogy*. Oxford: Oxford University Press.

Prabhu, N.S. (1990) There is no best method – Why? *TESOL Quarterly* 24/2: 161-76.

Prapaisit de Segovia, L. and D. M. Hardison. (2009) Implementing education reform: EFL teachers' perspectives. *ELT Journal* 63: 154-62.

Prime Minister's Office. (2011) *Vision 2020*. Available at http://www.pmo.gov.my/?menu=page&page=1898 (accessed 4 November 2011).

Punthumasen, P. (2007) *International program for teacher education: An approach to tackling problems of English education in Thailand*. Paper presented at the 11th UNESCO-APEID conference, 12-14 December 2007, Bangkok, Thailand.

Quirk, R. (1988) 'The question of standards in the international use of English', in P. H. Lowenberg (ed.). *Language spread and language policy: Issues, implications and case studies*. Washington, DC: Georgetown University Press.

Rasbash, J. R., Steele, F. A., Browne, W. J., and H. Goldstein. (2009) *A User's Guide to MLwiN, Version 2.10*. Bristol: Centre for Multilevel Modelling, University of Bristol.

Rea-Dickins, P. (1994) Evaluation and English Language Teaching. *Language Teaching* 27: 71-92.

Rea-Dickins, P. and P. Germaine. (1992) *Evaluation*. Oxford: Oxford University Press.

Rea-Dickins, P., Khamis, Z., and F. Olivero. (2011) 'Does English-medium instruction and examining lead to social and economic advantage? Promises and threats: a sub-Saharan case study', in E. J. Erling and P. Seargeant (eds.).

Rea-Dickins, P., Reid, M., and K. Karavas-Doukas. (1996) *Evaluation of PRINCE: October 1995-February 1996*. Poland: British Council.

Rea-Dickins, P., Yu, G., and O. Afitska. (2009) 'The consequences of examining through an unfamiliar language of instruction and its impact for school-age learners in sub-Saharan African school systems', in L. Taylor and C. J. Weir (eds.). *Language Testing Matters: Investigating the wider social and educational impact of assessment. Studies in Language Testing 31*. Cambridge: Cambridge University Press and Cambridge ESOL.

Reading is Fundamental. (2011) *Children's access to print material and education-related outcomes*. Available at www.rif.org/us/about/literacy-issues (accessed 26 July 2011).

Richards, J. C. and C. Lockhart. (1994) *Reflective teaching in second language classrooms*. New York: Cambridge University Press.

Richards, K. (2006) Being the Teacher: Identity and Classroom Conversation. *Applied Linguistics* 27/1: 51-77.

Rogers, E. M. (1983) *Diffusion of innovations*. New York: Free Press.

Rogers, E. M. (2003) *Diffusion of innovations* (Fifth edition). New York: Free Press.

Saunders, M. (2000) Report on the evaluation of Interculture Project Experience. Available from http://www.lancs.ac.uk/users/interculture/reports.htm (accessed 20 July 2011).

Schleicher, A. (2009) Lessons from the world. *Educational Leadership* 67/2: 50-55.

Schweisfurth, M. (2011) Learner-centred education in developing country contexts: from solution to problem? *International Journal of Educational Development* 3: 419-26.

Scriven, M. S. (1967) 'The methodology of evaluation', in R. W. Tyler, R. M. Gagne, and M. Scriven (eds.). *Perspectives of curriculum evaluation*. Chicago: Rand McNally.

Sharpe, R. and M. Oliver. (2007) 'Designing courses for e-learning', in H. Beetham and R. Sharpe (eds.).

Shaw, S. and N. Igneri. (2006) *Effectively Implementing a Blended Learning Approach*. Available at http://www.learningandskillsgroup.com/resources/ Effectively_Implementing_a_Blended_Learning_Approach_White_paper.pdf (accessed 20 August 2007).

Shohamy, E. (1997) Testing methods, testing consequences: Are they ethical? Are they fair? *Language Testing* 14: 340-49.

Shohamy, E. (2006) *Language Policy: Hidden agendas and new approaches*. Abingdon: Routledge

Short, D. and S. Fitzsimmons. (2007) *Double the work: Challenges and solutions to acquiring language and academic literacy for adolescent English language learners. A report to the Carnegie Corporation of New York*. Washington, DC: Alliance for Excellent Education.

Sikes, P. J. (1992) 'Imposed Change and the Experienced Teacher' in M. Fullan and A. Hargreaves (eds.).

Simola, H. (2005) The Finnish miracle of PISA: historical and sociological remarks on teaching and teacher education. *Comparative Education* 41: 455-70.

Smith, H. (1999) 'Managing ELT Projects: Identifying Best Practice', in C. Kennedy (ed.).

Spada, N. (1987) Relationships between instructional differences and learning outcomes: a process-product study of communicative language teaching. *Applied Linguistics* 8/2: 137-72.

Spolsky, B. (2004) *Language Policy*. Cambridge: Cambridge University Press.

Stenhouse, L. (1975) *An introduction to curriculum research and development*. London: Heinemann.

Stephenson, H. (1994) Management and participation in ELT projects. *English Language Teaching Journal* 48/3: 225-32.

Stoller, F. A. (1994) The diffusion of innovation in intensive ELT programmes. *Applied Linguistics* 15/3: 300-27.

Stoller, F. L. (2009) 'Innovation and effective leadership', in M. A. Christison and D. E. Murray (eds.).

Stoller, F. L. (2011) 'Catalyst for innovation', in M. A. Christison and F. L. Stoller (eds.).

Stronkhorst, R. and J. van den Akker. (2006) Effects of in-service education on improving science teaching in Swaziland. *International Journal of Science Education* 28: 1771-94.

Tan, H. and S. H. Chan. (2003) *Teaching Mathematics and Science in English: A perspective from Universiti Putra Malaysia*. Paper presented at ELTC ETeMS Conference 2003: Managing Curricular Change 2-4 December 2003.

Tan, P. K.W. (2005) The medium-of-instruction debate in Malaysia: English as a Malaysian language? *Language problems and language planning* 29/1: 47-66.

Thomas, S. M. and H. Goldstein. (2008) International comparative studies of achievement – re-examining the issues and impacts. *Assessment in Education* 15/3: 211-13.

Thomas, W. P. and V. P. Collier. (2002) *A national study of school effectiveness for language minority students' long-term academic achievement.* Santa Cruz, California: Center for Research on Education Diversity and Excellence, University of California Santa Cruz. Available at http://repositories.cdlib.org/crede/finalrpts/1_1_final (accessed 29 July 2011).

Toffler, A. (1970) *Future Shock.* New York: Random House.

Tomlinson, B. (1990) Managing change in Indonesian high schools. *ELT Journal* 44/1: 25-37.

Tribble, C. (2000) Designing evaluation into educational change processes. *ELT Journal* 54/4: 319-27.

Välijärvi, J., Linnakylä, P., Kupari, P., Reinikainen, P., and I. Arffman. (2002) *The Finnish success in PISA – and some reasons behind it.* Jyväskylä, Finland: Koulutuksen tutkimuslaitos.

Walker, A. and C. Dimmock. (2000) One size fits all? Teacher appraisal in a Chinese culture. *Journal of Personnel Evaluation in Education* 14: 155-78.

Wallace, M. (1994) *Training foreign language teachers: A reflective approach.* Cambridge: Cambridge University Press.

Walsh S. (2002) Construction or obstruction: teacher talk or learner involvement in the EFL classroom. *Language Teaching Research,* 6/1: 3-23.

Walsh S. (2006) *Investigating Classroom Discourse.* London, New York: Routledge.

Waters, A. (2009) Managing innovation in English language education. *Language Teaching* 42: 421-58.

Waters, A. and M. L. C. Vilches. (2001) Implementing ELT innovations: a needs analysis framework. *ELT Journal* 55/2: 133-41.

Waters, A. and M. L. C. Vilches. (2008) Factors affecting ELT reforms: the case of the Philippines Basic Education Curriculum. *RELC Journal* 39/1: 5-24.

Wedell, M. (2009) *Planning for educational change: Putting people and their contexts first.* London: Continuum.

Wedell, M. (2011a) 'More than just technology: English language teaching initiatives as complex educational changes', in H. Coleman (ed.).

Wedell, M. (2011b) 'Proficiency in English as a key to development? Helping teachers to help learners to succeed', in E. J. Erling and P. Seargeant (eds.).

Weir, C. and J. Roberts. (1994) *Evaluation in ELT*. Oxford: Blackwell.

Weiss, C. H. (1986) 'Towards the future of stakeholder approaches in evaluation', in E.R. House (ed.). *New Directions in Educational Evaluation*. Lewes: Falmer Press.

Weiss, C. H. (1997) How can theory-based evaluation make greater headway? *Evaluation Review* 21/4: 501-24.

Wells, G. (1999) *Dialogic Inquiry: Towards a Sociocultural Practice and Theory of Education*. Cambridge: Cambridge University Press.

Westbrook, K. (2008) The beginning of the end for blended learning? *IATEFL CALL Review,* Summer: 12-15.

White, R.V. (1987) Managing innovation. *ELT Journal.* 41/3: 211-8.

White, R. V. (1988) *The ELT Curriculum*. Oxford: Blackwell.

Widin, J. (2010) *Illegitimate Practices: Global English Language Education*. Clevedon: Multilingual Matters.

Woods, P. (2006) 'The hedgehog and the fox: two approaches to English for the military', in J. Edge (ed.). *Re-locating TESOL in an Age of Empire*. London: Palgrave Macmillan.

World Bank. (2005) *The LogFrame Handbook*. Washington, DC: World Bank. Available at http://www.wau.boku.ac.at/fileadmin/_/H81/H811/Skripten/811332/811332_G3_ log-framehandbook.pdf (accessed 18 November 2011).

Wright, T. (2002) 'Doing language awareness: issues for language study in language teacher education', in H. Trappes-Lomax and G. Ferguson (eds.). *Language in Language Teacher Education*. Amsterdam: John Benjamins.

Wysocka, M. (1989) *Rozwój mówienia i pisania w języku angielskim. (Developing English Speaking and Writing Skills)*. Katowice: Wydawnictwo Uniwersytetu Śląskiego.

Yang, S. C. (2001) Integrating computer-mediated tools into the language curriculum. *Journal of Computer Assisted Learning* 17: 85-93.

Yano, Y. (2001) World Englishes in 2000 and beyond. *World Englishes* 20/2: 119-31.

Yassin, S. M., Marsh D., Ong E. T., and Y. Y. Lai. (2009) Learners' perceptions towards the teaching of science through English in Malaysia: a quantitative analysis. *International CLIL Research Journal* 1/2: 49-59.

Young, R. and S. Lee. (1984) 'EFL curriculum reform and teachers' attitudes', in P. Larson, E. Judd, and D. Messerschmidt (eds.). *On TESOL* 84. Washington: TESOL.

Zikri, M. (1991) *CDELT language CDP and SDP: 1975–1991* (Manuscript).

Notes